EMPIRE OF DIRECT MAIL

D1521081

Empire of Direct Mail

How Conservative Marketing Persuaded Voters and Transformed the Grassroots

Takahito Moriyama

UNIVERSITY PRESS OF KANSAS

Published by the University Press of Kansas (Lawrence, Kansas 66045), which was organized by the Kansas Board of Regents and is operated and funded by Emporia State University, Fort Hays State University, Kansas State University, Pittsburg State University, the University of Kansas, and Wichita State University.

Library of Congress Cataloging-in-Publication Data
Names: Moriyama, Takahito, author.
Title: Empire of direct mail : how conservative marketing persuaded voters and transformed the grassroots / Takahito Moriyama.
Description: Lawrence, Kansas : University Press of Kansas, 2022 | Includes bibliographical references and index.
Identifiers: LCCN 2021050479
ISBN 9780700633418 (paperback)
ISBN 9780700633425 (ebook)
Subjects: LCSH: Viguerie, Richard A. | Republican Party (U.S. : 1854–)—History. | Advertising, Political—United States—History—20th century. | Advertising, Direct-mail—United States—History—20th century. | Direct-mail fund raising—United States—History—20th century. | Campaign literature—United States—History—20th century. | Conservatism—United States—History—20th century. | Political consultants—United States. | United States—Politics and government—1945–1989.
Classification: LCC JF2112.A4 M66 2022 | DDC 324.7/30973—dc23/eng/20220118
LC record available at https://lccn.loc.gov/2021050479.
British Library Cataloguing-in-Publication Data is available.

10 9 8 7 6 5 4 3 2 1

Cover image: An employee taking reel of computer tape off shelves at the Richard A. Viguerie Company in the 1970s. (Courtesy of U.S. News & World Report Magazine Photograph Collection, Library of Congress)

For my grandparents

CONTENTS

A photo gallery follows page 78

ACKNOWLEDGMENTS

Since I stumbled across the topic of political direct mail as an undergraduate, I have explored American history and politics. The research was a great journey, literally and figuratively, as I moved back and forth between Japan and the United States. This project would be impossible without the assistance of numerous people and institutions that I have encountered in the two countries over the years.

I appreciated that Toru Takenaka, Takao Fujikawa, Shigeru Akita, and other professors at Osaka University, offered generous support to me when I had not yet decided to make my way to academia. I am also grateful to professors at Kyoto University such as Masugi Shimada, Akio Kawashima, Jun Yoshida, Eisaku Kihira, to name just a few. In particular, Professor Shimada emotionally supported me and wielded profound influence by teaching American history as well as the excitement of cycling, which have become my lifetime job and hobby. I was lucky in Kyoto because I took a course in US history by G. Kurt Piehler. He encouraged me to go abroad to advance my research and helped me for years as a mentor at Florida State University where I completed my PhD. In the early stages of this research, Neil Jumonville, Michael Creswell, and Michael McVicar provided me with insights and criticisms. I am also indebted to Suzanne Sinke, Jennifer L. Koslow, Brad T. Gomez, and Alf Tomas Tønnessen who read the manuscript in its entirety. After I returned to Japan, I was able to move forward with publication at the University of Tokyo. While the coronavirus pandemic dramatically changed our lives, Yasuo Endo, Kenryu Hashikawa, and Kotaro Nakano provided me with circumstances under which I could put all my energy into the manuscript. At the University Press of Kansas, David Congdon gave me much advice in altering my PhD dissertation into a book for wider audiences.

This project has received the help of many other people. I would like to thank the staff of the Harry S. Truman, Dwight D. Eisenhower, Lyndon B. Johnson, Richard Nixon, Gerald R. Ford, Jimmy Carter, and Ronald Reagan presidential libraries. In addition, librarians were always supportive at the universities I visited, including Yale University, Brown University, Columbia University, Indiana University/Purdue University, Duke University, University of Arkansas,

University of Kansas, Arizona State University, University of Texas at Austin, and University of Wyoming. Especially significant for my research were the Hoover Institution Archives and the Library of Congress, which provided a number of materials concerning conservative activists and organizations. Looking back at these archival research trips reminds me of the fact that many people across the United States made contributions to my project.

I would not have achieved my research goals without the generous assistance of the Fulbright Scholar Program, which provided not merely financial support but also opportunities to socialize with other brilliant friends from around the world. The Alvin Achenbaum Travel Grant of Duke University, the research grant of the America–Japan Society, and that of the Harry S. Truman Library also made it possible for me to do research in several archives. I am grateful that I presented parts of this book in talks at the University of London, the University of Alabama, Lebanon Valley College, and the University of California, Berkeley, along with other places in which I received encouraging advice from scholars.

Last but not least, friends and family were essential to me. Since I was a master's student in Japan, it has been always thought-provoking to have conversations with Hideaki Kami. I was fortunate to benefit from the generosity of the "gang" in the Institute on World War II and the Human Experience at Florida State University. In the last few months at FSU, I truly enjoyed working with Huaqing, Shi, Gabriela Maduro, Gillian Morton, Julianna Witt, Andrew Flaxman, Bianca Pallo, Lee Morrison, Laran Dixon, Jenna Pope, Jessie Mrock, Allison Overholt, among other students. Some of them kindly proofread my dissertation quite carefully. Michael Kasper, then institute archivist, was among the most amiable and congenial persons I ever encountered in Florida (probably in the United States). I was also happy to share with Anne Marsh several stories about the Second World War. And Kurt, as the director of the institute and my mentor, patiently helped me. I can confidently say that the years in Florida were the most wonderful chapter of my life. No matter where I am in the world, Yasuhiro Moriyama, Yuri Moriyama, Hirokazu Moriyama, and Aya Omae have always helped me a lot, and it is my greatest pleasure to see my nephews and niece—Toru, Wataru, Sho, and Kokomi—growing up in Kochi, Japan.

EMPIRE OF DIRECT MAIL

Introduction

I N FALL 1978, RICHARD Viguerie invited a reporter to his office in Falls Church, Virginia. Viguerie rented three floors in a modern office building in the sprawling suburb of Washington, DC, where three hundred employees worked in the Richard A. Viguerie Company (RAVCO). One of the floors had a computer room guarded by two security systems. The room contained two giant IBM computers, two high-speed printers, and ten tape units for distributing millions of letters. An adjoining room, which was protected by even more elaborate security precautions that changed a combination lock every few days, stored three thousand rolls of magnetic tape that recorded the names and addresses of approximately fifteen million people who had been identified as likely donors to conservative causes. Grinning and pointing to the round cans of tape, Viguerie told the reporter, "If you're conservative, your name should be in there somewhere."[1]

The RAVCO was a consulting firm that engaged in political advertising and fundraising primarily for conservatism. Drawing on a huge database of personal information, Viguerie sent out computerized direct mailings from his office in north Virginia to conservatives around the nation. His appeals urged Americans to join battles revolving around single issues such as the Equal Rights Amendment, abortion, gun control, school busing, labor law reform, and the Panama Canal treaties. In election years, Viguerie's solicitation letters also called on recipients to support right-wing candidates including Senators Jesse Helms of North Carolina, Strom Thurmond of South Carolina, and Alabama Governor George Wallace. Millions of citizens received letters with a simulating personal touch, and hundreds of thousands of them sent back $10, $15, or $25 checks in response to Viguerie's letters. Grossing over $15 million a year, the RAVCO raised money to help conservative candidates and organizations in the late 1970s. The ten IBM magnetic tape units in Viguerie's office incessantly spun, adding new names, deleting others, and selecting those who would be responsive to future campaigns. The room with magnetic tapes was the nerve center of Viguerie's direct mail empire. He claimed that it was "the most important room in America for conservatism."[2]

Beginning in the early 1950s, conservative media activists like Viguerie propagated their antiliberal discourse through various media outlets. Along with right-wing intellectuals, White southerners, the Sunbelt's "suburban warriors," blue-collar workers, and conservative televangelists, these media professionals forged the conservative movement over the second half of the twentieth century. However, unlike grassroots activists who canvassed from door to door or prominent politicians who moved audiences in speeches, conservative advertisers mobilized people and lobbied lawmakers by sending messages from their offices in New York and Washington. This is a story of direct mail specialists who constructed conservative networks and created a new grassroots activism in twentieth-century American politics.

***

The impact of political direct mail, which is overshadowed by mass media such as the press and broadcasting, has been understudied thus far. Newspapers and magazines remained crucial in providing information throughout the twentieth century. Radio became increasingly popular among Americans and conveyed political messages by the 1930s. Later by the early 1950s when many households purchased television sets, political campaigners began to use television as a key medium in elections. Academic researchers have examined the effects of media in modern American politics with attention first and foremost to television.[3] Similarly, when it comes to conservative media, mass media always rivets much attention. When analyzing the role of right-wing media activists, researchers have addressed largely conservative publishers, talk radio hosts, and news anchors. Although scholars of right-wing media have dealt with various communication tools in politics, they accept a conventional wisdom that the press and broadcasting played central roles in the United States over the course of the late twentieth century, and more generally, that mass media was the main topic for political information campaigns.[4]

Computerized direct mail is a unique communications technology. The idea of direct mail was based on "personalization" and "selectivity," which derived from an advertising strategy called direct marketing that developed in the mid-century. Direct mail differed from broadcasting in that, instead of circulating the same information to the masses, it enabled campaigners to send personalized messages according to individual preferences. By selecting out likely customers and supporters, then focusing solicitation exclusively on them, direct mail could get messages to people more effectively than traditional media. The evolution of computer technology further transformed the outdated method of writing letters toward a sophisticated communication technique. As machines recorded a huge body of personal information, including magazine subscriptions and campaign donations, activists could discover prospective backers and carve out political niches more easily than before. Furthermore, whereas radio and television were regulated by the Federal Communications Commission, political direct mailings reached readers without being censored by officials, editors, or precinct leaders. In short, direct mail was distinctive from standardized broadcasting in mass society; it was a medium to connect grassroots individuals directly with the leadership in political campaigns and social movements.[5]

Political direct mail was particularly significant for the development of modern American conservatism. When antiliberal activists and intellectuals began to appear in the United States during the postwar era, they found themselves on the outskirts of the society. At that time, conservative voices were seldom heard as the great majority of Americans were satisfied with New Deal liberalism. The New Deal coalition was firmly established, the White House was held by Democrats or moderate Republicans like Dwight D. Eisenhower, the Supreme Court endorsed racial integration, and above all, the national mass media was dominantly liberal, leaving almost no political and cultural room for dissents of liberalism. Under these circumstances, direct mail provided conservatives with channels to gain support from and reach out to potential backers around the nation. By the 1980s, direct mail operatives helped build conservative coalitions by financing right-wing organizations and taking the initiative in crafting a political agenda. As a result, they also transformed the Republican Party from the party of moderates toward that of conservatives over the years.

The political importance of direct marketing was never confined to the conservative movement as liberals mobilized voters in newer but similar ways during the 1990s and beyond. Nowadays, marketing tactics have become the nuts and bolts of political campaigns by helping raise money, reach out to the electorate, and make good images of candidates, thus many people are recently talking about political consultants who are involved with "data mining," "microtargeting," "advertising," "branding," and other undertakings. Democrats and Republicans alike obviously benefit from these political marketing methods as, for example, Howard Dean and Barack Obama who successfully tapped the great number of individual contributions for their campaigns in the late 1990s and 2000s.[6] More recently, after Donald Trump won the 2016 presidential election, media at home and abroad covered the scandal of Cambridge Analytica, a consultant firm that reportedly acquired personal data from Facebook and influenced American voters. Therefore, we are likely to fasten on the rise of the internet in politics at the turn toward the twenty-first century without fully examining the development of direct mail politics back in the mid-twentieth century.[7]

This book systematically and critically explores the origins of big data politics by investigating how conservative direct mail emerged and how it influenced the rightward turn of the Republican Party from the 1950s through the 1970s. Moderate Republicans seized control of the GOP, and conservatives repeatedly failed to take over the party during the 1950s and 1960s. However, whereas more conservatives and Dixiecrats moved into the Republican Party in the late 1960s, right-wing media operatives called on Sunbelt suburbanites, working-class White people, and the Religious Right to endorse the party, ultimately reorganizing the GOP as an alignment of diverse White voters who emphasized private enterprise, social issues, racism, and patriotism. The metamorphosis took place partly due to successful campaigns of individual targeting media, through which political marketers collated and analyzed personal data and effectively sent political messages to voters beginning in the post–World War II period. Through examining the development of political media and the changes of political situation, this research inspects why conservatives and Republicans took advantage of direct mail politics more successfully than Democrats.

In addition to the transfiguration of political parties, computerized direct mail had a profound impact on the grassroots by affecting how ordinary Americans participated in politics. When people received solicitation letters, they did not just send back checks. Many letters housed in archives and libraries indicate that the grassroots who responded to direct mailings were never passive contributors, but active participants with their own voice. The number of conservatives gave financial and moral support to conservative campaigns by expressing who they were and why they endorsed the movement, while others sometimes refuted messages of direct mail even if they shared the antiliberal cause. These letters from rank-and-file conservatives demonstrate that political fragmentation was applicable not merely to the relationship between liberals and conservatives, but also to the conservative movement itself. But at the same time, those reactions from the grassroots suggest how direct mail successfully built up loosely connected networks of conservatism encompassing diverse political beliefs, which contributed to the 1980 Reagan Revolution. Far from being isolated and passive individuals, grassroots conservatives and right-wing messengers forged their movement in a different way from face-to-face relations and organization-based engagement.

Of course, many historians have delved into grassroots conservatives, describing vividly the enthusiasm of suburbanites in the Sunbelt, such as Orange

County, California, who built the conservative movement from the bottom up. The women and men in the modern suburbs participated in anticommunist groups like the John Birch Society, erected conservative bookstores around the area, and, as "kitchen-table" activists, enthusiastically supported Barry Goldwater in the 1964 election. Orange Countians also became zealous members of conservative megachurches, heralding the rise of the Religious Right at the national level beginning in the 1970s. By investigating these ordinary people discontent with liberalism, historians have disclosed how conservatism that emanated from neighborhoods and communities ended up turning national politics rightward.[8]

At the same time, direct mail opened up a new kind of grassroots activism. First, direct mail transformed a long-standing pattern of political contribution. By the early 1960s, campaign funds relied heavily on big money from a few of philanthropists and giant corporations. Yet direct mail made it possible for activists and organizations to amass small funds from a great number of individuals. Second, millions of small funds changed the organizational model of the social movements. Traditionally, movement organizations depended on membership fees for their finances, but the late 1960s witnessed the emergence of political groups that held fewer members and instead gained funds by means of direct mail. In a sense, sending small funds was a grassroots participation as ordinary people supported groups and candidates who shared a political cause. Yet simultaneously, direct mail politics offered political involvement without organizational membership or community engagement. While civil rights activists took to the streets and the New Left called for participatory democracy over the course of the sixties, conservative direct mail invented a distinctive meaning of the grassroots. It was *individualized grassroots*, which transformed grassroots mobilization from the building of face-to-face relationships toward the gathering of small involvements.

Direct mail effectively generated responses from individuals who had been unlikely to endorse conservatism. From the 1950s on, conservative consultants gradually undermined the New Deal coalition by sending out messages to people such as Democrats frustrated by the growing activist state, Republican supporters in the Solid South, religious minorities including Catholic and Jewish Americans, and finally working-class White people who felt isolated within the Democratic Party. New followers of conservatism were individuals who switched their political identity from Democrats to Republicans, despite the fact that their region, ethnicity, and class had conventionally been bases of liberalism. By contacting those grassroots supporters, direct mail specialists helped push for political realignment after the late 1960s. However, instead of establishing a new political party or national organization that courted the whole supporters, 1970s right-wing activists loosely linked diverse interests and focused on ad hoc political issues that could be shared by various groups. Indeed, tightly knit membership groups, such as the Birchers in the 1960s and the church-based Religious Right in the 1970s, remained active over the years. But direct mail certainly provided a new model of grassroots mobilization by segmenting individual voters and reorganizing them into a political movement.

This book also demonstrates that such individualized grassroots mobilization placed emotion in the foreground of conservative politics. In general, conservatism was frequently regarded as an irrational movement closely connected with angry emotion. In the aftermath of McCarthyism, the "consensus" scholars such as Daniel Bell and Richard Hofstadter observed the rise of the radical right in American society, explaining that the political phenomenon derived largely from psychological distress. Bell wrote in *The Radical Right* (1963) that conservatism was "the politics of frustration," which motivated those who were not able to comprehend the complexity of a modern society in the twentieth century. Likewise, Hofstadter pointed out the intense emotion and stupendous irrationality of "pseudo-conservatism," that frequently expressed negative emotions including anxiety, resentment, and rancor. Explaining that the psychological distress stemmed from "status anxieties" of those who were anxious over the fragility of their status in an increasingly changing American society, the consensus school took condescending attitudes toward the right-wing movement in which they observed emotion replacing reason.[9]

In particular, emotion characterized conservative direct mail that would accelerate political partisanship. When using direct mail in the midcentury, commercial ad agencies stressed the tradition of personal correspondence not only by conveying the information of products but also by writing intimately and intensifying the reader's emotion. Political media professionals shortly followed suit, turning intimacy into aggression as an effective strategy. Political mail highlighted such feelings as fear, anxiety, and hostility for contrasting "us" and "them" in the political arena. As such, emotional politics sped up political partisanship between Democrats and Republicans, and even among moderates and conservatives within the GOP. Again, Daniel Bell grew concerned that direct mail and political action committees that utilized the technology were breaking up an already fragmented politics, as conservative consultants like Viguerie actively deployed direct mail to attack liberals and moderates.[10] To be sure, political campaigns had always been emotional prior to the rise of direct mail, but the medium set out the systematic use of emotion in US politics. Thus, even when direct mail came to light, its political role was considered negative because the medium became a symbol of the conservative movement's emotional aspects beginning in the midcentury.

However, unlike what the consensus scholars and other historians asserted, emotional politics of the conservative movement was not necessarily irrational. From the beginning of political direct mail in the postwar years, operatives marshaled the technology by stoking negative emotion among letter recipients because they understood that it was the best way to persuade individuals to take action. Actually, although their messages were often incoherent and misinforming, conservative messengers deployed emotion for their political purposes in practical and competitive ways. Many intellectuals and pundits dismissed the outburst of fury and anxiety in politics as insane, but this study of direct mail will show that it was the result of the reasonable use of sentiment for mobilizing grassroots supporters. Political advertising agencies comprehended that offensive messages would attract attention in the 1950s, and conservative political consultants turned direct mailings ideological to raise more funds during the 1960s; then by the late 1970s, some religious conservatives marshaled emotional outcry as a competent strategy in politics. Although Democrats and liberals tended to stress hopes and ideals in their appeals, conservative activists surpassed their counterparts in direct mail mobilization. Right-wing ideological direct mail proved so competitive that even some liberals imitated conservatives' emotionalism by the 1980s. Thus, emotional politics would go on without right-wing extremists and demagogues because it is a systemic scheme that built on marketing and media strategies deeply rooted in American politics.

To explore the development of direct mail politics since the 1950s, *Empire of Direct Mail* focuses on several activists in New York City and Washington, DC. Yet it does not aim to make the case that these urban areas were as conservative as the Sunbelt.[11] Rather, the objective of this study is to argue that the two cities were significant for conservative direct mail because they were the capitals of media and politics. As the advertising industry developed on Madison Avenue beginning in the early twentieth century, New York attracted many media experts from around the nation. By the 1950s, these media operatives formed close relations with political parties and candidates, mobilizing Americans in other regions by sending messages. Indeed, Boston, Baltimore, and Chicago played key roles in providing media outlets, but New York occupied the center stage for political advertisement in the decades that this book deals with.[12]

Also, direct mail casts new light on the relationship between liberals and conservatives in their polemical politics. Despite vehement antiliberal rhetoric and hostile words, conservatives' direct mail actually relied on the structure constructed by the federal government and liberals. As the transfiguration of elections promoted the political use of mass media, which was effective but quite expensive, many became worried over the rise of campaign expenses and the issue of money in politics. There were a sequence of debates over campaign finance throughout the 1950s and 1960s. While Democrats tried to reform campaign regulations, conservatives resisted the alteration by claiming that it would violate the freedom of speech. Following the ideological disputes, Democrats amended the Federal Election Campaign Act in 1974 in an attempt to limit the amount of individual donation to candidates. However, this campaign finance reform by liberals ironically ended up boosting direct mail fundraising and catapulting Viguerie to political prominence in the late 1970s.

Through these analyses, this study examines the interplay between liberals and conservatives beyond the "red-blue binaries." Instead of the conservative "ascendancy," the 1960s and 1970s saw the complicated interactions between the two political forces. As modern conservatism accelerated reactionary movements, their anticommunist, antilabor, and antiliberal rhetoric led to intense partisan politics in the late twentieth century. But if one looks beneath the surface of the ideological conflicts, the left and right had in common certain movement cultures and organizational techniques. This book will explore how direct mail politics resulted from a cooptation of various actors, investigating how social movements, political parties, and the federal government caused a variety of changes, which set the stage for conservative media activism.

Chapter 1 surveys the transformation of political elections from the nineteenth century toward the mid-twentieth century. Political machines and party bosses, which played central roles in American political campaigns, were challenged by a series of progressive reforms designed to eradicate political corruption in the early twentieth century. These reforms paved the way for political consultants, the new political elite who introduced advertising techniques into political elections. This chapter also explains why the Republican Party would later surpass its counterpart in direct mail politics. The decline of political machines and the reliance solely on volunteers on the precinct level urged the GOP to build an intimate relationship with Madison Avenue. The Dwight Eisenhower and Adlai Stevenson campaigns in the presidential elections of 1952 and 1956 showed how new political campaigns replaced old-styled elections over the years. Simultaneously, the chapter investigates how journalists and intellectuals alerted the public as new communications and media professionals loomed large in US politics during the 1950s.

Chapter 2 devotes attention to the rise of direct mail outside of party politics in the midcentury. Along with the modernization of the US postal service and the advance of modern information technologies, commercial advertising agents altered direct mail from an ineffective communication tool toward a sophisticated advertising device in the 1950s. In these years, liberal, anticommunist, and conservative activists set out direct mail fundraising in New York. With shades of political orientations, these fundraisers co-worked to introduce direct mail's functions, such as selectivity, personalization, and intimacy, to political solicitation. Their direct mail fundraising activities demonstrated how the left and right interacted with each other in developing direct mail politics during the 1950s. However, the changing rhetoric of their direct mailings indicated that bipartisanship gradually gave way to partisanship in the latter part of the 1950s when the modern American conservative movement took shape.

Chapter 3 deals with the junction of party politics and grassroots movements, analyzing the first successful direct mail fundraising that the Barry Goldwater campaign implemented in the 1964 presidential election. As liberals dominated the mainstream media at that time, conservatives sought their own media to raise funds and gain support when conservative organizations and activists were involved with the Goldwater movement. Even if the Goldwater campaign resulted in a resounding defeat on Election Day, conservative political consultants in New York revolutionized campaign financing by amassing a remarkable amount of money from small donors. Marshaling the "air war" strategy, conservative fundraisers made a stark contrast to big money politics of the Democratic Party, as well as other right-wing organizations such as the John Birch Society that depended on the membership model of grassroots engagement.

Chapter 4 provides an exposition on the unfolding of direct mail politics from the mid-1960s to the early 1970s. Conservative mail fundraising increasingly developed in national elections over the years. But the chapter uncovers direct mail was not limited to conservative politics as moderate Republicans and liberal Democrats actively marshaled the political device. Despite the wide use of direct mail, conservative fundraising was more successful than liberal solicitation because Viguerie and other conservative activists elaborately institutionalized "ideological direct mail," which was intended to emphasize ideological conflict, partisanship, and emotion. The late 1960s also witnessed the reshaping of political consultancy. As political partisanship became more intense, the advertising industry started to withdraw from the political realm. The sea change resulted in the establishment of professional consultants solely for political advertising, and the central place of political consulting shifted from Madison Avenue toward the Beltway by the end of the decade.

Chapter 5 illuminates a historic irony when liberal campaign finance reforms consolidated the ascendancy of conservative direct mail fundraising in the 1970s. Charging money interests and political corruption of the Nixon administration, Democrats in Congress achieved the Federal Election Campaign Act (FECA) of 1971 and the Amendment to the FECA of 1974. Yet contribution limits of the campaign reforms benefited conservatives who collected the vast amount of funds from small contributors via direct mail. The chapter traces the process by which the campaign finance reforms took shape by the 1970s, surveying political scandals and congressional debates under three administrations. As television ads dramatically increased campaign expenditures, John F. Kennedy and Lyndon B. Johnson tackled money in politics, then Richard Nixon paradoxically assisted Democrats to pass reform legislation after the Watergate scandal stirred up debates over political corruption. While liberals contended that big money threatened American democracy, conservatives resisted the liberal reform by claiming that it would violate constitutional rights such as the freedom of expression. Despite the partisan disputes, the liberal reform unexpectedly benefited conservatives, and the change of the electoral system paved the way for the conservative victory in 1980.

Chapter 6 revolves around the New Right, a right-wing populist movement that Viguerie was engaged in during the 1970s. The first section of this chapter delves into the leadership, ideology, and media strategies of the New Right, comparing the distinction between 1960s and 1970s conservatives. Although the two generations of conservative activists shared many political issues, the New Right was an elitist movement defined by antielitism. A cadre of movement leaders in Washington coalesced diverse interests, including White southerners, blue-collar workers in the Rust Belt, and conservative Christians, into a "people's movement" against "the establishment" of big government, liberalism, and the big media. But the New Right in the Beltway mobilized conservatives through political advertising rather than organizing local chapters. Direct mail enabled the New Right to form the coalition by reaching out to each group with single issues, such as abortion, gun control, and the Panama Canal treaties. The second portion of the chapter narrows in on the 1976 and 1980 elections, investigating how the New Right assisted conservative candidates in their campaigns and paved the way for Reagan's presidency.

In the largest sense, this study analyzes the transforming nature of American civil society. Since Alexis de Tocqueville wrote his *Democracy in America* during the 1830s, many observers regarded the United States as a "nation of joiners" who organized voluntary associations to solve social and political problems. However, political scientist Robert Putnam and other intellectuals pointed out the "collapse of American community" after the 1960s when, Putnam claimed, participation in local groups and grassroots activities began to decline. If Putnam's argument found an echo at the end of the twentieth century, what changes took place in American politics during the latter part of the twentieth century? How did media influence ways in which American citizens were involved with politics, and how did liberals and conservatives affect the changes? The history of political direct mail narrates not only why conservatives rose over the years but also how the medium altered grassroots politics in the period between mass media and new media.[13]

In the "age of fracture," political direct mail was of historical significance.[14] Like commercial marketers categorized the market into specific groups of customers, direct mail consultants segmented voters in the process by which they identified stalwarts, sent personalized mailings, and carved out political niches. For the purpose of efficient mobilization, conservative media activists, especially the 1970s New Right, launched emotional messages and developed right-wing populism. In that sense, direct mail accelerated political divisions in the United States. But at the same time, direct mail and other communication devices have offered individuals opportunities for political participation by giving them new ways to express their political stances. The history of direct mail indicates both the possibilities and dangers of our information culture today.

CHAPTER 1

The Rise of Political Consultants

ROBERT HUMPHREYS WORKED FOR the Washington, DC, branch of the International News Service (INS) as a news editor from 1937 to 1944, during which time he built close relations with many Republicans on Capitol Hill. After he left the INS in Washington, Humphreys moved to New York City to become the national affairs editor of *Newsweek*. However, as the 1948 elections resulted in the Democratic majorities in both the House and the Senate, Speaker of the House Joe Martin asked the recognized newsman to return to DC. Assigned as director of public relations for House Republicans in 1949, Humphreys was engaged with public relations strategy for the GOP during the 1950s.[1]

Since Republican National Committee Chairman Arthur Summerfield had appointed Humphreys to direct publicity for the 1952 presidential election in January 1952, Humphreys had been crafting a blueprint for Dwight D. Eisenhower's campaign. Prepared in the standard format of a public relations agency, the plan outlined the basic campaign strategy, volunteer organization, radio and television programs, speeches, and advertising. After Eisenhower won the nomination at the Republican National Convention in July, Humphreys worked out the final version of the campaign plan in consultation with Eisenhower and his aides. Early in the morning of August 2, 1952, Humphreys arrived at the Brown Palace Hotel in Denver, Colorado. He was carrying several flip boards that many advertising agents used for presentation in the 1950s. The campaign plan was known among a handful of Republicans as "Document X," which was the first comprehensive strategy for national campaigning in American politics.[2]

The 1952 presidential election was of historic significance for several reasons. As the Korean War erupted in East Asia and Senator Joseph McCarthy accelerated fervent anticommunism at home, the election bookended New Deal and Fair Deal liberalism at the White House. Along with the ideological change in the early Cold War era, the year of 1952 marked a transformation of media strategies in political campaigning. Radio and television advertising increasingly played a crucial role in elections, and candidates of both parties—willingly and hesitantly—attempted to deploy new technologies of public relations. David Greenberg, for instance, mentioned that during the 1952 campaign Eisenhower and Adlai Stevenson faced a question of "whether and how to avail themselves of the newly sophisticated tools of what today we call 'spin'—in particular of television advertising."[3]

More importantly, the 1952 election was a critical moment when political consultants began to emerge as campaign managers at the national level. As the political scientist Larry Sabato defined, political consultant is "a campaign professional who is engaged primarily in the provision of advice and services" to their clients.[4] Exerting their expertise in public opinion polling, public relations, fundraising, speech writing, and other operations, political consultants were involved with campaign management and strategy to political candidates, interest groups, and other committees. These campaign professionals differentiated themselves from old-styled political machines and personal aides to candidates by employing scientific methods and introducing public relations techniques of the advertising industry. Madison Avenue provided knowledge for political candidates and parties, and by the early 1950s several advertising executives served as directors of the Democratic and Republican national committees. The growth of political consulting was so intimately related with the development of the advertising community in America that several scholars have pointed out political consultants were the "direct descendants" of the public relations professionals. The advent of political direct mail would not take place without political consultants in American elections.[5]

Beginning in the 1950s, several changes took place in national elections: the close partnership of politicians and the advertising industry, the resorting to commercial public relations expertise in electioneering, and the growth of expenditure for television advertisements. Newspaper editors and advertising agents joined the major party national committees, then media-savvy businesspersons introduced commercial techniques to political campaigns over the course of the 1950s. Furthermore, political consultants were engaged not only in publicity but also in comprehensive campaign management. To be sure, there had been many precedents of political consultancy, particularly at the local and state levels, prior to the 1950s. However, political consultant Humphreys distinguished himself from previous campaign advisers by wielding extensive power over national campaign so that resources, including money, time, and volunteers, would be allocated as effectively as possible. Thus, the 1950s was the period when political consultants centralized the process of national campaigning, creating a new, institutional relationship between politicians and the public.

The new political advertisers shortly attracted popular and scholarly attention. Novelists and journalists attended to the emerging advertising industry, describing advertisers as figures of popular admiration as well as controversy. Similar perspectives have arguably prescribed academic views of political advertising and media technology as many studies have emphasized ominous effects of political consultancy and its marketing strategies, such as belligerent messages and negative campaigns.[6] Pundits and researchers warned of the "commercialization" of American democracy, viewing political consulting as political entrepreneurship defined by businesslike rhetoric and pursuit of profit.[7] In *Anti-Intellectualism in American Life*, Richard Hofstadter articulated how intellectuals saw the relationship between business and politics. While exploring American anti-intellectuals, including politicians, the Religious Right, and conservative editors, among others, Hofstadter condemned business people who were diametrically different from intellectuals, saying the "circumstances of the industrial era in America gave the businessman a position among the foes of mind and culture so central and so powerful that other antagonists were crowded out of the picture."[8]

If we are to understand the significance of campaign professionals in the 1950s, we need to place them within a wider context of the development of political consulting from the early nineteenth to the mid-twentieth century. A sequence of electoral reforms affected American political campaigns in the first decades of the twentieth century. The progressive reforms undermined the conventional party structure, including political machines and party bosses, paving the way for the emergence of campaign professionals. Various actors served political candidates by involving themselves with propaganda, public opinion polling, fundraising, recruiting volunteers, and campaign management over the years. Yet particularly two transformations characterized the nature of political consultancy before the midcentury. Part-time advisers with nonscientific means who advised political candidates throughout the nineteenth century gave way to professional political consultants who employed modern and effective devices in campaigns by the 1930s. Simultaneously, the central actors in political consulting shifted from press editors toward advertising executives by the postwar era. Both major political parties were influenced by the electoral transformations beginning in the Progressive Era. However, they adjusted to the new electoral circumstances differently, according to their organizational structures as well as their ideological approaches to the mass society of the midcentury.

The Development of Political Consultancy

We can discover the precursors of political consultants in the colonial period and the Early Republic when personal friends and political associates helped candidates as unpaid volunteers. Among the first campaign advisers in eighteenth-century colonial America was an unnamed person who gave advice to George Washington that he purchase refreshments for the voters in the 1758 Virginia Colonial Assembly election. Thomas Jefferson was also assisted by an outstanding adviser. John Beckley, who had been the first clerk of the Virginia House of Delegates and later the first clerk of the House of Representatives, worked on behalf of Jefferson in the presidential campaigns. In 1796, Beckley set out the first massive media campaign in American history, circulating thousands of political handbills and over thirty thousand sample ballots. Although Jefferson failed to succeed Washington in 1796, his "media blitz" bore fruits in the 1800 presidential contest.[9]

The 1828 presidential election witnessed a remarkable evolution of political campaigning. John Quincy Adams and Andrew Jackson attempted to reach voters in the presidential contest, and various advisers joined the Jackson campaign under the direction of Martin Van Buren. The campaign staff was responsible for organizing public meetings, and the Jackson campaign managers harnessed mass meetings on a large scale for the first time in the United States.[10] The Adams and Jackson campaigns also actively used the press. Both campaigns contacted sympathetic publishers and distributed copies of their newspapers to disseminate favorable stories throughout the election. Congenial newspaper editors served the Jackson campaign as political advertisers, attempting to appeal to constituents in numerous ways. The observations suggested that since its beginning political consulting had a close connection with newspaper editors.[11]

Besides political public relations, press agents took an important part in surveying the trend of public opinion throughout the nineteenth century. The press editors attempted to gauge preelection sentiment of the electorate when they carried out "straw" polls, including clip-out questionnaires in their publications and ballots in subscription advertisements. Politicians depended on the reports by press reporters and editors, although they were nonscientific polls and unreliable sources. Political candidates also relied on field reports from precinct leaders and county chairmen. Precinct workers walked from door to door, asking potential voters about their impressions of candidates and politics, and precinct captains were expected to know the public opinion directly from the electorate and predict the outcome of elections. The rank and file at the precinct level were significant for political parties during election campaigns.[12]

But nobody arguably played a more important role than political machines and party bosses in waging political campaigns from the late nineteenth to the early twentieth century. Throughout the period, congressional candidates and those who ran for state and local offices were dependent on state and local party committees. The party organizations exercised the control over government jobs and wielded influence over immigrant communities in urban areas, and party bosses were able to raise funds, mobilize volunteers, and collect votes. Party committees, or old-fashioned political machines, were so dominant that they managed almost every dimension of political campaigning, ranging "from nominating candidates to mobilizing voters to cleaning up the remnants of the victory celebration."[13]

However, several changes affected the dominance of political machine over election during the Progressive Era. The increase of educational opportunities and the rise of the middle class subverted party bosses' power over their main constituents. A series of progressive reforms, including the adoption of the secret ballot, the direct primary, and civil service laws that led to the merit system, also diminished the influence of political machines over electioneering and government contracts. Designed to eradicate corruption, the progressive reforms rendered conventional forms of securing votes either obsolete or illegal. One commentator remarked in the 1908 presidential election, "The adoption of the secret ballot . . . has put an end to the ease and facility with which it used to be possible to . . . buy [votes] directly."[14] Woodrow Wilson, who severely criticized party bosses and their corruption, also made efforts to root out the secrecy of the congressional committee system. In his 1910 gubernatorial and 1912 presidential campaigns, Wilson highlighted publicity in pursuit of transparent elections and the direct form of public engagement. These campaign reforms shifted the nature of political elections from party-dominant toward candidate-centered campaigns, and political candidates could no longer rely solely on bosses and party organizations. The decline of the party machines' influence resulted in the increased significance of campaign strategists drawn from the personal circle of each candidate rather than party. Accordingly, individual politicians ardently recruited publicity professionals to sell the candidates to the voters.[15]

Both major parties attempted to adapt themselves to the new environment of political campaigns. The Democrats capitalized on the new political publicity quite successfully in the early twentieth century. In 1916, former newspaperman Robert W. Woolley directed the Bureau of Publicity of the Democratic National Committee (DNC), conducting an extensive publicity campaign. Woolley welcomed other public relations professionals, such as George Creel, who was well-known as a progressive journalist and became Woolley's special assistant. Paying attention to film as a new political instrument that visualized politicians' personality more vividly than prints did, Creel was in charge of the production of a campaign film titled *The President and His Cabinet in Action*. However, in the 1920 presidential election, the Republicans proved innovative in employing public relations techniques. Albert Lasker of the Lord & Thomas agency in Chicago, one of the nation's largest advertising firms, contributed to the victory of Warren G. Harding. Managing publicity for the 1920 campaign, Lasker set in motion a slogan "Wiggle and Wobble," launching signs and billboards with the slogan that portrayed Democrats as unscrupulous.[16]

In the years between the late eighteenth century and the 1920s, various people worked with political candidates in elections, but they were basically volunteers. While precinct captains built personal relations with their neighbors and party bosses secured votes by providing jobs for the constituents, editors and journalists served as nascent political consultants in promoting publicity and conducting polling through their publications. However, the part-time campaign advisers usually depended on nonscientific means of polling and face-to-face relations for fundraising. Prior to the developments of modern communication technologies and campaign techniques, the campaign advisers were minor, behind-the-scenes actors in politics.

The interwar period saw the transformation of political consultancy from amateurish advisers toward scientific professionals. Edward Bernays was among the key figures in the evolution. He began his career as an editor for a medical journal, then as a public relations agent working for Broadway shows in the 1910s. As a member of the Creel Committee, which was established to mobilize public opinion and promote Liberty Bonds during World War I, Bernays learned the political use of public relations under the Wilson administration. After the Great War, he founded his own public relations firm in 1921, while teaching the first college level course on public relations at New York University in 1923. Having spent time with his uncle, Sigmund Freud, Bernays drew on contemporary psychology when he established his theory of political advertising. Through his books, he indicated how political leaders could crystallize public opinion and engineer consent. For his educational activities and publications, Bernays was known as the "father of public relations," and many US presidents from Calvin Coolidge to Eisenhower called for Bernays's advice.[17]

Emil Hurja was another person who introduced scientific methods into politics in the 1930s. As a poll pilot in the service of Franklin D. Roosevelt, Hurja directed the first systematic political polling at the national level in the 1932 presidential contest, and later contributed to the landslide reelection of Roosevelt in 1936. Unlike amateur political consultants by the 1920s, Hurja's political polling was "guided by the newly developing science of public opinion polling and the political consulting business that would later grow from it." Born to a Finnish immigrant family in a mining town in the Upper Peninsula of Michigan, Hurja's interest in polling derived partly from mining. According to his biography, the political consultant's knowledge of sampling theory came from a mining expert's lectures. Hurja was also influenced by historian Frederick Jackson Turner, who demanded new methods to combine historical research with other studies such as economy, sociology, and statistics. Hurja revolutionized not only polling but also patronage in the Roosevelt presidency. Working under Harold Ickes, a Republican antimachine reformer who struggled to eliminate the spoil system in the Department of the Interior, Hurja provided political appointments for many New Deal loyalists and supporters in districts where Democrats faced their closest fights in congressional campaigns. Hurja's career demonstrated that political consulting grew under the influence of Progressivism and took the place of conventional political machines.[18]

Meanwhile, the first political consulting firm was established on the West Coast. In 1933, journalist Clement Whitaker met Leone Baxter, the manager of the chamber of commerce in Redding, California, and they founded the Campaigns, Inc. The team consulted campaigns for candidates, interest groups, and local businesses to win against their political opponents and ballot measures that menaced their interests. One of the most famous political actions in which Whitaker and Baxter were engaged was a campaign by American Medical Association (AMA) to defeat Harry Truman's national health plan in 1949. Following Governor Earl Warren's announcement of his plan for California's universal health care in January 1945, the California Medical Association hired Whitaker and Baxter, organizing a massive campaign against the proposed government-run health care program. Similarly, the duo cooperated with the AMA in framing President Truman's idea of national health insurance as a road to threatening socialism, then the Campaigns, Inc. coalesced the campaign to stop the national health care plan by bringing together diverse actors under the single banner. Until they faded away from the political consulting industry in the late 1950s, Whitaker and Baxter profoundly influenced American politics as they organized a variety of interests on behalf of the Republican Party. The Campaigns, Inc. was engaged in seventy-five campaigns from 1934 to 1958, winning seventy of them.[19]

By the mid-twentieth century, the main actors of political consultancy shifted from the press toward the advertising industry as the latter increasingly emerged as a significant partner of political candidates. The advertising business established an intimate relationship with the federal government during World War II when advertising executives collaborated in war propaganda campaigns.[20] Advertising agents in the postwar years explored a new market of political elections. Contemporary scholars associated political public relations with Madison Avenue. In his research on political advertising of the 1950s, political scientist Stanley Kelley found that advertising agencies exerted overwhelming influence on party propaganda, mentioning that the "present public relations departments of the Republican National Committee and the Republican Congressional Campaign Committee are, in effect, commercial public relations agencies performing political functions."[21]

Political consulting business developed throughout the first part of the twentieth century by replacing party bosses and political machines, which had slowly but gradually weakened since the Progressive Era. The old and new political forces were involved with elections in different ways. If bosses relied on immigrant communities and urban masses, political consultants were a cadre of campaign experts with scientific knowledge and professional methods. In addition, whereas local machines sustained political parties from the bottom up, political consultants took top-down approaches to achieve their goals effectively, working with political candidates, party committees, and interest groups. The Progressive reforms aimed at wiping out political corruption undermined party organizations and gave birth to a group of professionals who reached voters in new ways.

Political Consulting in the 1952 Presidential Election

In the early 1950s, Republicans employed advertising agencies more extensively than Democrats did. It was not necessarily because the GOP had an intimate relation with corporate interests, but rather because the progressive electoral reforms had a greater impact on Republicans.[22] While the Democratic Party could reach out to ethnic groups and mobilize the working class through labor unions since the 1930s, Republicans were heavily reliant on volunteers to carry out campaigns at the local level. A memorandum for Republicans succinctly pointed to this problem:

> The quarter-of-a-century political phenomenon which has seen the virtual elimination of city and courthouse political machines in both parties, together with the rise of civil service at all levels of government, has virtually destroyed effective party organization at the precinct level. . . . Today the

Democrat [*sic*] party depends on organized labor's professionals for precinct work; the Republican party depends on volunteers.[23]

For this reason, the Republican Party committees searched for new effective methods of raising funds, recruiting volunteers, and selling candidates more ardently than their counterparts. Republicans were keenly aware that the advertising industry on Madison Avenue was vital to elections in the era of new mass media. Guy G. Gabrielson, the RNC chairman in 1950, received a letter from Charles G. Thoma, who worked for Thoma & Gill Advertising in Newark, New Jersey. In his letter, Thoma urged Gabrielson to change the RNC's public relations strategy. "The Socialist-Democrats know what Republicans seemingly have never learned—that if you wish to win votes in an American election, you must talk the language of the common man.... The average American voter gives top preference to the sports page and the comic section of his newspaper. Political news, to interest him at all, must be on that level—colorful, sensational, and belligerent." Then the sender of this letter emphasized that the "matter of getting the Republican messages across is a job that should be planned and supervised by professional advertising men."[24]

By the 1952 presidential election, several newspaper editors and advertising executives, largely those in New York City, came together to the RNC, which was the nerve center for party campaigning. Emil Hurja, who had left the Roosevelt administration in 1936, became a Republican and sent advisory letters to Dwight Eisenhower in the early 1950s.[25] James Ellis of the Kudner Agency, Inc., who had worked with Senator Robert A. Taft in Ohio and brought about his sweeping reelection in 1950, was in charge of accounting for the Eisenhower campaign.[26] An iconic figure in the advertising industry of the 1950s, Rosser Reeves of the Ted Bates agency also participated in the campaign as campaign volunteer. More famously, Batten, Barton, Durstine and Osborn (BBD&O), the firm that had supervised advertisements for Thomas Dewey's unsuccessful campaign in 1948, played a central role in media strategies during the 1952 election. The BBD&O maximized the stage effects of Eisenhower's television speech and also promoted the barrage of spots, which were written by Reeves. Along with the RNC, the Citizens for Eisenhower Committee, a citizen group established to contribute to the Eisenhower campaign, also hired the advertising agency Young and Rubicam.[27]

Yet among these advertisers, Robert Humphreys was the key political consultant for the Eisenhower campaign because he created the first national campaign plan. There had been numerous examples of written campaign plans in state politics and congressional elections prior to the 1950s, but nobody had produced a blueprint for any campaigns at the national level. Judge Samuel I. Rosenman, one of Franklin D. Roosevelt's closest advisers during all his four presidential campaigns, recalled that no overall campaign plan was drawn up at that time.[28] In the words of James A. Farley, chairman of the DNC during the Roosevelt campaigns of 1932 and 1936, "[W]e had no definite campaign plan as such, during either of the two campaigns for the Presidency I managed for Mr. Roosevelt. We had in mind the way in which we would present the case for Mr. Roosevelt, and then we let it be governed by our day to day observations of the campaign itself."[29] The Democratic Party did not use any formal campaign plan to manage the Harry Truman campaign in 1948 nor Adlai Stevenson's campaigns of 1952 and 1956.[30] While the Democrats' campaign plans relied on each candidate's own decisions as well as local and state situations, Humphreys and the RNC provided a campaign plan called Document X to take central control over the entire process of the 1952 presidential election.

Document X targeted the "stay-at-homes," those who would go to the polls only when they were driven by discontent. Such voters contributed to the outcomes of several consequential elections, including the Harding campaign in the aftermath of World War I and Roosevelt's victory during the Great Depression. Humphreys calculated that, at the point of 1952, these "protest voters" outnumbered the independents by approximately forty-five million to an estimated three or four million; then he thought that if Eisenhower was to win the presidency, the Republican Party desperately needed to attract their attention.[31]

Humphreys set forth aggressive plans for the purpose of mobilizing the stay-at-homes, and his strategy was "Attack! Attack! and Attack!"[32] He demanded that the Republicans strenuously condemn the Democrats by claiming they made Americans, who used to be worried just about financial insecurity, fear for their national security in the postwar years. The campaign plan also called on Republican candidates to appeal to voters by asserting that Americans were confronted with government-sponsored inflation. Moreover, as the Cold War loomed large across the world, Humphreys recommended that candidates utilize national anxieties over communism, and that they mention that the growth of the federal government could result in the creation of a socialist state in the United States. Taking advantage of anticommunism at home and the Korean War abroad, Humphreys's Document X was designed to systematically evoke fear and anxiety among Americans in order to win the election.[33] Humphreys's plans set down the groundwork for offensive and emotional advertising drives in national political campaigns. "The Republican strategy for the presidential election of 1952—mapped by Robert Humphreys," as a political scientist pointed out, was "a classic example of an attack plan" by political consultants.[34]

Humphreys considered television the most important device for advertising the presidential candidate. Even if it was an extraordinarily expensive medium, televised advertising was a quite effective means of publicity. With the assist of other advertising professionals, the RNC televised major campaign speeches so that the public was able to listen to Eisenhower's policies, look at his appearance, and share the experience with other voters at the same time. Personal appearance was one of the key elements that Humphreys highlighted during the political contest, and he even suggested that public relations experts be assigned to each candidate at the national campaigns for the sole purpose of being alert to how a candidate was portrayed on television.[35] Other advertisers agreed with Humphreys on the significance of television for selling candidates. Invoking Thomas Dewey's broadcasting campaign in 1950, the TV Plans Board of the RNC pointed to the effectiveness of the "telethon," arguing that "No political figure who has staged a 'telethon' has ever lost an election yet."[36]

The striking impact of televised advertising was widely recognized. According to the Survey Research Center of the University of Michigan, the 1952 presidential campaign was "the first in which television played a major part." More people obtained campaign news through television during the 1952 race than ever before. Approximately 40 percent of the homes in the United States possessed television sets, but the Survey Research Center asserted that 53 percent of the population watched the campaign on TV. Furthermore, the center pointed out that many Americans regarded television as an informative source. Although television was available to only a minority of the population, it led other media in the number of persons who rated it most informative. Of those who actually watched the televised campaign, 59 percent answered that television was their most important information source.[37]

Expecting that television was the key to political advertising, the RNC spent a great amount of money on television drives. In the meeting on September 22, the TV Plans Board noted, "Just as commercial programs seek a perfect format and once discovered everything is poured into it, so it should be done in the TV presentation of General Eisenhower. Almost without exception TV industry programming heads agree on the TV method with which General Ike reaches and moves the people."[38] It was estimated that Republicans spent at least $800,000 for their spots, while Democrats expended only $77,000. Although the Republican Party usually overspent the Democratic Party in political campaigns, the RNC put heavier emphasis on televised ads in the 1952 presidential election.[39]

Democrats did not dismiss the importance of political advertisers in the 1952 presidential election. The DNC hired the Joseph Katz Company of Baltimore and New York. Katz had connections with Democrats in previous years as his Baltimore office had provided political advertisements for Democratic senatorial campaigns in Maryland, while the New York office assisted public relations for the Democratic Party in New York. In 1952, the Katz agency worked directly with the DNC by buying radio and television time and handling other media issues during the campaign.[40] Yet, while Eisenhower trusted his media consultants as significant advisers, Stevenson thought of them as a sort of technicians. According to political scientist Kathleen Hall Jamieson, Stevenson called a television consultant one night during the Democratic Convention in 1956 and asked him to fix the television set.[41]

Technological advances enhanced the role and status of advertising specialists in 1950s political campaigns. A Republican's report emphasized that "in an era of airplanes, automobiles, luxury trains, television, radio, motion pictures, newsreels, telephone, direct mail, 'slick' literature, billboards, and massive advertising techniques, political campaigning has become an extremely complex art requiring the employment of experts and skilled technicians to make the most effective use of all modern devices."[42] The 1952 election indicated the enlarged influence of political consultants such as Humphreys in the age of new mass media. However, political advertising was among diverse activities of consultants. Along with sending messages from the party committee headquarters, political consultants were engaged in organizing grassroots efforts.

Grassroots Mobilization and Direct Mail Fundraising in the 1950s

After the 1952 presidential election concluded with the victory of Eisenhower, Humphreys stayed in the RNC, directing the Eisenhower administration's publicity and GOP campaign strategy until 1960. In the 1956 contest again between Eisenhower and Stevenson, Humphreys planned to send "1 billion, 30 million messages, or more than 10 messages for each U.S. adult of voting age" at a cost of $2,200,000, which was the largest single item in the budget for the national campaign. It was "the greatest television campaign ever undertaken in so short a space of time," Humphreys stated.[43]

Along with mass media, political consultants developed two strategies for grassroots campaigns: women volunteers and mail fundraising. Humphreys not merely made use of radio, television, and film for public relations but also combined the mass media with volunteer mobilization in his extensive campaign

plans. In the early spring of 1954, leaders of Republican women's clubs came
to Washington from all over the country for a "Centennial Conference," in
which the women attended workshops on how to organize other women back
home into an army of volunteers. Each of the Republican women went back
to her local club with a neat fourteen-pound leatherette case containing a 35
mm film projector, which the Republican Congressional Campaign Committee
provided for free. Then female volunteers were able to hold political meetings
in their living rooms over coffee for an intimate group by showing campaign
films. Besides organizing the "coffee hours," women brought the projectors and
films into service clubs, women's clubs, civic organization meetings, libraries,
and churches. One Republican marveled at the grassroots campaign during the
1954 elections, saying that the volunteers toted campaign materials into "places
we never thought we could reach with a political message."[44]

Although the 1950s advertising industry was a male-dominated arena, Republican women took a part in advertising operations as well as grassroots activities.
The Republican Women in Industry and the Professions (RWIP), whose leadership included female advertising executives and public relations managers, sent a
letter to RNC Chairman Leonard W. Hall in June 1954. President of the RWIP
and a public relations promotion consultant herself, Kay Martin stressed contributions that ad women could make, claiming that the "Republican Party needed
an *organized* group of the top (mostly public relations) editors and advertising
women, who have offered to volunteer their time and best efforts to supplement
and work for the Party, it is this *very* minute." Martin went on to make her case
that the Eisenhower administration and its programs "needs to be interpreted
at grass-roots level *to* women."[45]

In response to these voices, Republican public relations professionals mapped
out a nationwide television rally of grassroots party workers with a special emphasis on women. Produced by the RNC in conjunction with members of the
Women's National Press Club and the Top Women Press Representatives of the
Nation, "Women Want to Know" was a TV program "designed for the special
tastes of the housewife." As a fifteen-minute, three-times-a-week series, the program showed the interactions of questions and answers among informed guests,
an inquisitive panel of experts, and a studio audience. The purpose of this series was to inform women of vital concerns to them, ranging from foremost
researchers in breast cancer, how their sons would be drafted, and to Geneviève
de Galard, a French nurse known as the "Angel of Dien Bien Phu." Reaching
out to housewives and female voters, "Women Want to Know" exemplified the
fusion of political advertising strategy and grassroots efforts.[46]

As historian Catherine Rymph has argued, "clubwomen" engaged in partisan politics by the 1950s. The National Federation of Republican Women promoted women's auxiliary role, and more women than ever before became an integral part in the Republican Party during the Eisenhower period. A 1950s survey demonstrated that women composed 56 percent of core GOP activists, while female activists were only 41 percent in the Democratic Party. The fifties also witnessed the decline of the American labor movement's influence at the local level. As trade unions shifted from radicalism of the 1930s toward moderation and practicality in the midcentury, American intellectuals such as C. Wright Mills and Seymour Martin Lipset were pessimistic about the political leadership of unions. Whereas the unions were integrated into a liberal coalition within the Democratic Party, they failed to mobilize white-collar workers in the years prior to the 1960s. At the same time, political consultants in the RNC successfully enlarged grassroots Republican forces by bringing women into political life.[47]

Mailing solicitation was another new dimension of grassroots campaigning throughout the 1950s. The popularization of advertising resulted in the swell of campaign budgets, which required unprecedented efforts to raise money. And both political advertising and fundraising affected the relationship between political parties and the electorate. When telecommunication became an important instrument in political campaigns, candidates and political consultants were confronted with financial issues throughout the 1950s. Television advertising was crucial for winning elections, but it was quite expensive. The expenditure on television advertising skyrocketed throughout the 1950s. In 1952, the first presidential campaign year for which political costs were calculated, the cost of television campaigns was $3 million. But the amount more than doubled to $6.6 million in 1956, growing further to $10.1 million in the 1960 race.[48] A memorandum in the early 1950s warned, "The problem was to find a sufficient amount of money to finance as much TV participation as possible and then work out a formula that would obtain maximum results for the member while treating all members on an equitable basis."[49] As such, the political use of mass media evoked a question of how to collect a war chest in campaigns.

In 1950, both Democratic and Republican campaign strategists made efforts to raise money in conventional ways. The DNC stressed the importance of personal contacts in fundraising. William M. Boyle Jr., chairman of the DNC that year, said that the key figure in the upcoming elections was "the precinct worker—the foot soldier of democracy—the man who makes the personal, human contact with the voter and discusses the issues with him and sees to it that he registers and votes."[50] This strategy worked properly as the Democratic

Party overwhelmed the GOP in fundraising in the off-year election; Democratic committees received $1,849,388 during the first eight months of 1950, while Republican committees obtained $759,298 over the same time.[51]

The RNC, too, clung tenaciously to old-fashioned fundraising in 1950. The political consultant responsible for the GOP's fundraising was Carlton G. Ketchum, founder of the Ketchum, Inc., which was the largest fundraising firm in America. As national finance director of the Republican Party from 1949 to 1957, he was credited with adopting an organized fundraising method to politics.[52] The finance committee under Ketchum emphasized face-to-face relations for fundraising campaigns in the 1950 campaigns. A fundraising manual in March 1950 stressed, "There is NO substitute for direct, personal solicitation, preferably by someone who knows the person he's asking to give. Telephone? Nowhere near as good. Letter? Seldom any good at all. When you write, you're asking for a turndown. When you present your case face to face, you're more than likely to make you point."[53]

For Ketchum, mailing was the least effective method for raising money. In his letters to state finance chairs in early March 1950, he claimed "Solicitation by letter? No! Moneyraising by letter is the least resultful [*sic*] of all methods. . . . The states with the best record of Party support, the biggest proportionate totals, are the ones that do least by letter, most by face-to-face selling."[54] Similarly, the Republican National Strategy Committee considered mailing a problem. In the 1950 congressional campaigns, it was reported that several supporters of Senator Taft wrote chain letter appeals. According to Louis Van N. Washburn of Massachusetts who received Taft's letter on this matter, although Taft was appreciative of his proponents' efforts, "he does not wish them to continue and thinks they are harmful to his campaign." Then Taft's campaign manager attempted to stop the chain letters.[55]

However, following its failure in 1950, the Republican Party exceeded the Democratic Party in their drive for campaign funds in the 1952 election. When the two parties released their reports about their national campaign funds on September 1, the Republicans had almost three times as much cash as the Democrats at hand; the RNC had a $509,709 balance while the DNC had $183,958. A journal article mentioned that the largest contribution to the GOP from June to August was made by the Texas Eisenhower Campaign Fund and other large contributors to the Republican group during the months, including John D. Rockefeller Jr. and other magnates in New York. Similarly, a report issued by the National Citizens for Eisenhower demonstrated that they were heavily dependent on the state of New York, whose donations amounted to approximately 54 percent of the total of $1,240,000 raised throughout 1952.[56]

In contrast to the Republicans' strategy to collect cash from large donors, the Democrats mobilized labor unions for its fundraising campaigns. Beardsley Ruml, a New York businessman and the chairman of the DNC's Finance Committee, revealed his plan of grassroots solicitation. The Democratic Party asked its supporters to donate at least five dollars for the 1952 campaign from October 8 to 15. When both Democrats and Republicans depended on big donations, Ruml's campaign aimed not only at raising funds but also at discovering a rich vein of small donors.[57] Yet a scandal marked this fundraising operation. The DNC received a number of small donations through labor unions, but newspapers reported that low-income workers were being forced to give their money against their will. "The money, collected in the guise of $2 and $3 'voluntary contributions,' has been exacted from the pockets of fearful unionists through threats."[58]

The GOP was not just a party of big money. Political consultants in the RNC and Citizens for Eisenhower were innovative in solicitation when they attempted to dig deeply for small contributions throughout the 1950s. One of their new instruments was direct mail, which had been used for polling and public relations. In the 1952 presidential election, Rosser Reeves of the Ted Bates Agency, who was among the most influential advertisers of the 1950s, decided which political issue was most crucial for American voters through mailing polls. After he obtained the mailing lists of *Reader's Digest*, the Eisenhower campaign sent different fundraising letters to ten groups of ten thousand individuals with each mail stressing a different issue. Then Rosser discovered that Americans overwhelmingly saw the Korean War as the most serious matter. This direct mail operation not only raised funds but also showed that voters would endorse General Eisenhower as the war hero who claimed he would bring peace to America.[59]

Walter Weintz, the circular manager of *Reader's Digest*, suggested how the volunteers of the National Citizens for Eisenhower Congressional Campaign could use direct mail. Stressing that direct mail was a new and effective method of advertising, Weintz explained why the political use of direct mail was important.

> So, why should you ever use direct mail? First of all, with direct mail you can hit everybody.... Secondly, it is the most expensive form of advertising, but it is also the most selective form.... Thirdly, it is the least expensive form of advertising in this respect; the effect you get from it costs you less than the effect you get by any other means.[60]

Direct mail was a good instrument for sending a message to many people. Moreover, unlike radio and television, direct mail was selective by finding responsive contributors. If appeal senders received letters from contributors, they could target those donors in following campaigns and raise funds more effectively.

In the 1954 congressional campaigns, unlike the RNC four years earlier, Republicans were willing to use mailing for the purpose of fundraising. Citizens for Eisenhower, which functioned as a national citizen organization for the Republicans in general, conducted fundraising campaigns by direct mail.[61] The organization searched for donors through the congressional report on the 1952 election for donors of less than $100, and a thorough list of contributors of $100 or more to the Eisenhower campaign. In addition, Citizens received a list of "best workers" for Citizens for Eisenhower–Nixon in 1952, and later made a "list of friends," which had been requested and submitted as a result of earlier appeals. The National Citizens for Eisenhower Congressional Committee sent seven letters to the 47,709 people named in the mailing lists from April to July.[62]

The 1954 finance report showed that Citizens received $85,830.73 through the direct mail solicitation with the cost of approximately $10,000 to $12,000, while they received $798,801.51 from all other solicitations.[63] The amount of funds raised by direct mail was smaller than that of other contributions. However, the Republican fundraising strategists discovered that, along with personal solicitation of big donations, they were able to rely on direct mail appeal for small contributions. In many states, although conventional ways of solicitation always raised more funds than direct mails did, the number of contributors through direct mail exceeded that of other solicitations.[64] With each contribution of $8.55 on average, the number of respondents amounted to 10,031 around the nation. The Citizen's report concluded that "those who had contributed over $100 in 1952 should be solicited personally by members of the Finance Committees, but that a mail appeal should be made to those who had contributed less than $100."[65]

Likewise, Democrats made efforts to collect small donations in 1954. The Joseph Katz Company produced advertisements for the DNC again in the 1954 elections, and the advertising accentuated small contributions. A newspaper ad demanded that voters help elect a Democratic Congress "by giving one dollar or five dollars," promising their contributions would be spent for newspaper advertisements and broadcasting. The ad also emphasized the drive was "a fight against four million dollars" that the GOP planned to spend in the race.[66] Stephen A. Mitchell, chairman of the DNC in 1954, made a plea for contribution in an ad in the *New York Times*: "[W]e have to depend on many small contributions from citizens who don't want anything for their money but good, effective government. Can you, will you, send us $2, $5, $10, $100, or more, to help carry on the campaign of 1954?"[67] More importantly, the DNC also published an advertisement titled "A New Declaration of Independence Needs Signing" during the 1954 congressional elections, calling on voters to sign checks to the committee.[68] The ad, with a picture displaying one check and a man's hands, demonstrated that Democrats adopted impersonal fundraising in addition to face-to-face relations.

Several Democrats also harnessed direct mail for fundraising by the end of the 1950s. After Mitchell left the DNC in 1956, he ran in the 1960 gubernatorial election of Illinois, during which he deployed massive campaigns of direct mail solicitation.[69] Hubert H. Humphrey too used direct mail for fundraising in his 1954 senatorial reelection. The Humphrey campaign dispatched the amount of direct mailings to the electorates and to specific groups, including farmers, school officials, and businessmen. However, even when some Democrats employed mailing solicitation, they persisted in their ideal of face-to-face grassroots campaign, believing that personal relationships had a great impact on voters' behaviors. Humphrey's campaign director Herbert J. Waters said that "the major dependence was placed on personal work rather than mailings, with organized door-to-door literature distribution."[70]

Democrats were trailing Republicans in employing political consulting for their party during the 1950s. The *New Republic* reported that while the Republican Congressional Campaign Committee launched several political advertising campaigns in 1954, the Democrats were never a match for their opponents, noting, "There will be no 'secret weapon,' no 'saturation,' and very few 'services' or Madison Avenue consultants."[71] No Democrats more clearly expressed hesitation about accepting Madison Avenue than Stevenson. When he contended with Eisenhower in 1952 and 1956, the presidential candidate incessantly denounced Republicans' advertising politics.

Why did Democrats lag behind their counterparts in introducing innovative techniques from Madison Avenue throughout the 1950s? As previously mentioned, as electoral reforms since the Progressive Era reduced the influence of political machines, political consultants offered alternative campaigning methods for Republicans, whereas Democrats could mobilize labor unions for elections. Furthermore, as David Greenberg suggested, Democrats of the 1950s were concerned over anti-intellectualism of mass media and the advertising business. The increasing popularity of television, the rise of consumer capitalism, and the new elite of business managers were "discouraging to liberals weaned on the visions of reason and refinement that Stevenson embodied."[72] The emergence of political consultants transformed campaigning in the postwar years, and it simultaneously stirred up debates over American democracy.

Criticism of Political Salesmanship

It was evident that political consultants introduced business culture into politics. In his plan for the 1952 national campaign, Robert Humphreys stressed the importance of "salesmanship" when he argued that candidates were required to learn multiple know-hows of salesmen "who would normally be welcomed visitors in almost one hundred per cent of the living-rooms of America." Leonard W. Hall, chairman of the RNC from 1953 to 1957, agreed with Humphreys, saying, "You sell your candidates and your programs the way a business sells its products."[73] Humphreys and other advertising executives in the RNC advised Eisenhower to take business techniques for selling himself to voters as effectively as he could.

The RNC continued to adopt Humphreys's strategy following the 1952 election. After Eisenhower won the presidency, the committee maintained that the effective way for political public relations was to use "the weapon of attack." It further remarked that Republicans needed to bring to the fore their message that the Roosevelt and Truman administrations led Americans into a socialized form of government and that the Eisenhower administration relied on the principles of the founders of the United States. The committee emphasized that aggressive messages were necessary to contrast Republicans with previous Democratic administrations, adding, "In other words, we need a 'selling job.'"[74] As a memorandum entitled "Political Salesmanship" clarified, selling the party's viewpoint was a key concept well into the 1954 congressional elections. The memorandum demonstrated that attack, affirm and compare, and repetition were three basic approaches to successful political salesmanship: "It is the first of these, attack, that makes the front pages and the radio and TV newscasts. It is the second of these, affirm and compare, that tells the voter that he is getting a better product than he used to get. It is the third of these, repetition, which closes the sale."[75]

Journalists shortly began to point out that the Republican Party drew on public relations methods from the business community. *Sponsor*, a trade magazine for broadcasting, radio, and television advertising buyers, covered Republicans' media strategy in the March 1952 issue. Analyzing how campaign managers directed the Thomas Dewey campaign with the support of the New York Republican Committee in the 1948 presidential election, and the Robert Taft campaign in the 1950 senatorial election, the article boldly stated that a "political candidate is a product."[76] The *New Republic* in 1954 penned that Republicans planned "'the biggest off-year campaign in history'—with the ad-men in charge." Dubbing Humphreys's campaign strategy in the year as "Operation Huckster," the writer of this article worried that Republicans would be "merchandized" as the Republican Congressional Campaign Committee and the Citizens for Eisenhower looked for guidance from Madison Avenue.[77]

Several political scientists of the 1950s shared journalists' concerns over the merchandization of political parties. Stanley Kelley's pioneering study of professional political consultants disclosed the problems of adverting business in politics. Surveying the roles of public relations professionals in electioneering, public opinion, policy making, and other activities, Kelley argued that the growing influence of political consultants could radically transform the characteristics of American politics. In the eyes of Kelley, political advertisers were changing the relationship between the public and politics through the mass media rather than personal ties to voters. Furthermore, he believed that the change of communications altered the conventional decentralized structure of a political party, offering national leaders alternative avenues to reach the electorate and providing party leadership with political power independent of local organizations. In his 1956 monograph, Kelley expressed that the "central concern of this book is the public relations man—his role in contemporary American politics and the consequences of his activities for our political life."[78]

Edward M. Glick similarly traced the transformation of political campaigns from the 1930s through the 1950s. Glick obtained his PhD in political science in 1960 by writing his dissertation on the Republican Party's strategy of the 1958 campaign. In his article, Glick observed that as GOP strategists approached Madison Avenue, Republican candidates built up partnerships with the commercial public relations specialists, while adopting an advertising-type approach to the use of the mass media, especially television. As a result, Glick emphasized, Republican politicians resorted to commercial-type advertising gimmicks. Glick also mentioned that many pundits criticized the Eisenhower administration in adopting the commercial techniques, which stressed the importance of approaching voters with irrational messages. Asking "Can Government be merchandized?," political scientists were concerned about how advertising influenced American politics.[79]

Glick and Kelley touched on the possible influences of consultants on political decision making in the 1950s. Although Glick acknowledged that the rise of commercial expertise in politics could threaten American democracy, he did not overemphasize the role of political advertising specialists in the decision-making process. In Glick's analysis, politicians, instead of advertising executives, had the ultimate responsibility for campaign strategy. When Humphreys drafted national campaign plans in 1952 and 1956, the Republican Strategy Committee dominated by politicians revised and approved his blueprints. Therefore, Glick argued, even if public relations experts infiltrated the higher echelons during the 1950s, they were influential advisers, rather than final decision makers.[80] Alternatively, Kelley was more pessimistic. He observed that public relations agents went beyond their original roles in the middle of the twentieth century. If they began as technicians, Kelley noted, their status was elevated in the business world as they became vice presidents or chief executives in their companies. Then the political scientist warned, "It is hard to see why the same trends which have brought the public relations man into political life will not also push him upward in political decision making."[81]

The image of advertisers as menacing American democracy became the mainstream in narratives of political consultants by the end of the 1950s, and it was deeply rooted in skepticism to the advertising business in the postwar years. In 1946, Frederic Wakeman's *The Hucksters* laid the groundwork for a typical perception of public relations people as it described a struggle between a heroic, creative, and competent protagonist and the advertising world. A World War II veteran Victor Norman returns home and gets a job for radio production. But soon he is disappointed with the radio public relations, which is repetitive, monotonous, and strictly prescribed by previous models. When Victor attempts to break new ground in advertising practice, other businesspeople consider his behavior a taboo and see him as mad. The advertising business that Wakeman depicted was a world with no room for creative genius. Similarly, *The Man in Gray Flannel Suit*, a 1955 novel by Sloan Wilson and a 1956 drama film based on the book, built up a vision of the advertising community in the period of conformity. Tom Rath is a public relations man at a broadcasting company and commutes from his home in a suburb of Connecticut. He is not necessarily satisfied with his circumstances; his salary is insufficient and colleagues are annoying. Still, Tom does not have other visions beyond working within the public relations business. Despite several problems in his life, the protagonist in Wilson's novel is basically content with his job and company. Cultural products on the advertising agency in the 1940s and 1950s constructed the popular perception of dull advertising agencies.[82]

These portrayals of advertisers in literature were closely associated with sociological criticism of mass society. David Riesman's *The Lonely Crowd* in 1950 was one of the most influential works on changing characteristics of American society in the postwar years. Riesman argued that while the "inner-directed" persons attempted to pursue traditional ideals such as individualism, the newly emergent "other-directed" persons adjusted their own behaviors and ideas to those surrounding them. According to Riesman, the "other-directed" character was a product of affluence and complacency in postwar America, and the personality was dominant among city dwellers, the upper middle class, and especially businessmen at big companies. In 1956, William H. Whyte analyzed a similar type of character in his book *The Organization Man.* Whyte asserted that the "organization man" believed less in Protestant ethics than in "social ethics," which accentuated a sense of belonging. The social ethics justified social pressure on individuals, dismissing any conflicts between individuals and organization. Finding numerous organization men among those in bureaucracy and mega companies, Whyte maintained that the suburb was a hotbed of the new ideology. If Victor Norman in *The Hucksters* is an "inner-directed" person at odds with other "other-directed" advertisers, Tom Rath in *The Man in Gray Flannel Suit* is a typical "organization man."[83]

Contending that these new types of individuals were obedient to organization and social pressure, critics of mass society captured popular anxieties over cadres of manipulative elites. Vance Packard's *The Hidden Persuaders* sparked controversies over the scientific methodologies of advertising. Citing the studies by Kelley, Riesman, and Whyte, Packard maintained that the Eisenhower campaign had used emotional and irrational methods to influence voters' decision making during the presidential elections of 1952 and 1956. The 1957 best seller provoked outrage at fraud and promoted conspiratorial ideas that advertisers manipulated the public through their subliminal advertising.[84]

Given that commercial ad professionals allegedly had expertise to maneuver public opinion, Kelley, Glick, and other political scientists of the 1950s were alarmed at the rise of political consultants. The criticism of mass society defined some politicians' attitude to advertising executives. When he accepted the presidential nomination at the Democratic National Convention in 1956, Stevenson expressed his concern over political advertising.

The men who run the Eisenhower Administration evidently believe that the minds of Americans can be manipulated by shows and slogans and the arts of advertising. And that conviction will, I dare say, be backed up by the greatest torrent of money ever poured out to influence an American election, poured out by men who fear nothing so much as change and who want everything to stay as it is—only more so.[85]

In contrast to Stevenson's speech, the reality was that the expertise of advertising politics was imperative in mid-twentieth-century American politics. Political consulting in the United States experienced developments throughout the nineteenth and early twentieth centuries. The rise of the middle class and the promotion of progressive reforms had undermined the influence of political machines and party bosses over their constituents by the middle of the twentieth century. The electoral transformations steadily led to candidate-centered and publicity-driven campaigns, which made political consulting more important for politicians than ever before. Professional political consultants with scientific methods superseded part-time advisers in the first part of the twentieth century. Moreover, while editors and journalists managed campaigns for polling and publicity from the nineteenth century through the first part of the twentieth century, commercial advertisers came to occupy center stage in political public relations. As a consequence, the advertising industry, especially Madison Avenue agencies, established a close relationship with politicians by the 1950s. Although both major parties adopted new techniques of campaigning over the years, it was the Republicans who rode the wave in the presidential election of 1952.

Mailing solicitation dramatically emerged with the rise of political consultants during the 1950s. The traditional and seemingly ineffective way to raise funds was transformed by the hands of public relations professionals into a necessary technique in the modern period. Indeed, direct mailing was not so important in the decade when television became increasingly dominant for sending messages, and face-to-face contacts remained the most reliable strategy for fundraising. Still, the fact that the GOP began to explore political direct mail in the postwar years would be crucial for the relationship between Republicans and conservatives, and the rightward turn of American politics in the 1970s.

CHAPTER 2

The Development of Political Direct Mail

FTER WORKING WITH POLITICAL consultant Robert Humphreys at the Republican National Committee (RNC), Arthur Summerfield resigned as the RNC chairman and was appointed by President Dwight D. Eisenhower to his cabinet as postmaster general of the United States in 1953. Summerfield was pleased by the new position because his father had been working as a letter carrier in Pinconning, Michigan, and the family had lived next door to a post office for many years. But he was simultaneously confused by messy operations of the US Postal Service (USPS). As he recalled, the Post Office Department in the early 1950s employed no single certified public accountant without any plans to develop efficiencies nor systematic training programs for more than five hundred thousand employees.[1]

The USPS went through a transformation from the 1950s to the 1960s. As political consultants adopted commercial advertising techniques for new electioneering, so did Postmaster General Summerfield modernize the postal services by introducing "the economical equipment used by businesses that must account for every penny of costs—modern conveyors, lift trucks, tying machines, label-printing machines, and many other devices new to postal operation."[2] Summerfield also proudly announced the plan of "missile mail"; on June 8, 1959, the US Navy submarine USS *Barbero* fired a Regulus I missile that landed with three thousand letters at the Naval Auxiliary Air Station in Mayport, Florida. Summerfield was quoted as saying that this project was "of historic significance to the peoples of the entire world." "Before man reaches the moon," he said, "mail will be delivered within hours from New York to California, to England, to India or to Australia by guided missiles." (However, the launch in 1959 ended up as the first and last missile mail experiment.)[3] In the early 1960s, the postal service rode the "wave of the future" as it offered facsimile mail in 1960, which instantaneously transmitted messages across the continent with the privacy perfectly preserved. Furthermore, the subsequent Postmaster General J. Edward Day adopted the Zoning Improvement Plan, or the zip code system, in 1963. The zip codes were originally designed for streamlining mail delivery, but the new system enormously contributed to the evolution of mass marketing because it was critical to quickly and effectively pinpoint potential customers.[4]

Direct mail politics developed at the intersection of the advertising industry, political consulting, and the conservative movement during the 1950s and early 1960s. The years witnessed a revolution of mailing from *mass* mail toward *personalized* mail as technological innovations made it easier for marketers to reach out to individuals, rather than groups of people, according to personal tastes. Until the early 1950s, ad agents had used letters largely for mass advertisements: mail-order catalogues were dispatched to a cluster of customers for the purpose of transmitting the same message at one time. In this sense, mass mail functioned in the same manner as the mass media including the press, radio, and television. At the same time, direct mail appeared as a personalized medium targeting particular groups of individuals. Advertising agencies accumulated a huge body of information on each customer's preference, then compiled mailing lists to select out specific customers who were likely to purchase their products. The features of personalization and selectivity differentiated direct mail from other media forms as advertisers considered the new medium to be more flexible and efficient than conventional mass mail. As commercial advertisers began to pay attention to direct mail during the 1950s, so did political consultants in political parties and social movements. While Republicans zealously needed political consultants' expertise on media operation, conservative activists ardently searched for their own channels of communication. In the postwar years, conservatism was a peripheral movement in American society. Modern American conservatism began to take shape as an organized movement when William F. Buckley Jr. established the magazine *National Review* in 1955 to assemble antiliberal intellectuals and Robert Welch founded the John Birch Society in 1958, which became the largest grassroots anticommunist organization in the nation. These conservative groups financially depended on membership fees, big donations from philanthropists, and funds raised by conservative direct mail consultants. Direct mail provided conservative fundraisers with a new approach to collect small contributions from a great number of individuals in a period when liberal politics and the mainstream media had almost no room for right-wing activists.

Demonstrating both conflicts and interactions between liberals and conservatives in direct mail politics, three political consultants were engaged with mail fundraising in New York City during the 1950s and 1960s. Among the first direct mail fundraisers, Harold L. Oram founded his own consulting firm and committed himself to liberal and anticommunist organizations after the

Second World War. Working with Oram throughout the 1950s, Marvin Lieb-man learned how to raise funds via mail and to organize political movements. Unlike Oram's dedication to liberal causes, Liebman devoted his energies to conservative anticommunist movements, engaging with Buckley's *National Review* and other right-wing groups. Finally, Richard A. Viguerie joined Liebman's fundraising campaigns in the early 1960s, and cut his teeth before becoming the central figure of conservative direct mail in the following decades. Although conservatives were more successful than liberals in direct mail solicitation, a commonality of the three consultants indicates that the development of direct mail politics was characterized by the nuanced relationship between the left and right. Over the course of the 1950s, political consultants attempted to use direct mail through bipartisan efforts to include both liberals and conservatives under the banner of anticommunism. However, direct mail politics became more par-tisan as the conservative movement gathered steam by the early 1960s.

From Mass Mail to Direct Mail

A few commercial advertisers knew of direct mail in the mid-twentieth century, but at first they never regarded it as profitable. "In the 1940's and 1950's direct mail had little intelligence," said Lester Wunderman, a prominent advertiser known as the "father of direct marketing." He was one of the first to devote attention to direct mail advertising immediately after World War II. However, as the US postal system did not yet use zip codes and the advertising industry did not actively employ computers at that time, direct mail worked poorly with mailing lists recording little information about customers except their names. Wunderman later remembered, "The system wasn't very sophisticated."[5] Other advertisers similarly pointed to the inferior status of mailing in the advertising community, saying that "it is not at all usual for a representative of a national advertising agency to be concerned with Direct Mail—except, perhaps, reluc-tantly."[6] Several entrepreneurs tried out direct mailing before putting it into practice, but as an advertiser lamented, "[T]he fact is that countless millions of letters and mailing pieces are sent out every year without benefit of tests."[7] Direct mail might have been sufficient as a local medium when small letter shops employed it in towns and cities, but advertisers failed to handle the medium on a national scale. Another reason why mail advertising did not work was that agencies used it in the same way as mass media. Advertising agencies dispatched direct mailings—or mass mailings—with uniform information to a mass of customers, but they had smaller impact on the market than radio and television advertisements did.[8] Wunderman mentioned the lack of success, saying that, in the 1940s and early 1950s, "[in] an age of mass production, mass media, mass marketing and mass consumption, mail for a time was wrongfully positioned as a mass medium."[9]

However, several innovators gradually discovered ways to use direct mail more skillfully during the 1950s. If direct mail "is properly understood and appropriately used," an advertising agency opined in 1953, it could be "a national advertising medium possessing special characteristics of selectivity and personalization."[10] In the shadow of the mass media, direct mailing did not work well if advertising firms sent out standardized letters to their customers. Instead, as an association of direct mail advertisers observed, messengers set out to deploy direct mail as a "vehicle for transmitting an advertiser's message . . . by controlled distribution direct to selected individuals."[11] Some agencies realized that they needed to "fragment" the market to identify specific groups of persons who shared common characteristics. In doing so, direct mail appealed to prospects with words that were "phrased in very explicit, very meaningful, very personal terms."[12] Wunderman clearly contrasted direct mail with mass media, arguing, "Radio and television are truly mass media. They blindly reach out for everyone—without selection and discrimination. . . . Direct mail must increasingly use its power to address specific individuals of known demography and characteristics, if it is to come to full flower."[13] As such, by pinpointing selected individuals suitable for specific products without wasting effort on the people who would never buy the products, advertisers expected that they could get "higher readership than any other form of advertising."[14]

Intimacy, which is closely associated with the functions of personalization and selectivity, also characterized direct mail advertising. Direct mail pioneer Wunderman intriguingly put the medium in a tradition of personal correspondence such as essays, poetries, and love letters, which "made letter writing more than just a way of giving news, keeping in touch or building relationships."[15] Similarly, one advertising agent highlighted the effect of direct mail to intensify readers' emotion. Quoting Charles W. Eliot's poems, "Carrier of news and knowledge" and "Messengers of sympathy and love," that are inscribed at the corners of the mail post office in Washington, DC, the advertisers pointed to mail's dual roles of communication and intimacy, and anticipated the growth of direct mail advertisements.[16] By the end of the 1950s, as advertisers meticulously analyzed, classified, and identified groups of consumers, they used direct mail advertising quite distinctively from the mass media: direct mail advertisers approached people through selectivity and intimacy instead of standardization.

Wunderman maintained that the changed nature of direct mail shifting from mass toward personal marketing was not isolated from the transformation of America from a mass society into a postindustrial society. Wunderman contended that the mass media dominated communication in an age characterized by mass production, mass consumption, and mass marketing. Newspaper, radio, and television advertising flourished throughout the 1950s, and back then they were much less expensive than in the following decades. Drawing on Daniel Bell's study, Wunderman asserted that the 1960s witnessed the postindustrial revolution that shook "the foundations of direct mail, other business and all of our lives." As the baby boom generation grew up in the postwar years, they sought the alternatives to the mass culture and influenced consumption patterns. "The era of mass everything" did not fit what the baby boomers desired, Wunderman believed.[17]

Wunderman predicted that the revolution of communication technologies would result in an age of individualization. "[We] are living in an age of repersonalization and individuation," he said. "Automation, which we feared as being anti-people, has become pro-person. . . . Our automated, computerized, electronic, information society has created opportunities for personalized, individualized selling, which will surely replace mass marketing." Wunderman particularly stressed that computers caused a seismic change in marketing and advertising. When computers recorded detailed information on hundreds of millions of consumers, the advertising theorist forecasted that new forms of marketing would evolve into direct marketing "where the advertising and buying become a single action."[18] Another advertiser made a similar case that direct mail metamorphosed consumers from a mass to individuals, claiming that "there just aren't any masses any more. People today are individuals. . . . Difficult, suspicious, slow with a dollar, hard-headed, and even ornery individuals—as a lot of politicians found out just the day before yesterday."[19]

Whereas visionary advertising agencies were creating new strategies in the postwar period, the federal government played a role in paving the way for the new marketing. The zip code was another element that altered the nature of direct mail, becoming part of the growing information industry. When the Post Office Department introduced the zip code in the early 1960s, the Advertising Council appointed Wunderman's company as the volunteer agency for the department. Although marketers and advertisers would benefit from the zip code later, the community of direct mail advertisers initially resisted the new idea. But the Post Office Department's extraordinary efforts to persuade the public and the generous media budget of the Advertising Council overcame the resistance.

Following its adoption in 1963, the advertising community reorganized their database of customers based on the zip code, then it turned out the new technique facilitated the distribution of mail and information. Combining census data and polling information, marketing companies shortly utilized zip codes for targeting individual consumers according to their preferences and lifestyles.[20]

Also known as "microtargeting," direct marketing would develop into diverse advertising technologies including telephone marketing, outreach based on precinct data, and cable television advertising, among others. But, as political scientist R. Kenneth Godwin pointed out, direct mail was the most profitable and efficient of these.[21] Some political activists turned their attention to the new commercial tool. For instance, Billy James Hargis, an ultraconservative evangelist in Oklahoma, actively employed direct mail for his anticommunist activities in the early Cold War period.[22] However, it was on Madison Avenue, the center of the American advertising industry, that direct mail politics flourished during the 1950s and 1960s.

Harold L. Oram and Liberal Anticommunism

The change of mail advertising throughout the 1950s and 1960s gradually influenced political consultants. Whereas radio and television were the mainstream of advertising in these decades, several consultants in New York City began to bring mail advertising into the political arena.[23] Harold Leon Oram was a pioneer of political direct mail on Madison Avenue. Born in 1907 in Butler, Pennsylvania, to an immigrant family who had migrated from the Austro-Hungarian Empire, Oram was initially educated in his hometown, then studied history and economics in the University of Miami in Florida for two years. After graduating, Oram stepped into the world of journalism, moving to Texas where he was involved with a weekly newspaper called the *Fort Worth Monitor*. However, as the newspaper was unsuccessful, Oram left for New York to work for other newspapers in Hartsdale and Brooklyn while he earned a degree in law from New York Law School in 1934.[24] From then on, Oram's activities were based in New York City.

Oram's career as a political activist commenced in 1936 when dictatorship and warfare loomed large in Europe. As the Spanish Civil War erupted, he joined the North American Committee to Aid Spanish Democracy in favor of the Loyalists. Oram also joined the Spanish Refugee Relief Campaign, in which as the director of publicity and fundraising he made efforts to raise aid for Spanish refugees who left Spain after Francisco Franco rose to power.[25] In September

1939, Oram founded his own fundraising company called Consultants in Fund Raising, which was soon renamed Harold L. Oram, Inc. Before he enlisted in the army in 1942, he was responsible for funding projects to aid refugees and fight fascism in Europe. For instance, the Emergency Rescue Committee was engaged in assisting anti-Nazi intellectuals and activists. Oram's clients before World War II included the National Association for the Advancement of Colored People Legal Defense and Educational Fund.

After he came back from military service in 1946, Oram continued to involve himself with refugee relief and liberal activism. As the Cold War intensified from the late 1940s, Oram's attention shifted from antifascism to anticommunism with his interests extending to East Asia. Among the most notable examples of his philanthropic activities in the postwar era were the fundraising campaigns for Aid Refugee Chinese Intellectuals (ARCI), American Friends of Vietnam, and Committee of One Million, all of which were programs to aid anticommunists in East Asia. Simultaneously, Oram remained involved with activities for European refugees, collaborating with the Citizen's Committee for Displaced Persons, which was aimed at securing "emergency legislation permitting the United States to admit its fair share of Europe's displaced persons." Oram also dedicated efforts to endorsing the United Nations by fundraising for the American Association for the United Nations (AAUN). His stance as a liberal anticommunist was evident as letters on behalf of these organizations had the signatures of prominent Democratic figures such as James A. Farley and Eleanor Roosevelt.[26]

Oram rose to prominence as a guru of mail fundraising in postwar politics, drawing on ideas and methodologies from commercial mail advertisers. In his letter to a client in May 1947, Oram indicated that he had raised approximately $775,000 after returning from the army in January 1946. Breaking down this total, he revealed that most of the money came from mail solicitation: $475,000 was raised through mailings, $175,000 through dinner and luncheon meetings, $60,000 by one telegraphic appeal, $50,000 through personal solicitation, and $15,000 via advertisements. In this letter, Oram strongly recommended fundraising via "the mass media appeals," which were solicitation by telegraph, mailing, and advertising, adding that "[s]uch a mass media campaign which is the only one I can recommend as having any possibility of success in the brief time, involves a considerable expense in comparison to an organized appeal by personal approach to a carefully selected list of large donors."[27] Although Oram regarded mail fundraising as a mass media approach, his solicitation methods relied on selectivity that direct marketers emphasized in the 1950s.

Oram's techniques of mail fundraising also built on the intimate approach of direct marketing. The sense of urgency characterized fundraising letters sent by the Harold L. Oram, Inc. Appeals usually began with the following words: "Every American is faced by the challenge of impending war, for many of us the possibility of the third great war in our lifetime."[28] Another appeal similarly urged letter receivers to take some actions by stating, "We believe that the rate of change in the modern world has produced a new predicament for man. Greater changes are coming in the future than any we have experienced. This Age of Change may be marked by violence and chaos, or it may be an Age of Reason."[29] While emphasizing the menace of the Cold War and the rapid transformations of the modern age, Oram's mailings impelled readers to take action, claiming that their choices were crucial for the world. One of his fundraising letters said, "Today we are making a historic choice which, in the end, will determine the fate of all mankind. By our words and our actions, we are deciding irreparably for war or for peace." The appeal also stressed, "We are today entering a most dangerous period. Recent events are already threatening to divide the world into two hostile camps."[30] As political scientists have pointed out, threatening language is important for direct mail because it effectively urges readers to take immediate action. Emotion, researchers have argued, is a key element. "The message has to be extreme, has to be overblown; it really has to be kind of rough."[31]

Whereas gloomy anticommunism dominated Oram's solicitation letters, nonpartisanship characterized Oram's fundraising campaigns. As President Harry Truman announced that he would attempt to contain Soviet's threats to Greece and Turkey in May 1947, ideological tensions increasingly grew between the United States and the Soviet Union. Nevertheless, Oram's appeal of September 2, 1947, on behalf of the AAUN, called for the cooperation of America with Russia. "We are today entering a most dangerous period," said the letter, but it added that the success of the United Nations as a universal organization hinged on Soviet–American cooperation from the outset. The only way to prevent warfare, Oram's letter stressed, was to convince Russian leaders that "cooperation, rather than antagonism, between the West and the East, is in their own interest."[32] Another mailing for the AAUN went so far as to say that a third world war was "more probable so long as our country is confused and divided by partisan passion."[33] One solicitation appeal on behalf of the Center for the Study of Democratic Institutions highlighted nonpartisanship as it stated that anybody was entitled to join programs for democracy. "We have ignored the labels of 'right-wing' and 'left-wing.' We have secured the participation of Catholics, Protestants, Jews, secularists, men who call themselves 'radicals' and others who regard themselves as 'conservatives.'" Oram and his clients had no qualms about involving any religious and ideological groups in their campaigns. The appeal also boasted that the center had visitors from Western Europe, Latin America, South Asia, and even the Soviet Union.[34]

Over the course of the 1950s and 1960s, Oram was working together with diverse agencies. Oram sent out his solicitation letters to government, businesses, foundations, and many individuals as potential donors for anticommunist causes. His clients were not only anticommunists such as Walter H. Judd, a conservative anticommunist congressman who supported the Chinese nationalist government, but also liberal activists and politicians including the Reverend Martin Luther King Jr., William Fulbright, and George McGovern, and a long list of others.[35] According to Henry Goldstein, the current president of the Oram, Inc., the firm has served "liberal and left-wing counter-cultural organizations."[36] In the course of his philanthropic activities, Oram developed manifold fundraising techniques. He was responsible for direct mail appeals and also credited as the first to employ full-page advertisements in newspapers such as the *New York Times*. Moreover, he assembled and compiled lists of donors by using *Who's Who* as a mailing list. Using cutting-edge information technology, Oram accumulated the required data to seek potential contributors and made political mailing more efficient than ever before. Oram remained involved with liberal politics throughout his career of political consulting, yet his fundraising laid the groundwork for direct mail politics, including both liberals and conservatives.

Marvin Liebman and Conservative Anticommunism

In the early 1950s, Marvin Liebman took a step into direct mail politics on Madison Avenue. Born in 1923 in Brooklyn, New York, the young Jewish American was a communist in his youth. As a high school student in Brooklyn, Liebman was invited by his civics teacher to the American Students Union where he took part in far-left politics. Shortly, he joined the Young Communist League, which was an affiliate of the American Youth Congress that had many other communist youth fronts. The young Liebman became more profoundly engaged in pre–World War II communism when he came under the discipline of the Communist Party. He helped craft propaganda for the party, socialized with left-wing writers, and developed his affections for art and politics. "I was good at politics," Liebman later said, "and the Communists were putting on the best political show. I fell in them."[37]

Liebman enrolled at New York University. Yet he shortly left the university and plunged himself into the circle of the literary left in Greenwich Village. As the United States joined World War II, Liebman was drafted into the US Army Air Corps in 1942, serving in the army in North Africa and Italy until 1945. By the end of the war, Liebman became engaged with Zionism. In 1946, he was associated with the American League for a Free Palestine in Europe and Palestine. By early 1947, an anti-imperialist impulse pushed him to sign on with an Israeli military group known as the Irgun, whose aims were to liberate Palestine from British rule and to relocate Jewish refugees from Europe. After returning to the United States, Liebman helped raise money for the American League for a Free Palestine, then he became a fundraiser for the United Jewish Appeal (UJA), a successful charitable organization founded by Jewish Americans, and the American Fund for Israel Institutions. The UJA sent Liebman to its fund-raising school, opening the door for his political consulting career.[38]

While Liebman developed his activism following World War II, his communist fervor faded away. In 1946, the Communist Party leader Earl Browder was dismissed from the party hierarchy after being accused of his attempt to achieve the cooperation between capitalists and communists during the war. Liebman, who adored Browder as a mentor and hero, realized that it was ideologically and emotionally hard to shift smoothly from the Popular Front to the Cold War. But it did not mean that his passion for politics died out. In 1948, Liebman headed for California and joined the campaign of Henry Wallace, whom he admired. At the same time when Liebman was engaged in this political campaign, he pursued his desire to be an artist and was temporarily employed as a screenwriter in Hollywood. Liebman's odyssey to the West Coast was short as he came back home to Brooklyn in 1951. When he reached New York, the May Day parade was held. Walking along with many other participants, however, Liebman noticed that he was "bored by the slogans, by the songs, and most of all, by the desperate earnestness."[39]

Following a suggestion by a member of Americans for Democratic Action in Los Angeles, Liebman visited Harold L. Oram, Inc. immediately after he returned to New York. Oram decided to employ the young ex-communist, saying, "I just may be able to turn you from an agitator into a fund-raiser."[40] In his autobiography, Liebman recalled that he had learned all he knew about fundraising when he was working with Oram. The walls of Oram's office were lined with metal shelves and drawers holding thousands of three-by-five cards, and each one was hand-typed with a name, address, and other pertinent information. Even though almost everything was done by hand and time consuming at the time, this approach was relatively successful. Liebman not only learned Oram's solicitation methods but also improved them. Understanding that personalization was the key to successful direct mailing, Liebman came up with two ideas to make envelopes look more personal. He had volunteers at the office hand-write the addresses so that recipients would pay special attention to the appeals, and also affixed a first-class stamp instead of a Pitney-Bowes postage imprint. Working with Liebman during the 1950s, Oram regarded the young fundraiser's adroitness so highly that he promoted Liebman to vice president of Harold L. Oram, Inc.[41]

Bipartisanship defined Liebman's direct mail fundraising in the early 1950s. In the first years at Oram's fundraising firm, Liebman had many occasions to work with liberals, partly due to Oram's liberal policy and probably also because of Liebman's own experience of converting from communism. The first project Oram gave him was raising funds for the Liberal Party, the political arm of two major New York labor unions, the International Ladies' Garment Workers Union (ILGWU) and the Amalgamated Hatters Union. Liebman sent out approximately seventeen thousand letters to raise funds. He had no hesitation in working with liberals to develop a large network of anticommunists. He said, "[W]henever I organized a 'conservative' or 'anticommunist' group, I followed Oram's example and tried to include as many 'liberals' as I could on the letterhead to create the broadest possible base of support." The signature of an anticommunist organization with which Oram and Liebman were involved clearly demonstrated diverse supporters. It included poets Conrad Aiken and Siegfried Sassoon, cellist Pablo Casals, novelist John Dos Passos, psychologist Carl Jung, architect Walter Gropius, physicist Robert Oppenheimer, philosopher Bertrand Russell, historian Arthur Schlesinger, and the American Socialist Party leader Norman Thomas, to name only the most notable.[42]

But Liebman's activities at Oram, Inc. were linked primarily to anticommunism. As the second project for Liebman, Oram put him in charge of solicitation for the International Rescue Committee (IRC). Having been dedicated to antifascism and rescuing refugees from Nazi Germany during the Second World War, the IRC transformed itself toward a liberal and anticommunist organization, giving emergency assistance to over one hundred thousand people from Eastern Europe communist regimes, including East Germany, Czechoslovakia, Yugoslavia, Poland, and Hungary. Oram's firm raised money for the IRC by means of mail, telegraph, advertising, and other ways. Oram sent Liebman to California to arrange fundraising meetings for Elinor Lipper, who had published a book on her seven-year experiences in Soviet prison camps. Liebman flew to the West and set up a large rally, which San Francisco mayor and other local notables attended, and the IRC successfully raised funds by the time Lipper completed her West Coast tour.[43]

Another anticommunist organization for which Liebman raised funds was the Aid Refugee Chinese Intellectuals (ARCI). Founded in 1952, the chief aims of the ARCI included resettlement, reemployment, and rehabilitation for Chinese intellectuals who had left the People's Republic of China. In 1952, Liebman founded offices in New York City, Hong Kong, and Taiwan, then initiated the operations to help refugees. With financial support from the CIA, the ARCI helped over 15,000 Chinese intellectuals leave the mainland for Hong Kong, 14,000 college graduates and their families relocate to Taiwan, and 2,500 refugees relocate in the United States and 1,000 in other countries. Unlike the two previous solicitation drives for the Liberal Party and the IRC, Liebman not only raised funds but also organized the project. He prepared an outline of the necessary steps and created the format based largely on his knowledge of how the left was organized. The establishment of the ARCI also provided Liebman with an opportunity to enlarge his network with other anticommunists as he allied with such figures as anticommunist Congressman Walter Judd and Christopher Emmet, who was Oram's friend and a staunch anticommunist.[44]

Solicitation for the ARCI indicated the nature of Harold L. Oram, Inc., demonstrating how diverse individuals and institutions were involved in its fundraising networks. To arouse sympathy among American intellectuals, the ARCI sent appeals to university presidents around the nation. Meanwhile, the organization also called on many citizens, politicians, and philanthropists to donate money for Chinese refugees. Many recipients sent back small checks such as $1, $3, or $5, while others donated a larger amount of money such as $750. The Lilly Endowment, a philanthropic institution that sent $25,000 to the ARCI, was one of the big contributors on Oram's mailing list.[45] Liebman also mailed out appeals to foundations including the Ford Foundation, the Rockefeller Foundation, the Carnegie Corporation, the Pew Memorial Foundation, and the Rockefeller Brothers Fund. The federal government, too, was one of the most important sponsors for the ARCI as the Department of State poured $250,000 into the ARCI. Sending out solicitation letters to sundry individuals and institutions, direct mail fundraising by Oram, Inc. was dependent on both small and large contributions.[46]

The respondents sent back not only checks but also letters to express their own voices. Several contributors opined in their letters that financial aid was not enough to fight communism. A recipient of the ARCI's appeal claimed that the organization could give Chinese refugees "a chance to protect their own form of government," saying, "Instead of starving in Hong Kong they might welcome the chance to be given uniforms and equipment and be transferred to the Korean front to defend their ideals and pull a lot of our boys out of there."[47] Another person made a similar case in his letter by arguing, "There is no question in my mind but that we should have used all these anti-Communists in Formosa, Hong Kong or elsewhere—long ago in the fight in Korea, as they wanted to be used."[48] These responses revealed that several supporters wanted more action rather than philanthropic assistance in order to win the Cold War in East Asia.

Within the ARCI, the same controversies revolved around what it ought to do for anticommunist activities. As the organization grew in size, tensions and conflicts appeared between the "philanthropist" sponsors and the "activist" anticommunists. The philanthropists, including Oram and most of the directors, were the mainstream of the ARCI. And Liebman and other activists were frustrated by the philanthropic majority, believing that the ARCI as a political organization could overthrow Communist China by assisting armed forces from Taiwan under the leadership of Chiang Kai-shek. Liebman attempted to persuade other directors to change the group's aim, sending a memorandum to the ARCI executive committee. In the memo, Liebman stressed that the emergency or "newness" of the problem was essential for successful fundraising. He claimed that initial efforts to resettle Chinese refugees had been once urgent for many Americans, but "it has lost its novelty for the people who are our potential supporters." Therefore, he suggested the ARCI required an approach to help the Chinese refugees "in every way possible to reconstruct a free society."[49] However, Oram and many members did not change their humanitarian approach. They restated the ARCI's aims and objectives to reconfirm that all of the organization's projects "shall be concerned with resettlement or be directly contributory to facilitating as rapidly as possible the primary aim of resettlement."[50]

While Oram was engaged in fundraising for liberal causes, Liebman gradually leaned toward more activist and conservative anticommunism throughout the 1950s. In 1953, Liebman started to organize a new anticommunist conservative group while he continued to work at Oram, Inc. Following the armistice of the Korean War in July, Liebman set up a small meeting at New York's University Club in September. Along with several members of the ARCI, Liebman, Emmet, Judd, and Charles Edison, the inventor Thomas Edison's son and former New Jersey governor, discussed new problems after the war. Their primary concern was the issue of whether the international community should recognize the People's Republic of China as the legitimate regime of China, and whether

the United Nations should admit it. The members of the meeting tried to stem
the wave of communism in Asia by denying Communist China's admission to
the United Nations. Liebman and other participants decided that the goal of
the organization was to influence public opinion through the media, publishing
their own newsletter and booklets and using radio spots and newspaper ads.
They also planned lobbying activities to promote their campaign. Setting up a
headquarters on West 40th Street in New York, Liebman named the new organization the Committee of One Million. Then, as usual, Liebman initiated
mail solicitation.[51]

Appeals of the Committee of One Million suggested that bipartisanship still
characterized Liebman's fundraising after he shifted toward activist anticommunism. An appeal contended, "The Democrat and the Republican parties . . . have
a unique opportunity to take the issue of the admission of Communist China
to the United Nations out of American partisan politics." Adding that such
bipartisan action would prove the solidity of American sentiments on the issue,
Liebman tried to take inclusive approaches to anticommunism.[52] Another letter
similarly held that the relationship of the United States with the People's Republic of China was unique because "it commands almost universal bi-partisan
agreement." The letter emphasized that the bipartisanship was true under any
circumstances, suggesting this particular issue was of supreme importance for
American foreign policy.[53] Direct mailings of the committee incessantly stressed
that the policy against the People's Republic of China was "so widely supported
as our policy" in the United States that "every major American organization"
adopted expressions against Communist China and "all the American people"
refuted the appeasement of communism in East Asia.[54] Starting in 1953, the
Committee of One Million dispatched direct mail campaigns to call for support among Americans.

Over two hundred recipients responded to the first appeal and signed its
statement: forty-nine members of Congress, including twenty-three Democrats,
coupled with twelve governors, thirty-three business magnates, twenty retired
generals and admirals, fourteen religious leaders, and twenty-two scientists and
educators. Many other individuals followed suit. One letter was sent to the
Committee of One Million by a mother who lost her son in the Korean War.
The mother joined the organization primarily due to the POW issue. While
the son was fighting on the Korean Peninsula as a member of the 45th Infantry
Division, he was reported "missing in action" on November 30, 1952. Believing
that her son was captured by Chinese communists, the mother condemned that
the People's Republic of China for not announcing he was dead or whether he

was a prisoner. Furthermore, she claimed that the United States joined in this effort "to wipe out the reality of my son."[55]

The Committee of One Million made efforts to mobilize the "grass roots sentiments" of American anticommunism in various ways. On October 22, 1953, the committee started a public campaign to distribute approximately 240,000 copies of a petition that the People's Republic of China shall not be admitted to the UN, and received about 150,000 signatures by January 1954. The committee finally sent the signed petition with the 1,032,017 signatures to President Eisenhower in 1955. The organization mentioned that their petition campaign gave impetus to similar drives in other countries including Canada, the Philippines, and Indonesia.[56] Liebman also launched full-page advertisements in nationally known newspapers such as the *New York Times* and the *Washington Post*.[57] In 1956, the Committee of One Million was working to have both Democratic and Republican national conventions adopt a joint plank against any move for recognition of China or resumption of trade with her. The committee set out a greater campaign by sending out a propaganda kit to every person who ran for federal office and arranging conferences at universities to promote the anti-Beijing campaign among intellectuals and students.[58]

Liebman's activist anticommunism went along with the transformation of modern conservatism's foreign policy from isolationism to fervent anticommunism overseas. In the mid-1940s, conservative Republicans, particularly Senator Robert Taft, had challenged the strategy of interventionism by voting against American participation in the International Monetary Fund, the World Bank, and the North Atlantic Treaty Organization. Conservative Republicans in both houses also attempted to repudiate the Bretton Woods arrangements, a $3.75 billion loan for the recovery of Britain, and the Marshall Plan, all of which looked to the conservatives like the expansion of the federal government on a global scale. However, with the armistice of the Korean War and the death of Senator Taft in July 1953, conservative politicians began to highlight engaged nationalism. Senator William Knowland of California took a leading role in making conservatives fervent Cold War warriors, and conservatives became more hawkish than ever in American foreign policy.[59]

Liebman's political consulting converged on the formation of intellectual conservatism advanced by William F. Buckley. Buckley figured in modern American conservatism when he published his book *God and Man at Yale* in 1951 while he was still a student at Yale University. *Time* magazine writer Willi Schlamm, who conceived the idea of a new conservative journal, approached Buckley and asked him to become the journal's editor in chief. They began to organize an intellectual forum for American conservatives by recruiting anticommunists, libertarians opposing big government in favor of individual liberties and the free enterprise system, and conservatives embracing religious and traditional values.[60]

Buckley and Schlamm made efforts to collect funds for the undertaking. According to Liebman, in 1955 Oram received Buckley's solicitation letter for his new magazine project, and Oram asked Liebman to meet with the young conservative. Although he was impressed by Buckley's vigor and intelligence, Liebman thought that the idea of publishing a new conservative journal would be unsuccessful due to the scarcity of a conservative audience in the mid-1950s.[61] Since Buckley founded *National Review* (initially called *National Weekly*) in late 1955, the enterprise was financially shaky all the time. Upon launching *National Review*, Buckley borrowed $100,000 from his father and received donations from Massachusetts candy manufacturer Robert Welch, Southern California's oil magnate Henry Salvatori, Eastern Airlines CEO Eddie Rickenbacker, and other conservative businesspeople. Nevertheless, Buckley's magazine was continually short of cash, and he attempted to cover the deficits by soliciting tax-exempt donations for nonprofit groups, which he then turned over to *National Review*.[62]

Still, *National Review* slowly established itself as a force in modern American conservatism as it gradually gave shape to ideas alternative to liberalism. At first, the average circulation of the magazine was relatively small with the readership reaching 30,000 in 1960, while Billy Graham's *Christianity Today* had a paid circulation of 150,000 by the early 1960s. Yet *National Review* emerged as a forum of opinion and disputation, contributing to the fusion of eclectic conservative philosophies, such as anticommunism, traditionalism, and libertarianism, which had common goals but sometimes conflicted with each other. Contributors to Buckley's magazine included ex-Marxist anticommunists, such as Whittaker Chambers, James Burnham, and Frank Meyer, as well as traditionalists like Russell Kirk. Many *National Review* editors and writers were Catholic, including Buckley himself and L. Brent Bozell, while Jewish Americans appeared on the original masthead of the journal. As *National Review* provided channels of communication and opportunities to discuss conservatism from different strands of ideas, the magazine formed a conservative intellectual establishment, serving as the backbone of the conservative movement.[63]

Liebman became Buckley's close friend shortly after they met. In 1957, he founded his own public relations firm, Marvin Liebman Associates, Inc., in New York. Known as the "wizard of direct mail fundraising," Liebman assisted Buckley as the publicity arm of *National Review*, actively raising money for anticommunism and the nascent conservative movement in general. Buckley and Liebman collaborated in organizing several conservative groups during the 1960s. After Fidel Castro established the communist regime in Cuba, the two conservative activists organized the Committee for the Monroe Doctrine to defend America's right to intervene militarily in the island nation and other countries of the Western Hemisphere. Liebman and Buckley also created the National Committee Against the Treaty of Moscow that opposed ratification of the treaty to ban the testing of nuclear weapons.[64] In his political career, Liebman's personality as a political entrepreneur was notable, working behind the scenes rather than moving forward to the center stage. He noted, "Part of the style I had developed was to keep out of the limelight and let other more prestigious people carry my plans. These techniques not only proved effective, it gave me an invigorating sense of power over events."[65]

Young Americans for Freedom (YAF) was another organization Buckley and Liebman founded.[66] As conservative students organized the Youth for Goldwater movement in May 1960, the *National Review* circle offered operational support for the youth. The political journal ran advertisements soliciting financial aid for the young conservatives. Elder conservatives also supported the leadership of newly emerging activists. For instance, David Franke, a student at Delmar Community College in Corpus Christi, Texas, who worked as an editor of *The Individualist* published by the Intercollegiate Society of Individualists (ISI), was hired as an intern at *National Review*. Liebman hired Doug Caddy at the Marvin Liebman Associates shortly after he graduated from Georgetown in the spring of 1960. Buckley realized that conservatives needed to develop conservatism from an intellectual circle toward a social movement by organizing conservative students across the country.[67]

Buckley issued a call for a meeting to form a new organization for the youth at his estate in Sharon, Connecticut. From September 9 to 11, 1960, approximately one hundred young conservatives gathered at the Sharon conference, in which the young people managed discussions but the *National Review* crowd indirectly influenced the participants. Caddy carried out much of the planning at the conference, Franke took the lead in discussions about the organization, and Bozell, Buckley's brother-in-law, gave a speech titled "Why a Conservative Political Youth Organization Is Needed," emphasizing the necessity of political movements in conservative politics.[68] M. Stanton Evans, editor of the *Indianapolis News*, drafted the "Sharon Statement," which represented YAF's three strands of ideologies. It stressed traditionalism, stating that "individual use of his God-given free will" was fundamental to humankind. The statement also reflected libertarian confidence in the free market and small government. But at the same time, it claimed America's mission to fight against worldwide commu-nism, which seemed to contradict the principle of limiting government. Fusing the three ideologies, the Sharon Statement declared the establishment of YAF and marked the emergence of a student activist movement in conservatism, like the Port Huron Statement in 1962 for the formation of Students for a Demo-cratic Society on the left.[69]

Liebman was intimately associated with YAF from its foundation. He pro-vided his office facilities when Caddy organized the Sharon conference. After YAF was established, Liebman not only offered his office on lower Madison Ave-nue for the national board but also gave financial support for the young activists. When YAF set out to publish its magazine, the *New Guard*, in March 1961, Liebman supported the publication with logistics. *National Review* publisher William A. Rusher was concerned that Liebman spoiled YAF members like "a rich and adoring uncle."[70] Meanwhile, despite Liebman's generosity, some YAF activists were frustrated with the elder mentor, claiming that Liebman embez-zled YAF's funds for his other fundraising enterprises. After the internal conflict occurred within the youth organization, Liebman resigned in January 1962.[71]

As a political consultant, Liebman continued to be engaged in conservatism by raising funds and organizing other groups. Although the Committee of One Million, *National Review*, and YAF were confronted with financial crises over the years, these groups promoted the rise of the conservative movement in American society. YAF grew to a national vehicle for young conservatives discontented with liberal politics, opening the way for a new generation of right-wing activists to enter the political arena. Among the new conservatives was a Texan who would be a central figure of conservatism as the prominent direct mail fundraiser by the 1970s.

Richard A. Viguerie and Conservatism in the Early 1960s

While Liebman had learned fundraising for the anticommunist cause by work-ing with the liberal Oram, Richard Viguerie developed his direct mail solici-tation solely for conservative politics.[72] Viguerie's autobiography demonstrates that he shared a similar background with many other young conservatives of the 1960s, and simultaneously he had a peculiar identity as a political consultant. Viguerie was born to a Catholic family outside Houston, Texas, in 1933. His parents were of Louisiana French descent, and his mother retained a little of her Cajun accent. The Viguerie family had earned its living in real estate in south Louisiana, but they had lost almost everything in the financial panic of the early

1920s. Viguerie's parents moved to Texas in 1929 immediately before the Great Depression. According to Viguerie, his family had little higher education. His father had no college education while his mother had one year of college. Despite his educational background, Viguerie's father became a manager of Shell Oil Co. Viguerie himself went to Texas A&I and then to the University of Houston, where he received his BS in political science with a minor in economics. Dreaming to be a politician in Washington, Viguerie first wanted to be an engineer because he thought that he could make a great deal of money. But once he realized he was not good at algebra, his aims shifted toward law. However, after getting many Cs and Ds, Viguerie decided to enlist in the US Army Reserve program in March 1957 and served six months of active duty at Fort Chaffee, Arkansas. At the end of the 1960s, he got a job as a clerk in an oil company.[73]

Anticommunism was kindled in Viguerie's mind during the 1950s through the influence of political figures such as Douglas MacArthur and Joseph McCarthy. He worked for the Eisenhower campaign in 1952 and 1956 as chairman of the Harris County Young Republicans. An anecdote showed that the conservative cause was more important than party politics for Viguerie. One day he invited Jack Cox, a solid conservative Democrat in Texas, to speak at a Young Republicans barbecue. While several people criticized Viguerie because Cox was not a Republican, Viguerie claimed that he did not understand why they accused him. He involved himself in conservative politics again in 1960, when he was named Harris County campaign chairman for Republican John Tower who challenged Lyndon Johnson for a seat in the US Senate. Viguerie helped write one-page fundraising letters for the Republican candidate. Tower ended up losing the election, receiving 41 percent of the vote, but he won the special election for Johnson's old seat in early 1961.[74]

In 1961, Viguerie responded to a classified advertisement in *National Review*, which required four field men, and he decided to move from Texas to New York. At first, Viguerie met with *National Review* publisher William A. Rusher. Rusher interviewed Viguerie for the position as executive secretary of Young Americans for Freedom. And then Rusher introduced Viguerie to Liebman, who offered his office to YAF and would become Viguerie's mentor for fundraising. As Viguerie was learning how to effectively collect money and gain support during the early 1960s, the young political fundraiser became known as "the 'new' Liebman" in conservative circles.[75]

Viguerie's ideological, religious, and social backgrounds—anticommunism, Catholicism, the South, and relatively poor educational level—were shared by many other conservatives in the 1960s.[76] However, a unique feature of Viguerie's

activity was notable during this time in YAF. Viguerie was surprised to find that
the organization, not one year old, was $20,000 in debt with only two thousand
paid-up members, although YAF claimed a membership of twenty-five thousand, and just a couple of weeks' operating money remained on hand. So he
got involved in making the student group financially successful.[77] In his words,
"Plenty of young conservatives were boning up on conservative philosophy, and
many others were studying the technique of political organization. Nobody . . .
was studying how to *sell* conservatism to the American people." Viguerie acknowledged that he was not able to be a prominent political intellectual. He was
instead determined to "stick to your brand" and to be the best "marketer" in conservative politics. Therefore, he perused many books on marketing and psychology rather than politics or political philosophy. He even confessed that he barely
read *National Review* or *Human Events*.[78] Viguerie as a political consultant used
rhetoric, including several commercial vocabularies such as "sell," "market," and
"branding." By doing so, he forged his identity as a political consultant, bridging
politics with business through rhetoric and methodology.

With his unique orientation toward political advertising within the conservative movement in the early 1960s, it was not accidental that Viguerie shortly
noticed the potential of direct mail. His direct mailings for YAF showed his
inclination for political business as well as the conservative movement. From
1961 to 1963, as administrative secretary of YAF, Viguerie dispatched letters several times.[79] A mailing in November 1961, for example, recommended that YAF
members subscribe to *National Review* and purchase *Revolt on the Campus* written by M. Stanton Evans, who had drafted the Sharon Statement when YAF was
founded in 1961. Advertising the political magazine and monograph as the best
conservative publications in scope and literary quality, Viguerie's letter stressed
the significance of distributing conservative philosophies to individuals, noting,
"In the past, conservatives have not been as effective as they might have been,
because they failed to *sell themselves* and their point of view on a personal basis
to all segments of the population."[80] Another mailing of March 22, 1962, also
claimed that what the United States needed was "dynamic young conservative
leadership capable of *selling conservative ideas* to the American voter," as it reported that more than 180,000 conservatives gathered in Madison Square Garden on March 2, 1962, for the "Rally for World Liberation from Communism"
sponsored by YAF.[81] The New York City rally had major addresses delivered by
well-known conservatives such as senators Barry Goldwater, Strom Thurmond,
and John Tower, and delegations represented a young generation of American
conservatives from many universities. Viguerie's other direct mailings informed

YAF members of the organization's activities, including producing anticommunist films, establishing local chapters around the country, and staging demonstrations in several states. His appeals at the same time called for donations to sustain these undertakings. "YAF's treasury is now empty and the entire future of Young Americans for Freedom is endangered. If additional contributions are not forthcoming immediately from our past supporters, our work may have to cease."[82]

As YAF aimed at promoting conservatism on campuses, Viguerie's direct mailings also highlighted conservatives' struggles with the dominance of liberalism in American universities. One of the main targets of YAF was the National Student Association (NSA), a national confederation of college student governments dominated by liberals.[83] A direct mailing to YAF members raised the question, "Are American students really moving to the left?" "But the NSA is in real trouble," the letter claimed, and mentioned that YAF had launched a nationwide campaign to drive NSA off of the campuses, creating a report on the NSA and urging schools to withdraw from "the far left-wing" organization.[84] Saying "Young Americans for Freedom is engaged in a critical battle with the left-wing professors in our nation's colleges and universities for the minds of our youth," another solicitation appeal emphasized the necessity of organizing young conservatives to resist the influence of "the left-wingers."[85] Even though YAF attempted to remain a nonpartisan organization without commitment to the Republican Party, partisan rhetoric characterized its activities and direct mail politics that emphasized ideological battles between liberalism and conservatism in American politics.

***

Imported from the advertising industry on Madison Avenue, direct mail was increasingly colored by partisanship in American politics throughout the 1950s. New York political consultants who were not affiliated with political parties, such as Harold Oram, Marvin Liebman, and Richard Viguerie, demonstrated how direct mail politics developed in the hands of both liberals and conservatives in the postwar years. Fundraisers initially employed the medium for bipartisan drives or purposes that leftists and rightists could share. Yet coupled with the resurgence of the conservative movement, ideological struggles came to characterize direct mail politics by the time Viguerie started his solicitation activities in New York in the early 1960s. However, nothing revealed as clearly the ideological conflicts between liberals and conservatives during the sixties as the Goldwater movement in the presidential election of 1964.

CHAPTER 3

The Presidential Election of 1964

B
ARRY M. GOLDWATER'S ESTATE stood in Paradise Valley, a wealthy suburb near Phoenix, Arizona. Naming the home *Be-Nun-I-Kin*, "the house atop the hill" in the Navajo language, Goldwater used to enjoy a panoramic view of Camelback Mountain and the bleak red desert from its terrace. The main room was a sunken library-living room that held a small collection of books on Arizona and Indian lore. This space also had the owner's desk and ham radio facilities with which he could monitor aviation frequencies and get complete weather reports. A stone wall in the living room opened for a movie projector and a screen was lowered automatically from the ceiling. Outside, a US flag flew from a pole that electronically raised the flag at dawn and lowered it at sunset. "Senator Goldwater loves gadgets, and his home and grounds are filled with them," a newspaper reporter remarked.[1]

The 1964 election was a historic moment for modern US conservatism as right-wing groups animated grassroots conservatives who had been scattered and unorganized in American society. When the conservative movement went national during the postwar years, "grassroots" became a magic word for conservatives to confirm their movement's authenticity. Conservative activists have asserted that they started at the political fringes immediately after the Second World War and rose from grassroots to national prominence.[2] From the late 1950s to the mid-1960s, the John Birch Society (JBS) played a central role as the largest grassroots anticommunist group in organizing local chapters across the nation, calling on its members to influence other neighborhood associations, and supporting conservative candidates like Goldwater in election cycles. Although the founder Robert H. W. Welch's extreme conspiracy theories were frequently controversial, even among conservatives, the JBS provided many antiliberals with opportunities to take action for conservative causes. As such right-wing organizations contacted millions of men and women to endorse Goldwater in 1964, activists could depict modern American conservatism as a people's movement arising from the bottom up, which would lead to the "Reagan Revolution" in 1980.

But at the same time, the Goldwater movement was also historic as the first political campaign successful at deploying targeted advertising in presidential elections. The first conservative candidate on the Republican ticket, Goldwater employed modern information technologies including computerized direct mail. Goldwater compiled lists of contributors to his campaign beginning with his first senatorial race of 1952, then his campaign managers systematically constructed an IBM computer-stored database of conservative voters by 1964. Local activists and political consultants made efforts to raise funds and reach out to voters on Goldwater's behalf, while also sending the information of conservative prospects to the campaign headquarters. The data of individual donors increasingly swelled during the campaign, attracting large numbers of small contributions with some even just one dollar. The Goldwater backers revealed that they were discontent with liberalism, and after Election Day, the campaign handed down lists of supporters to the conservative movement. The mailing lists were a legacy of the Goldwater campaign, which would arouse grassroots conservative Americans in ensuing decades.

The Goldwater campaign did more than build up the conservative movement, as its alternative media strategy created a new kind of grassroots activism by revolutionizing fundraising activities. Direct mail's function of selectivity made it possible for conservatives to carve out political niches, exploring conservative prospects and enlarging the financial base for the conservative movement. Consequently, direct mail brought great numbers of small donations to the Goldwater campaign, then transformed a long-standing pattern of political contribution from "fat cat money" by the few of giant businesses and wealthy philanthropists toward small funds from ordinary people. In a sense, direct mail fundraising democratized campaign finance by altering political donation into a more usual behavior than ever among the grassroots. But this sort of "grassroots" activity in direct mail politics was quite different from the tradition of American associational democracy, in which people organized voluntary groups, interacted with each other in person, and shored up democracy from the local level. Political direct mail redefined grassroots mobilization as the gathering of small involvements, which was distinctive from the building of face-to-face relationships in the traditional sense.

Among diverse groups and activists involved with the Goldwater movement in the 1964 race, two forces relied on the different types of grassroots mobilization, struggling with each other within the conservative movement. On the one hand, the JBS drummed up support for Goldwater by mobilizing ordinary people in conventional ways: the organization established many local chapters particularly in the Sunbelt, encouraged its members to join the Goldwater campaign, and promoted face-to-face political engagement such as door-to-door canvassing and running local events. On the other hand, right-wing media activists in New York successfully gathered moral and financial support from the grassroots. If the JBS was a major grassroots conservative organization in the mid-1960s, William F. Buckley Jr.'s *National Review* was the key magazine for conservative intellectuals, offering a platform for writers and philosophers to shape American conservatism, when the majority of mass media dominated by liberals criticized Goldwater throughout the presidential race. Buckley and other media-savvy consultants in New York City, such as Marvin Liebman, actively drew on marketing strategies from Madison Avenue, wringing small money from the large numbers of individual donors and providing avenues for those citizens to participate in conservative politics. While the JBS organized the grassroots on a traditional model of local associations, New York consultants employed direct mailings to mobilize conservatives through loose networks. The conflict between the two conservative factions has been interpreted as an internal strife for "respectable" conservatism. But at the same time, it was also a clash of two sorts of grassroots activism.[3]

Barry Goldwater Prior to the 1960s

Barry Goldwater's political belief was inextricably connected with his circumstances. When Goldwater was born in 1909, Arizona was still a remote territory. The population was small and the environment was brutal. Local politicians and economic interests traditionally assumed that the economy of arid Arizona was dependent largely on four C's: cotton, copper, cattle, and climate. Far away from the Northeast geographically and mentally, political culture in Arizona stressed individualism, free enterprise, and small government. Goldwater belonged to the business elite of Phoenix as a member of the owner family of local department stores in Arizona. Since his early career, Goldwater emphasized probusiness principles, antiliberalism, and individual liberty, perceiving a big government and labor unions as threats to American freedom. As Franklin D. Roosevelt promoted liberalism as a solution to the Great Depression during the 1930s, Goldwater regarded the growth of the federal government as menacing what he believed to be the principles of Arizona as well as the United States. However, in the middle of the twentieth century, Arizona was dramatically transformed from an agricultural area toward part of the modern Sunbelt. In attempts to maximize the benefits of industrialization and the inflow of population, local elites made Arizona a new frontier for businesses. They implemented policies such as fewer taxes and antilabor restrictions to make Arizona attractive to businesses. In Arizona, where the majority of registered voters were Democrats, Goldwater joined the efforts in altering the Phoenix Chamber of Commerce, city hall, and the Arizona Republican Party into instruments for antiliberals before he won a seat in the US Senate in 1952.[4]

Stephen C. Shadegg was a political consultant who directed the Goldwater campaign in the 1950s. Moving from Southern California to Arizona in 1932, Shadegg had worked as a freelance writer for radio production, newspapers, and Hollywood screen plays. When he settled in the Phoenix business community, Shadegg became engaged in local politics as a campaign manager beginning in 1938. Shadegg led the campaign of Democratic Senator Carl Hayden in 1950, and Goldwater asked the consultant to manage his campaign in 1952. Shadegg was in charge of various tasks. He prepared the scripts for radio and television, wrote speeches, and produced campaign literature for Goldwater. Working together in political elections throughout the 1950s, Shadegg became known as Goldwater's "alter ego."[5]

Shadegg actively attempted to sell Goldwater as an innovative statesman through political advertisements. "The man is not the product of any political machine," a pamphlet emphasized. The message acclaimed Goldwater for his entrepreneurship, saying that in his family business, "New styles were introduced. New values were offered. New methods of advertising and merchandising were employed, and Barry Goldwater demonstrated his ability as a business man."[6] Shadegg's campaign literature also advertised Goldwater's political beliefs, such as individualism, faith, and freedom. By contrasting liberalism with his political philosophies, the campaign also attacked the New Deal. A newspaper advertising noted, "Fear has been the catch word of the new dealers. . . . This nation was founded on faith in Almighty God and in man's destiny. . . . *Fear* is the *tool* of *tyranny* . . . *faith* is the *weapon* of *freedom*."[7] Still another campaign advertisement of Goldwater specifically targeted his opponent Ernest McFarland, incumbent Arizona senator, by focusing on the Korean War. "Ask yourself this question: 'Do I want to handicap Eisenhower's positive and decisive efforts toward Peace in Korea and toward Decency and Thrift in government by saddling him with a Trumanite senator (McFarland) who, modeled by years of blind political servitude to the Truman Machine, will oppose Ike's every move?'"[8]

In tandem with newspaper and radio advertising, political mail was a significant weapon used by Shadegg. As Robert Humphreys at the Republican National Committee stressed the importance of the stay-at-homes in the 1952 presidential race, Shadegg was convinced that crucial voters were the "Indifferents," those who did not vote whatsoever or voted only in response to an emotional appeal. For the purpose of reaching out to the inactive voters, the campaign obtained lists of registered voters in each precinct, sending out fifty thousand selected mailings to Democrats who were the majority in the state. The letters and postcards urged the recipients to cross the party line in favor of the new Republican candidate. However, many people still doubted the effects of political mailing. Shadegg remembered that a Republican leader in Arizona told him that it was a waste of time to send postcards in order to persuade Democrats to vote for Goldwater. The actual impact of the mailings was unclear, but Shadegg suggested that many voters went to the polls with his postcards, and the Goldwater campaign continued to employ mailing solicitation in subsequent elections.[9]

Few people expected that Goldwater would win his first senate election. In 1952, he was not merely a political neophyte but also challenged McFarland, a two-term experienced Democratic politician and Senate majority leader. Goldwater defeated the Democrat in part because he rode the wave of Dwight Eisenhower's popularity. Whereas Eisenhower was highly regarded as a World War II hero by Americans, President Harry Truman's unpopularity obviously affected Democratic candidates. Shadegg recalled that Goldwater won the 1952 race because of "Democratic softness towards Communism, the corruption in Government and the Truman failure to win the war in Korea."[10] But another reason for Goldwater's slim victory was that Joseph McCarthy had campaigned against McFarland in the 1952 election. Since McCarthy had visited Arizona for health reasons in the 1940s, Goldwater had been his personal friend. Even when President Eisenhower charged McCarthyism, Goldwater continued to endorse his colleague and later wrote, "I couldn't approve of some of the charges McCarthy was making, but there was a tremendous amount of evidence to support his allegations."[11] Although Goldwater was not ideologically a vehement anticommunist, the freshman senator was close to the Republican Party's right wing, like Robert Taft.

Senator Goldwater gradually emerged as a critic of Eisenhower's modern Republicanism. When the president offered his vision in which the business community and labor unions cooperated in favor of national economic prosperity, Goldwater criticized such moderate policies as a compromise with New Deal liberalism. He gained national visibility as chairman of the Senator Republican Campaign Committee, traveling extensively throughout the United States to deliver speeches. On the road and on the Senate floor, Goldwater charged Eisenhower's support for the welfare state. Furthermore, whereas Republicans lost seats in the 1954 midterm election, the Arizonan's fame was elevated as an anti-labor conservative during his fights with trade unions. Serving on the Labor and Public Welfare Committee, Goldwater attacked what he called "compulsory" unionism of the Congress of Industrial Organizations-Political Action Committee (CIO-PAC), which had poured a great deal of money into Democrats in the 1954 election. Goldwater also trained his fire on labor leaders. With the conservative Democrat John McClellan on the Select Committee on Improper Activities in the Labor or Management Field, also known as the Rackets Committee, Goldwater castigated Jimmy Hoffa who wielded powerful influence on the Teamsters unions. When Goldwater targeted Walter Reuther, president of the United Auto Workers, during the 1950s Kohler strikes, the face-off catapulted the Arizona senator into national fame among conservatives, while trade unions deemed Goldwater as a big enemy by the late 1950s.[12]

In the 1958 reelection campaign, Goldwater and Shadegg intensely marshaled political direct mail. The candidate and political consultant had prepared lists of Goldwater's supporters since his 1952 senatorial contest by compiling the information on voters throughout Arizona. Goldwater wrote to Shadegg in 1954, "My mailing list, which I am keeping extremely active and up to date, now numbers over 30,000 names," and the number of names on his list grew to 50,000 by 1956.[13] In July 1958, a political consultant wrote to Goldwater, stressing that direct mail could reach his supporters more effectively than mass media. "It has been proven, that a direct mail program can be the most important single item of your campaign. Too much money is spent by too many hopeful candidates, shot-gunning their messages through a mass media; messages that should be aimed at a segment of the populace."[14] Shadegg organized and used the information on Arizonan voters. The Goldwater campaign sent out mailings to the constituency with the names of such groups as "Friends of Barry Goldwater," "Physicians for Barry Goldwater," "Democrats for Arizona," "Lawyers for Goldwater Committee," "Attorneys for Goldwater Committee," and "Bi-Partisan Small Business Committee for Barry Goldwater."[15]

While gathering voters' information, Goldwater and Shadegg also began to use state-of-the-art technology for direct mailing. "You and I are living in an age of electronics," declared a pamphlet of Goldwater's campaign, depicting how the campaign staff employed computer technology in their efforts to reach out to voters during the 1958 senatorial election. An IBM machine scanned punch cards and reproduced each voter's address on an envelope exactly as the name appeared on the voting records in the county. As the machine printed thousands of labels every hour, it was much more time effective than handwriting.[16] In a time when many political candidates did not yet employ mass media such as radio and television in their campaigns, Goldwater and his campaign staff did not have qualms about testing the cutting edge of campaign technologies.

Shadegg deployed direct mail for multiple purposes in 1958, claiming that the mail campaigns were "extremely satisfactory."[17] In the early stage, Shadegg used direct mail for public opinion polling. He sent mailings to seven or eight hundred people in Arizona and asked them to fill out a questionnaire regarding issues that they were concerned with. Shadegg's direct mail also urged the receivers to send their friends questionnaires. "It's most important," the political consultant stressed in his letter, "to address our attention to those issues which are currently occupying public concern."[18] As in the previous election, Shadegg planned to mail out approximately 150,000 postcards to voters. Moreover, he distributed a letter from Goldwater and two "I'm for Barry" stickers to every registered Republican in the state. The letter encouraged the readers to put a sticker on their cars and to ask their friends to use the other. According to Shadegg's memoir, five days after the stickers were mailed, he witnessed many vehicles had the stickers; and ten days after the distribution, he observed cars with the stickers in parking lots and shopping centers in the greater Phoenix area.[19]

Indeed, Goldwater's direct mail articulated his political principles, such as the private enterprise system and personal freedom of the individual, remarking "I have opposed Bigness—Big Spending, Big Government, Big Business, Big Unions."[20] However, direct mail of the Goldwater campaign distributed different messages suited for each group of voters. Small business was one of the major bases for Goldwater. The Goldwater campaign sent out a letter with the signature of John Ong, president of Ong Insurance Agency in Phoenix. Enumerating several reasons why he supported Goldwater, Ong stressed how the senator had contributed to the mining industry, cotton farming, and military installations in Arizona. But Ong highly regarded Goldwater's role particularly in strengthening government functions such as "the Small Business Administration, helping small business firms to create new jobs for Arizonans."[21] In another letter, the Goldwater campaign crafted an elaborate rhetoric concerning the relationship of the federal government with small business. The letter was delivered to an employee of a developer in Phoenix. It acclaimed the homes that he had built under the Federal Housing Administration and Veterans Administration programs, saying, "This has been an interesting and a commendable example of private enterprise prospering with government encouragement but without the unfavorable side effects and the burden upon taxpayers that results from government subsidies." In other words, despite Goldwater's idea against big government, the direct mailing for the developer acknowledged the effects of "government encouragement" that benefited small businesses.[22]

Like he had attempted in 1952, the senator tried to reach anyone who could support his conservatism without regard to party affiliation. "Whether you are Democrat or Republican, I hope that we can be together in this effort to retain decency in our government."[23] In another appeal, a group called Democrats for Arizona stated that they supported the Republican senator with a message against labor unions and Ernest McFarland. "Ex-Senator McFarland has lived on the public payrolls of our State and Nation for almost thirty years. He has never been a vigorous or forthright leader. He accepted a $4,000 check from Jimmy Hoffa's Teamsters Union in return for his promise to support the Teamsters efforts to destroy a section of the Arizona law, and then he conveniently forgot to report that check, claiming he didn't know about it, and blaming his campaign manager."[24] In Arizona with the "Jeffersonian" democratic tradition, which emphasized entrepreneurial individualism and opposition to governmental regulations, antiunion messages were significant when Goldwater made efforts in reaching beyond his own party. Shadegg also distributed direct mailings that enclosed copies of Goldwater's speech in Detroit, where he vehemently criticized labor unions. "You will remember it was this speech which produced the hysterical outcry from Mr. Reuther, 'Barry should see a psychiatrist, he is not sane.'"[25]

While Goldwater attacked trade unions during his first term, unions and the mainstream media denounced the senator, labeling him as an irrational politician. A Republican in Pima County, Arizona, described a typical impression about Goldwater, especially his antiunion opinion. "You wonder what people back here think of Goldwater. The most any of us can ascertain from newspaper, radio, and TV is that he is a destroyer.... Now I've watched him on TV and this is the only impression I can get."[26] In counterattacking the barrage of condemnation, Shadegg launched a direct mail campaign for revising negative images of Goldwater. His political opponents claimed that Goldwater was anti-Semitic, saying that Goldwater did not employ any Jews in his department store business. A letter from the Goldwater campaign headquarters denied the rumor: "This is not true. Goldwaters [sic] application blanks do not ask for any information on religious affiliations or racial background."[27]

Jewish Americans were a group that Goldwater's direct mail aimed at in the 1958 race. The campaign dispatched mailings to the Jewish community to call for their support. The solicitation was designed to convince Jewish Americans that Goldwater should be reelected by highlighting what the senator had achieved for minorities at home and abroad. To be sure, as the letter admitted, Goldwater "is a conservative while many Jews traditionally align themselves with professed 'liberal' candidates." But it maintained that his record demonstrated that he had consistently voted for the "extension of human rights." The letter listed what Goldwater had done: He had voted for admission of more refugees from Europe; he had spoken against the persecution of minorities in Russia; he had taken a stand against colonialism; he had visited Israel and expressed admiration for the development of the nation; he supported the civil rights legislation to pass the US Congress; among others.[28]

In these direct mail drives during the 1958 senatorial election, the Goldwater campaign properly used different languages for each group and individual in Arizona so that his messages effectively generated responses. Shadegg asserted the direct mail campaign contributed to the impression that "Goldwater supporters were in the majority" among Arizonan voters, and Goldwater successfully won the reelection in 1958.[29]

The Goldwater Movement

Conservative activists showed signs of interest when the Arizona senator emerged as a rising star of conservatism. Several editors of the *Los Angeles Times* turned their attention to Goldwater. In late 1959, managing editor Nick Williams invited the Arizona senator to write a regular column for the newspaper. After discussing the project with Shadegg, Goldwater accepted the offer, and Shadegg served as a ghostwriter.[30] With his columns in the most influential newspaper in Southern California, many people noticed the name of Barry Goldwater. Clarence Manion, a conservative broadcaster famous for his radio talk show, *Manion Forum*, planned to publish a book to propagate Goldwater's conservative principles. Ghostwritten by L. Brent Bozell, William F. Buckley's brother-in-law, *The Conscience of a Conservative* became a best seller. With three and a half million hardback and paperback copies sold after its publication in April 1960, the book was reviewed not only by conservative magazines including *National Review* and *Human Events*, but also in such established newspapers as the *Chicago Tribune*, the *Washington Post*, and *Barron's*. The book catapulted Goldwater into national fame among conservative Americans.[31]

Whereas publishers disseminated Goldwater's political philosophies and mass media spotlighted the senator, conservative activists rallied support for the newly emerging politician. Conservative university students organized the National Youth for Goldwater for Vice President after the Republican Party nominated Richard Nixon as the presidential candidate in 1960. Manion and

Bozell, too, formed "Americans for Goldwater" to establish conservatism as an alternative ideology to liberalism. Although Goldwater withdrew from the race for the presidential nomination at the Republican National Convention on July 25, he arose as a new standard-bearer of modern American conservatism.[32]

The 1964 presidential election witnessed two conservative factions with different approaches to the grassroots. On one hand, as the first right-wing force, the John Birch Society (JBS) was a significant but controversial group for the grassroots efforts to draft Goldwater as well as the conservative movement in general. Robert Welch, a candy manufacturer in Massachusetts, founded the society to prevent what he perceived to be a communist subversion within the United States. Established in December 1958, the JBS increasingly developed into a national organization, taking firm roots especially in the Southwest. Many local chapters mushroomed in Southern California, and middle-class men and women in wealthy suburbs participated in the conservative crusade while several business magnates joined and financed it. On the other hand, when the JBS emerged as a national conservative organization, intellectuals and the national media lambasted the founder for his conspiracy theories. Welch assumed that communists had infiltrated the federal government and, in his book *The Politician*, he went so far as to claim that President Eisenhower was a communist agent. Therefore, many pundits and journalists called the Birchers "extremists" or the "ultra-right," and framed the conservative movement itself in those terms throughout the 1964 election.[33]

Despite his conspiracy theories and radical ideas, Welch structured his institution on an American tradition as the "nation of joiners." Believing that it was significant to connect individuals at the local level, Welch ardently encouraged Birchers to build small local chapters around the country. Conservative women and men organized individual chapters in their neighborhoods, gathering regularly in members' houses. In each chapter, the Birchers watched short films, listened to lectures, and at times joined letter-writing campaigns. Through formal and informal networks of family, friends, and associates, the members shared information and recruited new participants. Welch also encouraged JBS members to infiltrate local school boards and town commissions to spread conservative ideas in their neighborhoods. "We are not," Welch said, "so loosely and tenuously held together that we resemble a gaseous fog far more than a solid body."[34] The JBS was dependent on a grassroots model that the rank and file were tightly connected and mobilized by dense grassroots networks.

In addition, JBS members established bookstores as public places for conservative grassroots readers. In his 1958 *Blue Book*, Welch called for "reading rooms" operated by local members of the Birch Society. Some volunteers opened JBS reading rooms, but other members founded their own independent "patriotic bookstores" to deepen grassroots conservatism in local areas. As historian Michelle Nickerson demonstrated, these bookstores spread across the Los Angeles area, and female members of the JBS played a crucial role in opening the settings. By trading right-wing books, magazines, and newsletters, the JBS earned more than funds. The organization also constructed a collective identity as modern conservatives when they read, discussed, and circulated conservative literature. On the aspects of structure, recruitment, and activism, the John Birch Society was premised on face-to-face grassroots relationship.[35]

Meanwhile, as the second force within the conservative movement, several activists in New York were giving shape to a Draft Goldwater campaign. William Rusher, F. Clifton White, and John Ashbrook were political allies since they had joined the Young Republican National Federation during the 1950s, pushing the Republican apparatus to the right. They remained active in conservative politics well into the 1960s as Rusher was involved with Buckley's *National Review* as its publisher, White worked as a political consultant in New York, and Ashbrook was a congressman from Ohio. In the early 1960s, they were seeking a candidate for the 1964 presidential election who could turn the GOP into a vehicle for conservatives. White would later recall that they had known of Goldwater back in 1953. There had been a meeting of the Young Republicans in Colorado in the spring of the year, and Rusher had attended it and told White in New York, "I've just seen a man from out of the West that I think is going to be great. . . . Barry Goldwater, the Senator from Arizona."[36] They organized the Draft Goldwater Committee on October 8, 1961, to encourage the senator to run for president even though he was not yet willing to be nominated. Appointing state chairmen and running political operations at the precinct level, White took the lead in organizing the citizen movement and mobilized grassroots conservatives across the nation.[37]

However, a cacophony lurked in the relationship between Goldwater and grassroots conservatives from the scratch. Goldwater indeed endorsed conservative philosophies that resonated with conservative activists. But his mercurial personality did not always go along with the conservative movement. His close friends well understood Goldwater's "versatility." Having worked with him in the 1952 and 1958 senatorial campaigns, Shadegg observed a gap between the politician and conservative activists, saying that Goldwater "is not an inflexible reactionary conservative. . . . Goldwater won't be pushed to the right, he won't become an inflexible, die-hard uncompromising conservative, because this is not his nature."[38] The crack grew into a rift between Goldwater and conservative activists, as well as among right-wing organizations, in the 1964 presidential race.[39]

The 1964 Presidential Election

While White and other conservative activists in New York established the Draft Goldwater Committee, a coterie of Goldwater's intimate allies organized another committee on his behalf. After the 1962 midterm election concluded, a group of Arizonan supporters founded a national Goldwater for President Committee with headquarters in Phoenix, setting out to raise funds, print campaign materials, and create charters in other states.[40] In the summer and fall of 1963, White and many activists of the Draft Goldwater Committee independently drummed up support in the precincts without encouragement from Senator Goldwater. When Goldwater finally announced that he would run for president on January 3, 1964, the National Goldwater for President Committee absorbed White's Draft Goldwater Committee, and Goldwater's old friends seized control of the campaign.[41]

When Goldwater took over the draft committee, the candidate designated his close friends to the key positions in the campaign. Instead of Clifton White, Goldwater gave the responsibility for campaign management to Denison Kitchel, appointing him as general director of the Goldwater for President Committee. Another key man in the campaign was Dean Burch, a Tucson attorney who had worked with the senator as his administrative aide. Goldwater also designated Richard Kleindienst as codirector of field operations, and Daniel Gainey and G. R. Herberger to the Finance Committee. Kitchel and Kleindienst were lawyers in Phoenix, while Gainey was a Minnesotan businessman who owned ranches in Arizona, and Herberger was a department store owner and a land developer in the state. Although Kitchel and Kleindienst had some political experience, working in the Arizona Republican State Committee, they were not prominent in national politics.[42] Considered "political amateurs who worked like professionals" by the mass media, the "Arizona Mafia" took the place of conservative activists in the campaign after July.[43]

William J. Baroody was a central figure in the inner circle of Goldwater's campaign. Baroody, son of a Lebanese immigrant and economist, had reshaped the American Enterprise Institute (AEI), initially named American Enterprise Association, from a small nonprofit organization toward an influential think tank in Washington, DC. Inviting conservative scholars as full-time and part-time researchers, the AEI provided members of Congress and the public

with academic analysis of current public policy or legislation. Although Baroody identified himself as neither a conservative nor a liberal, he emphasized
economic enterprise, property rights, and religious values. Sharing several political philosophies, Goldwater and Baroody were personally close. In August
1964 Baroody explained, "Senator Goldwater and I have been friendly for a long
time. He goes to my daughters' weddings and I go to his daughters' weddings."[44]

Kitchel invited Baroody to the Goldwater campaign as he expected the organizing genius would be helpful. Particularly after Goldwater's nomination in
San Francisco, his old advisers gave way to a brain trust recruited by Baroody.
Lee Edwards, a YAF activist and director of public information of the Goldwater campaign, mentioned Baroody's role in 1964. According to Edwards, a small
group "headed up by Baroody" crafted Goldwater's acceptance speech, which
sparked controversies over the conservative's radicalism when Goldwater stated,
"I would remind you that extremism in the defense of liberty is no vice. And
let me remind you also that moderation in the pursuit of justice is no virtue."
Edwards and other conservatives had not reviewed the draft before the candidate read it at the Republican National Convention. Baroody's strong leadership
or behind-the-scenes power play alienated many within the campaign, and the
small circle, including Kitchel and Baroody, contributed to the yawning gap
between the Goldwater campaign headquarters and grassroots conservatives.[45]

The Goldwater campaign headquarters, Sunbelt grassroots conservatives like
JBS members, and New York political consultants took different approaches in
voter outreach. A handbook of the Goldwater campaign headquarters stressed
newspaper, radio, and television as effective ways for political advertising. But
at the same time, it noted that canvassing "was a most important method used
in increasing membership."[46] Similarly, another campaign manual emphasized
that successful fundraising would be accomplished "through personal contact
by someone known to the person being contacted."[47] As a traditional and reliable
way, the handbooks encouraged campaign workers and volunteers to build up
face-to-face relations in their neighborhoods by walking from door to door and
making direct contact with people.

Vital grassroots efforts have been accounted as a remarkable characteristic
of the 1964 Goldwater campaign. Such a grassroots activism for Goldwater was
noticeable in the Sunbelt, particularly Southern California. One of its examples was "Operation Q," which Southern Californians carried out to nominate
Goldwater as a presidential candidate in the state primary. In March, his supporters invited their friends for coffee at their homes, while other volunteers
canvassed houses in Orange County suburbs, asking them to fill in nominating

petitions. Conservative women and men successfully gathered more than eighty-six thousand signatures, much over the necessary thirteen thousand names, in three days. Besides, in the week before the primary, Goldwater's campaign managers and Clifton White organized a vast drive to get out the vote. With lists of voters in California and detailed maps of Republicans, volunteers contacted many supporters to confirm that they had already cast a vote.[48] Popular culture also played a role in grassroots conservative activism. In the summer of 1964, Fred Schwartz, a prominent anticommunist in Southern California and founder of Christian Anti-Communism Crusade, recruited a folksinger, Janet Greene. Schwartz announced that he would ask the singer to write anticommunist songs so that her voice and guitar "blend to produce satirical folk-type tunes attacking Communism, beatnik demonstrators and the Castro regime in Cuba" at rallies around the nation.[49]

However, the Birchers were the most active group in the Goldwater movement at the community level. Especially after the Republican National Convention in San Francisco in July, an increasing number of JBS members penetrated the campaign. Robert Welch did not directly refer to Goldwater, but he encouraged his followers to work hard for "the candidates of your choice." In the October 1964 issue of *Bulletin*, the group's newsletter, Welch urged the Birchers to take efforts in recruitment by organizing more presentation meetings in the weeks before the general election.[50] The Birchers were profoundly involved with the Goldwater campaign as individuals. Whereas some of the members played roles in the leadership and membership of the California Republican Assembly, others participated in conservative groups such as Young Americans for Freedom. The Birchers took part in the Goldwater campaign not merely because they were dedicated to the conservative candidate; they also used the campaign as an opportunity for their own propaganda and recruitment. The impact of the 1964 election on the JBS was evident in the Sunbelt. In the latter part of the 1960s, the membership of the JBS continued to grow, and several JBS members became officers of Republican organizations such as the California Young Republican organization and the California Republican Assembly.[51]

While grassroots conservatives actively worked for Goldwater across the Sunbelt, the candidate's managers and activists were engaged in compiling a giant database of conservative supporters. Despite the psychological distance between the Arizona Mafia and New York activists, the two camps together constructed a database of conservative Americans via fundraising drives throughout the 1964 election. Harry Rosenzweig, an intimate friend of Goldwater for more than fifty years, served as Arizona finance chairman of the Goldwater campaign. From

1963 to 1964, Rosenzweig directed fundraising initially for Goldwater's 1964 Senate race, then for the presidential campaign, by sending mailings in and outside Arizona. The solicitation campaign also served as public opinion polling. In an appeal of October 17, 1963, the campaign staff stressed, "What we are trying to do, Seth, is to set up a file of persons interested enough in the Senator to be willing to support him financially. At the present time, of course, we are raising funds for his campaign as the Senator from Arizona, however, as Harry [Rosenzweig] says, it is easy to see which way the wind is blowing, and if the Senator and his advisors decide the wind is right, we soon may be contacting people on a national basis for financial assistance in a campaign of national scope." In replying to this appeal, a person in Cleveland, Ohio, sent back a check for $25 and a list of names of people who were expected to be interested in supporting Goldwater.[52] In this way, the mailing lists increasingly grew as the Goldwater campaign expanded the network nationwide.

As in the 1958 senatorial election, Goldwater and his aides used innovative machines for political purposes in 1964. The staff in Arizona mentioned, "Through IBM computer-stored data, we can make them available to Senator Goldwater and the Republican Party, if and when the Senator becomes a candidate, our network of people ready to go to work in every area for his election."[53] The Goldwater for President headquarters in Washington, DC, also boasted about the IBM data processing system. A campaigning handbook of the Goldwater campaign stressed the role of computers, noting, "When a filled-out petition is received at National Headquarters, we will assign a membership number to each new applicant and have all of the information punched into IBM cards. These cards will then be converted to magnetic tape for use on any IBM computer."[54] The novel electronic apparatus functioned effectively in raising money and finding prospective conservatives at the local level.

New York conservative activists joined the fundraising campaign on behalf of Goldwater. After the Arizonan circle took over the national Goldwater for President campaign by August, Clifton White shifted his efforts toward activities in New York State. New York conservatives attempted to cooperate with the national Goldwater movement while also distinguishing their grassroots mobilization from the national headquarters of the Goldwater campaign and the Republican National Committee. In their view, the Goldwater movement in New York was "not concerned with formal Republican Party campaign efforts; rather it is concerned with independent and/or 'citizens' efforts.... If a national 'citizens'' Goldwater movement is established from Washington, we will work as closely as possible with this."[55]

New York was critical for the 1964 Goldwater campaign. Big donors in the region, including the New York metropolitan area and Pennsylvania, had usually given funds to the Republican Party since 1936. However, avoiding Goldwater's conservatism and his radical right followers, many Republicans gave practically nothing to the candidate in the 1964 election.[56] Under the circumstances that Goldwaterites were not able to resort to the conventional sources of political funds, New York conservatives struggled to open up a new channel for campaign finance.

Marvin Liebman, a Madison Avenue political consultant associated with Buckley's *National Review* and YAF, was responsible for operating a grassroots fundraising campaign in the state of New York during the 1964 general election.[57] Liebman was involved with "organizing and mailing a fund raising appeal" to New Yorkers and "stimulating and directing local grass-roots fund raising activities throughout the state utilizing our 'stock' sales technique," while simultaneously running other types of local fundraising efforts including dinners, luncheons, and others.[58] Liebman put together the names and addresses from various prime lists, such as the membership of YAF and the Conservative Party of New York State, contributors to several anticommunist and conservative groups, and subscribers to conservative magazines including *National Review, Human Events*, and *America's Future*.[59] He sent each of the possible supporters a direct mailing, which held a letter, a piece of Goldwater literature, a sheet giving a short biography of each delegate and a picture, and a slip of blue paper announcing local political events and rallies.[60]

Many individuals replied to the solicitation letters from the national Goldwater campaign and New York activists. In their replies, several citizens pointed out the rise of grassroots conservative support whom they witnessed. Ernest Hillman, a retired businessman in Pittsburgh, was a contributor to the Goldwater campaign. Sending his check for $500 to the finance committee in Washington, DC, he mentioned the enthusiastic movement for Goldwater increasingly grew but the grassroots supporters were at times out of control. "I am very happy to do this because I have long been an admirer of Senator Goldwater. . . . However, I am firmly convinced that there is a tremendous and ever growing demand, from the grassroots and the uncontrolled voter, for Barry Goldwater for President. There is more interest right now in the next election for President by the individual voter than I have ever seen before."[61] William Morris of Tuscumbia, Alabama, also highlighted the support of "ordinary men" for Goldwater. Noting that he had a conversation with another person about governmental fiscal policies, Morris endorsed Goldwater's attack on the federal government because the conservative did "bring the notice of the common man that the continual depreciation of the buying power of the dollar is being a strictly governmental mismanagement."[62] Morris donated funds to Goldwater so frequently that the campaign staff said, "Your money is coming in faster than my Gal Friday can keep track of it!"[63]

Other contributors made donations due to their concerns over the Cold War. A. L. Hall, a grower and shipper of fancy-leaved caladium bulbs in Lake Placid, Florida, sent his check for $500. "I am not a wealthy man, but I am a veteran of both world wars, having spent two years in the 26th Division, mostly in France in the 1st War and 2 1/2 years in the [South] & Central Pacific in the 2nd world war, and I feel that we are in more dangers right now of losing our liberty & our way of life than at any time during my life."[64] Leon R. Clausen, who lived in Racine, Wisconsin, was concerned with "internationalism" and "pro-communism" under Democrats and moderate Republicans since the 1930s:

> I am enclosing a check to further help because I believe, for the first time in thirty years, we have an opportunity to vote for a candidate who is not running out of the same stable as the Democratic Internationalist stooges who have been scuttling the United States of America. The Internationalists, pro-Communists, and phony liberal conspirators who have been running the show for the last three decades may think they are smart in undermining this country, but actually they are dumb beyond description. They are like the individual who burns down his house with the family in it in order to clear the ground for a new structure which is more to his liking."[65]

While many conservative Americans financially supported Goldwater by sending checks, some grassroots conservatives accused the candidate of his radical words. Marvin Liebman Associates, Inc. sent out direct mailings over the signature of E. V. Rickenbacker on October 17. Rickenbacker, a former chairman of the board of Eastern Airlines, winner of the Congressional Medal of Honor, and World War I flying ace, solicited contributions from the members of the Fighter Aces Association. Under the name of "Fighting Aces for Goldwater," the statement in the direct mail invoked Goldwater's famous speech at the Republican Convention, "extremism in the defense of liberty is no vice," and claimed that military pilots were "extremists" by likening military services to enthusiastic political activism. The statement called on former pilots to take action for Goldwater, saying, "The undersigned were called upon by the Nation to take 'extreme' action in time of war. In the service of our country we took the lives of the enemy—the most 'extreme' action one man can take against another."[66]

Several former pilots furiously reacted to this appeal. "I have been, and am, a Republican all my life, and what I consider to be a conservative," wrote a man called Doug Campbell. Yet he also wrote that he would always cast a vote for Republicans except when voting for president because he felt that "when one votes for a President, one is trying to vote for an individual who has demonstrated that he has good judgement. In my opinion, Mr. Goldwater does not qualify under this heading." Another former pilot articulated his anti-Goldwater attitude. John M. Smith of Washington, DC, pointed to what Goldwater said when a reporter asked him how to define political extremism: "When asked what his own definition was, Goldwater responded that to him extremism meant Fascism, Nazism, Communism or something similar. This was the same man who only minutes before had spoken in defense of extremism." Smith went on, "If your solicitation of support for Senator Goldwater indicates a policy of the Fighter Aces Association, then I as a member strongly protest." He protested particularly the use of the phase "Fighting Aces for Goldwater" because the name might mislead the public into thinking that the organization took an official position. These voices suggested that some conservatives considered Goldwater an inappropriate candidate for conservatism.[67]

The distinctiveness between "extreme" and "respectable" conservatives was a sensitive issue throughout the 1964 race. The John Birch Society was incessantly controversial in the conservative movement because it was the icon of the radical right. To be sure, the JBS was the largest grassroots organization of conservatism in the 1960s. But the conspiracy theories of the founder Robert Welch were problematic and dangerous for many conservatives, who were afraid that the lunatic ideas could taint their movement as a whole. Taking it on themselves to save respectable conservatism from extremism, the *National Review* crowd attempted to exclude the JBS leader from the conservative movement. In 1962, William F. Buckley had openly criticized Welch for his "silliness and injustice of utterance."[68] YAF, the university student organization under the auspices of *National Review*, was also alarmed at the emergence of the Birch Society within the movement. Although there were JBS sympathizers in the organization, YAF members frequently suffered from internal conflicts with the JBS and other right-wing group during the 1964 campaign.[69]

The conservatives' concern was appropriate. Democrats vehemently attacked Goldwater by emphasizing his image as an extremist during the general election. For this purpose, they employed television as the main medium for political advertising. On March 19, 1964, Lyndon Johnson signed a contract with Doyle Dane Bernbach (DDB), a Madison Avenue agency that had been famous for its TV spots

for Volkswagen, "Think Small." In consultation with Tony Schwartz, a sound engineer in Hell's Kitchen, DDB created an ad for the Johnson campaign. Plucking
the petals from a daisy, a little girl awkwardly counts, "one, two, three, four, five,
seven, six, six, eight, nine." Then, the girl's innocent voice is changed into a baleful
adult's countdown. At zero, the camera zooms in on her eye, on which the explo-
sion of an atomic bomb is reflected. The famous "daisy ad" appeared just once on
September 7; nevertheless the spot deeply etched the fear of nuclear annihilation
in the popular mind. The spot did not mention Goldwater's name or words. Yet,
along with other antinuclear ads, the daisy commercial reminded many viewers of
Goldwater's remark about dropping atomic weapons on Vietnam, reinforcing his
image as an extreme politician unsuitable for the US presidency.[70]

The advertising operatives of the Johnson campaign also capitalized on moderate Republicans' sentiment against Goldwater so as to widen the fissure within
the Republican Party. In a four-minute ad titled "Confessions of a Republican,"
actor William Bogert playing a Republican explains why Goldwater scares him.
Suggesting the emergence of the "weird groups" among Goldwater supporters,
such as the JBS and the Ku Klux Klan, the character in this commercial con-
fesses that he and other Republicans want to leave their party if the radical right
takes over the Republican Party. Such ads aimed to split the GOP by pointing
to the anti-Goldwater emotions of many Republicans. But at the same time,
those spots were designed to avoid criticism of negative campaigns. In 1964,
negative advertising was already controversial and deemed unfair. By making
Republicans show their frustrations, the ads effectively obscured the association
of Johnson and Democrats with the anti-Goldwater campaigns.[71]

The Goldwater campaign, too, launched massive television drives in attempt to evade the Johnson campaign's negative advertising. On September
18, Goldwater's first paid televised speech aired, which was written by Charles
Lichenstein who handled much of the Goldwater campaign's advertising. The
thirty-minute address, however, worsened the public image of the conservative
candidate, rather than countered the anti-Goldwater advertising. Goldwater
began the speech by repeating the Johnson campaign's charges that he was "im-
pulsive, imprudent, and trigger-happy." The televised address ended up making an impression that the Republican candidate was on the defensive. Stephen
Shadegg, who served as a regional director for western states in 1964, said, "No
one was happy with the speech."[72] Lichenstein further produced other television programs, including the "Conversation at Gettysburg" that displayed the
talk between Dwight Eisenhower and Goldwater. But the Goldwater campaign
could not effectively overturn the label of extremism put forward by Democrats'
advertisements.[73]

Goldwater supporters did not necessarily expect that the conservative candidate would win the 1964 presidential election. Before Goldwater was nominated by the Republican Party, Ralph W. Applegate in Chicago, Illinois, donated money four times to the campaign by the end of May. As the California primary in June was around the corner, the insurance businessman in Chicago said, "California seems to be the big test and if he can win this one, with the [Henry Cabot] Lodge and [Nelson] Rockefeller forces in coalition against him, he should make the grade." But at the same time, he wrote that the result of the election did not matter: "If nominated, Barry may not win, but LBJ will know that he has been in a political campaign." Even after the election ended up with the landslide victory of Johnson, Goldwater supporters were optimistic. "The loss of the election was due to the great number of people who were either uninformed or misinformed. The solution and cure to our problem is for each one of us to inform two people. That will win."[74]

***

The 1964 presidential election resulted in Lyndon Johnson's landslide victory. In the popular vote, President Johnson gained 61 percent while Goldwater obtained 39 percent with a margin of 15,951,220 votes; Johnson won 486 votes of the Electoral College and Goldwater only 52 votes. Goldwater's conservatism resonated among enthusiastic grassroots supporters in the Sunbelt, but on Election Day, he won just six states, his home state and five others in the Deep South.[75] Goldwater remarked that the 1964 contest was "a choice, not an echo." The choice was clear-cut and simple for conservatives. Goldwater was the first conservative candidate, neither liberal nor moderate Republican. But conservatives were definitely the minority of voters, and most Americans still endorsed the successor of John F. Kennedy and liberal politics in the mid-1960s.

With the benefit of hindsight, however, the Goldwater campaign paved the way for the advancement of conservative politics in the years to come. First and foremost, conservatives constructed a collective identity throughout the election period. As anticommunist organizations contacted millions of people, those ordinary people realized the existence of an antiliberal voice in the United States. For quite a few conservative activists, the 1964 election was the starting point of their political activism as the Goldwater campaign introduced them to the conservative movement.[76] Also, the nomination of Goldwater at the GOP national convention was an unprecedented achievement for modern conservatives. It was the attainment that 1950s right-wing Republicans, such as Robert Taft and Joseph McCarthy, had attempted to no avail, suggesting that conservatives could possibly take over a major party as their own vehicle in the future.[77] Furthermore, grassroots supporters demonstrated that it was possible for the Republican Party to make further inroads into the South, the Southwest, and the West. As Kevin Phillips would point out, the "emerging Republican majority," which centered in the South, the West, and in the urban-suburban districts, appeared by the 1968 presidential election. The sea change had taken place in 1964.[78]

In the context of electoral politics, television was the dominant medium from the 1950s onward. Goldwater's campaign failed to change his image as an extremist that liberal media constructed, but it did not mean that the campaign headquarters dismissed the central role of mass media in politics. In 1964, the Republican Party spent a larger amount of money in political broadcasting. When Democrats used approximately $11 million for broadcasts, including radio and television, Republicans spent $13 million, spending 63 percent of the total money for the presidential election. Nevertheless, unlike the Democratic Party, the GOP concluded the campaign without a deficit.[79]

Despite or because of this fact that television became the central device of communication in elections, direct mail emerged as an indispensable tool for campaign finance. As both parties poured more money into political advertising, particularly expensive television spots, raising funds became a matter of urgency for politicians. Political scientist Dan Nimmo argued that direct mail fundraising drives modified a long-term pattern in American politics. Campaign funds used to depend on large contributors of $500 or more. In 1960, the Nixon campaign solicited approximately forty thousand individual donations. Four years later, however, the Goldwater campaign received funds from 650,000 people, collecting $5.8 million from the contributors by sending fifteen million letters. Many of the individual contributions were small such as $1 or $5. In the 1964 election, 28 percent of the Republicans' income came from donations of $500 or more, while such big contributions occupied 69 percent of the Democrats' campaign finance. Television campaigns, including Ronald Reagan's televised speech known as "A Time for Choosing," also contributed to collecting the small donations. Congressional Quarterly, Inc. estimated that Republicans raised over $2 million by television campaigns, while their direct mail collected over $5 million, almost one-third of the Goldwater campaign's war chest. A report of Congressional Quarterly, Inc. noted, "For the first time in national politics, direct mail and television appeals for funds proved fully successful."[80]

Grassroots conservatives were definitely the central driving force behind the Goldwater movement. Coupled with mailing drives, the Goldwater campaign mobilized a great number of volunteer workers in a traditional way. Goldwater's campaign handbook stressed newspaper, radio, and television as devices for advertising, but noted canvassing was "a most important method used in increasing membership."[81] Mobilized by grassroots organizations like the JBS, four million women and men distributed publications and walked from door to door, contacting twelve million households. The army of volunteers demonstrated their enthusiastic devotion to Goldwater, but also sparked controversy among conservatives. In the wake of the election, the *Register*, a conservative newspaper in Orange County, California, carried a resident's voice. The man claimed, "Personally, I feel the defeat was necessary and vital for the conservative cause. Too many Goldwater supporters became headstrong after their victory in San Francisco and as a result developed a lack of understanding, sympathy and compassions.... The election was lost not so much by Goldwater and the conservative philosophy. It was lost by his zealous grass roots supporters."[82]

In addition to the fervent door-to-door canvassing and other conventional field operations, however, direct mail shaped a new sort of grassroots mobilization. Whereas the JBS-type crusaders eagerly supported Goldwater, direct mail consultants constructed loosely connected networks of conservatives, amassing a large number of small funds instead of building face-to-face involvements. As a major political consequence of the Goldwater campaign, *National Review* publisher William Rusher remarked, "It sensitized large numbers of previously dormant conservatives, turned them into political activists, and introduced them to each other through direct-mail techniques."[83] Direct mail not only provided an alternative way for reaching out to voters. But the medium also transformed political engagement, opening up a new way for ordinary people to participate in politics by making small contributions as well as giving voice directly to the campaign. Distinguished from broadcasting that was designed to send messages to the masses, direct mail was a medium to promote the interactions between political leaders and the grassroots. Goldwater's list of 221,000 contributors turned into a legacy for the Republican Party and the conservative movement by broadening the GOP's financial base and exploring a new source of funds for conservative organizations.[84]

With direct mail, conservative political consultants successfully explored a new terrain of the electorate by circulating personalized messages and emotional appeals. Goldwater's campaign managers sought to gain votes by targeting politically indifferent voters, dissents among Democrats, ethnic groups like Jewish Americans who voted largely for Democratic politicians, and so on. Unlike mass media disseminating the same information to the masses, direct mail sent out personalized messages to each group on the basis of their political preferences. In those direct mailings, Goldwater was represented as a fighter against big unions for Arizonan Democrats, a champion of human rights for White ethnicities, and in the eyes of Arizonan small businesses, an adept politician who brought federal funds to the local economy. In order to draw enthusiasm from individuals who had never participated in conservative politics, political consultants also conveyed emotional messages in uncensored direct mailings. Following the strategy of 1950s political advertisers, conservative media activists deployed aggressive, "good and evil" rhetoric. Even though these passionate messages caused antipathy from liberals and even some conservatives, the strategy of stoking furious sentiments emanated from political marketers' rational use of emotion. In the Goldwater campaign, the new grassroots activism went hand in hand with personalization and emotion.

Because the strategies of direct mail and broadcast advertising were aimed at inflaming emotions to promote voters' political actions, the Goldwater campaign in 1964 spurred political partisanship in American politics. A mailing from a conservative group declared, "We believe that our voting population deserves an honest choice of candidates—not a liberal vs a liberal, but a CONSERVATIVE vs a liberal."[85] Harold Oram, who had engaged in direct mail fundraising for liberal organizations and worked with Marvin Liebman during the 1950s, realized that things had changed. As conservatism gathered steam in the 1964 presidential election, he lamented, "We are living in a period of political upheaval and partisan agitation."[86] Partisanship in direct mail politics highlighted the distinction between liberals and conservatives. But it also accelerated the conflicts within the conservative movement after the 1964 election.

Harold Oram in his office in November 1956. Oram was among the first political consultants who marshaled direct mail for fundraising in the post-World War II period. (Courtesy of the Oram Group, Inc. Records, Ruth Lilly Special Collections and Archives, IUPUI)

Barry Goldwater using his HAM radio. Goldwater loved gadgets and actively employed state-of-the-art technologies for his political campaigns since the 1950s. (Courtesy of Arizona State University Library)

Barry Goldwater in Newark, New Jersey, during the 1964 presidential election. In the background, there was a billboard ad with his slogan, "In your heart you know he's right." Goldwater used the slogan to combat the negative image as an extremist. (Courtesy of Arizona State University Library)

An employee taking reel of computer tape off shelves at the
Richard A. Viguerie Company in the 1970s. (Courtesy of U.S. News &
World Report Magazine Photograph Collection, Library of Congress)

An office room of the Richard A. Viguerie Company, including tape drives,
printers, computers, and other electronic equipment. (Courtesy of U.S. News &
World Report Magazine Photograph Collection, Library of Congress)

Paul Weyrich was an activist of the New Right. Like Richard Viguerie,
Weyrich contributed to the rightward turn of national politics
throughout the 1970s by co-founding the Heritage Foundation in 1973,
and the Moral Majority with Jerry Falwell in 1979. (Paul M. Weyrich
Papers, American Heritage Center, University of Wyoming)

CHAPTER 4

After Goldwater

RICHARD A. VIGUERIE VISITED the office of the clerk of the House of Representatives for several weeks after the 1964 presidential election. In December 1964, Viguerie resigned from Young Americans for Freedom (YAF) where he had worked as a fundraiser, then established his own direct mail firm, the Richard A. Viguerie Company (RAVCO). His new consulting company initially had just YAF as the major client, which he lost within a few years. After founding the RAVCO in Falls Church, Virginia, Viguerie went down to the office of the clerk that housed the files of those who had contributed $50 or more to the Barry Goldwater campaign. In the mid-1960s, such information was open to the public, but photocopying was prohibited. So Viguerie, and several women he had hired, copied down the names and addresses of Goldwater supporters across the nation, compiling a handwritten list of 12,500 donors. It was the beginning of his well-known direct mail list, "without which I wouldn't be in business today," as Viguerie would later recall.[1]

In direct mail politics of the 1960s, Viguerie rose to prominence as the most successful political fundraiser of the time. The conservative consultant has claimed that he was the pioneer of direct mail solicitation, insisting that almost nobody paid attention to the significance of the promising medium at that time. In fact, however, the mid-1960s witnessed a burst of direct mail fundraising as many other conservatives, moderates in the RNC, and even Democrats mailed out solicitation letters. Nevertheless Viguerie handled direct mail most effectively, not because other activists and candidates dismissed the political medium, but because he was keenly aware that partisanship, ideology, and emotion were the keys to the success of political direct mail. To borrow Viguerie's words, he elaborately institutionalized "ideological direct mail" to stand out in the highly competitive market.[2] In this sense, the evolution of direct mail politics went hand in hand with the development of partisanship, factionalism, and offensive ad campaigns.

Direct mail not only raised political funds but also impacted the organizational structure of the Republican Party and conservative groups in the 1960s.

While Viguerie set up his new direct mail firm primarily for the conservative movement, Republican leaders sought to rebuild the party. On the heels of Goldwater's debacle on November 3, 1964, moderate and conservative wings seriously divided the Republican Party. Grassroots conservatives built their strength through local chapters in the South and Southwest as the John Birch Society (JBS) made some important strides in Republican organizations such as the Young Republicans. However, out of fear that "the radical right" might take over the Grand Old Party, moderate Republicans reorganized the party in the mid-1960s. Party leaders entrusted Ray C. Bliss, a newly elected chairman of the Republican National Committee (RNC), with the task of reforming the party structure following the 1964 election. The chairman constructed the "Bliss model," the blueprint for party organization based on professional staff, systematic fundraising, extensive voter outreach, and the integration of national, state, and local party committees. Bliss's reform laid the groundwork for party organization for Republicans, and later for Democrats alike, in the 1960s and beyond.[3]

As moderates and conservatives struggled to gain control of the Republican Party after 1964, fundraising became one of the most significant foci for the intraparty conflicts. As Bliss stressed the "nuts and bolts" strategy, which focused on basic tasks such as precinct organization, finances, and the selection of attractive candidates, he attempted to concentrate fundraising operations under the RNC in order to stabilize and expand the party's financial base. Yet conservative political consultants, such as Viguerie and his direct mail mentor Marvin Liebman, developed direct mail solicitation solely for conservative causes. The fundraising activities of conservatives intensified tensions within the Republican Party because their solicitation drives resulted in the diffusion of financial power and widened ideological divisions within the party. As such, direct mail politics developed in connection with Republican intraparty partisanship in the latter part of the 1960s.

Simultaneously, direct mail played a major role in branding conservatism in the 1960s by offering a channel to bypass what they believed was a liberal-dominated national media. Several conservative "splinter" groups arose to mobilize conservative individuals after the Goldwater campaign. These groups needed to tackle the label of "the radical right" that liberal media and intellectuals had given to the conservative movement. And the organizations faced the question of how to differentiate themselves from the JBS founder Robert Welch, whose conspiracy theory and fierce grassroots activities provided liberals with opportunities to portray conservatives as "extremists" or "fanatics." The American Conservative Union (ACU), which Liebman and

William F. Buckley Jr. established to direct the conservative movement in the post-Goldwater era, was at odds with the JBS as well as Republican moderates, and criticized them through publications and direct mail.

The branding of conservatism was accompanied by a transformation in mobilization style, which diverted from grassroots activism. Historians have interpreted the contest within the conservative movement as a struggle for "respectability" that was quintessential for conservatives to gain wider support in American society. As Frank Meyer, a columnist in *National Review* and a leading theorist of modern American conservatism, argued, "the establishment of responsible leadership" was the primary concern of many conservative activists in the mid-1960s.[4] But more fundamentally, the competition within the conservative movement demonstrated that the ACU and political consultants turned away from the grassroots movement on the JBS model by transforming the relationship of conservative leaders with the rank and file. Instead of organizing local chapters and financing itself with membership fees, the ACU depended on direct mailing for raising money and generating support across the nation. Since the Goldwater movement, direct mail promoted the shift from face-to-face membership toward masses of individual contributions within the conservative movement. The widespread use of direct mail by moderates and liberals reinforced the newly defined "grassroots" activism in American politics as the accumulation of individual contributions, rather than direct interactions at the local level.

Liberals lagged behind conservatives in direct mail fundraising partly due to their complacency. The 1964 race seemingly reconfirmed the ascendancy of liberalism since the 1930s, and the national mass media, including prominent newspapers, radio, and television, largely endorsed liberal policies. Yet visionary Democrats, such as George McGovern and Eugene McCarthy, devoted attention to political direct mail by the end of the 1960s. Liberals' mailings contrasted with conservatives' emotional appeals by using more positive rhetoric for raising money. The 1960s witnessed the expansion and diversity of direct mail politics but ended up demonstrating that emotion and populism attracted more money.

Reorganizing the Republican Party

In the wake of Goldwater's resounding defeat, Republican leaders set out to reform the RNC. Indeed, there was little criticism of Dean Burch, a member of Goldwater's "Arizona Mafia" and the chairman of the RNC in the 1964 campaign. But several Republicans thought that they needed to remove him because they believed that it was a necessary symbolic step toward a reorganization of the party on the national and state levels. As an RNC member mentioned, nearly every Republican state committee was divided over the issue of Goldwater, and many Republicans were worried about Goldwater's continued influence on the party apparatus through Burch. For such concerned Republicans, the assignment of a new chairman was obligatory for the unity of the party.[5]

Raymond C. Bliss was elected as the director of the RNC in 1965. Bliss had served as the Republican state chairman in Ohio for sixteen years and transformed the state party from an ailing organization into "one of the best-oiled political organizations in the nation."[6] Beginning as a volunteer of the mayoralty campaign of 1931, Bliss climbed up the ladder of state politics step by step. While maintaining his insurance and real estate business in Akron, Ohio, he helped Republican candidates as a precinct committeeman and then a member of the State Central Committee by 1944. After Republicans went through a devastating defeat in 1948, Senator Robert A. Taft and other party leaders in Ohio asked Bliss to become state chairman, and he showed his genius for party organization, using advanced techniques such as confidential polling. By the time of the 1964 presidential election, the Ohioan became preeminent in the Republican Party as "the organizational man."[7]

Additionally, Republican leaders considered Bliss the best choice for rebuilding the party due to his nonideological position. "Most people know that I have been a desk chairman in Ohio," Bliss explained in his typical practical tone. He had worked largely behind the scenes in Ohio and stated that he would continue this stance in Washington, adding, "I have always felt that as chairman it was my duty to build up others."[8] When former president Dwight Eisenhower asked him to become national chairman, Bliss clarified again his focus on pragmatic tasks in the RNC by saying, "I don't want to get into degrees of Republicanism. Once a man is nominated, I will support him."[9] As David S. Broder of the *New York Times Magazine* observed, such modesty was one of the reasons why his colleagues regarded Bliss as a "safe man" when the Republican Party was ideologically divided.[10]

As national chairman, Bliss devoted most of his energy to fostering the unity of the Republican Party, as he directed the vital areas of fundraising and party organization in ways that his predecessors had never done. Having learned lessons from his experience in Ohio, Bliss firmly believed that unified fundraising was important so that "donors are not repeatedly solicited by a succession of party committees."[11] More critically, Bliss asserted that the unified fundraising was necessary for integrating the party on the local, state, and national levels.

Prior to the 1960s, the RNC had had few reliable resources and depended on state committees. In Ohio, Bliss had insisted on his right as state chairman to allocate funds among candidates and state and county committees. Affirming that party interests were undermined by officeholders who became too profoundly indebted to particular big contributors, Bliss battled against any candidates and donors who tried to short-circuit the official channel of campaign finance. "Establishing the national chairmanship as a similar financial fulcrum," a *New York Times Magazine* article pointed out, "will be Bliss's first and most important test in Washington."[12]

Bliss reinforced the financial capacity of the Republican Party with direct mail as the backbone of the party solicitation. Back in 1962, the RNC had launched a direct mail "sustaining membership" program to collect money from small contributors. This program brought $500,000 to the party coffers in its first year, and in 1963 netted over $1.2 million, which was 45 percent of all money available to the national committee that year. Assigning General Lucius D. Clay as financial chairman in 1965, Bliss enormously expanded the RNC's direct mail programs. The RNC under Bliss raised $4 million in 1965, and later in 1966 $7.1 million, a record for a midterm election year. By 1967, Bliss's programs of direct mail solicitation offered 82 percent of the funds raised by the RNC. Direct mail provided a reliable, sustainable, and substantial revenue source, which was indispensable for a permanent, professional, and service-oriented national party headquarters. By the late 1960s, Bliss succeeded in constructing a financially independent national headquarters, reducing state party dominance over the national committee as the RNC no longer relied on state party assessments for revenue. Now, the national committee headquarters reversed the flow of money by allotting revenues to candidates and state committees.[13]

Bliss cautiously continued to be ideologically neutral in order to keep the party unified. Although he opposed Goldwater's nomination in 1964, Bliss stated that Goldwaterites had their place in the party, saying, "Certainly I consider Goldwater and his people must be in the spirit of his party. We need to hold the party together."[14] Bliss's innovative strategy of fundraising also helped promote his shift away from ideological debates within the party. In a meeting with Republican state chairmen in January 1966, for example, the most extensively discussed item was a report on the Michigan state committee's use of a computer to process its fundraising. "That item, uninteresting in itself, speaks volumes about the shift in the mood" of the RNC, an article in the *New York Times* reported.[15] Contemporary reporters and pundits found that Bliss averted the focus of the GOP from the ideological arguments of the 1964 campaign toward the practical necessities

of preparing for ensuing elections. The focus on technologies, such as computerized direct mail solicitation, was important not only for integrating national
and state committees, but also for maintaining Republicans' unity regardless of
their ideologies following the Goldwater campaign.

Republican leaders and mass media expected that Bliss would lead the RNC
as a nonideological manager. However, as David Broder of the *New York Times*
accurately mentioned, this prediction was incorrect. Bliss had strong views on
the condition of the Republican Party and on his role as national chairman that
"inevitably will produce conflict."[16] Despite Bliss's efforts to integrate moderates
and conservatives in the party, conservatives doubted his blueprint. "Bliss' job
is to hold the Republican Party together as best he can," William F. Buckley Jr.
wrote, "But such an uneasy alliance will not save the GOP."[17] For Buckley, it
was merely a hallucination that conservatives and moderates worked together by
putting ideological differences aside. "Ecumenism is in the air, but so, the world
continues to discover, is sectarianism," observed Buckley.[18]

Conflicts between Bliss and conservatives began immediately after his assignment as national chairman. Because Bliss emphasized party finance as the
foundation of his organization strategy, Bliss brought his Ohio colleagues to the
RNC, replacing committee members who had been selected by Goldwater with
his "Ohio Mafia."[19] Furthermore, in order to prevent the diffusion of funds in
the Republican Party, Bliss needed to deal with in-party and side-party organizations, which mushroomed after the 1964 campaign. Among conservative
splinter groups was the Free Society Association (FSA), which Denison Kitchel,
Goldwater's campaign manager, founded to organize Goldwater supporters after
the election. When establishing the conservative group, Kitchel used $150,000
from the treasury of the Citizens for Goldwater–Miller that was inaccessible to
the RNC, and then launched solicitation drives that diverted Republicans into
third-party efforts.[20] Such a movement did not go unnoticed by Bliss and other
party leaders. Bliss rejected any attempts to diffuse the money and energy of the
Republican Party, saying he was "against political splinter groups in general and
against Barry Goldwater's Free Society Association in particular."[21]

The American Conservative Union

The Free Society Association was not the only conservative organization that
annoyed the Republican Party in the mid-1960s. When the 1964 presidential
election resulted in the crashing defeat of Barry Goldwater, conservative political consultants were quick to organize a post-Goldwater movement. "Splinter"

groups mushroomed to mobilize conservatives around the nation, and the American Conservative Union emerged shortly thereafter as the most preeminent group in the conservative movement.

Anticipating that Goldwater could not win the presidential election, Robert Bauman, chairman of Young Americans for Freedom, called political consultant Marvin Liebman in October 1964. The young activist maintained that conservatives needed to turn the expected defeat into grounds for their movement by founding "a conservative umbrella group." Liebman, who had helped establish YAF for student conservatives four years earlier, was pleased because he also had conceived the idea of "a senior organization" of YAF to augment the conservative movement.[22] The young activist and consultant contacted conservative politicians about the creation of their new group. They sent a letter to Congressman Donald C. Bruce of Indiana just the day after the election, suggesting the formation of a new political organization to be known as the American Conservative Union (ACU). Liebman and Bauman explained that the general objectives of the ACU included "consolidating the over-all strength of the American conservative movement through unified leadership and action," "molding public opinion," and "stimulating and directing responsible political action."[23]

In early December, Liebman invited several conservative leaders to the ACU's founding meeting that was to be held at the Statler-Hilton Hotel in Washington, DC, on December 18 and 19, claiming, "There are literally millions of American citizens who seek conservative leadership in the months and years ahead."[24] Due to his close relationship with Liebman as a fellow conservative activist, William F. Buckley Jr. received the invitation and attended the meeting. Other participants in the founding meeting included William A. Rusher, the publisher of Buckley's *National Review*; Frank Meyer, an editor and writer for the magazine; and John Dos Passos, an ex-communist conservative novelist. At the ACU first meeting, Bruce was elected chairman with Congressman John Ashbrook of Ohio as vice chairman.[25]

The participation of these activists, intellectuals, and politicians in the ACU was crucial to its objectives to "mobilize the moral, political and intellectual leadership of the American conservative movement."[26] The presence of the two lawmakers in leadership positions confirmed the connection of the new conservative organization with the Republican Party. The ACU's proposal made it clear that one of the most immediate tasks for the conservative organization was the revitalization of the two-party system. The "Republican Party must be brought to life," the memo announced, by providing "new and positive leadership, new creative programs, a new image." While endorsing the Republican

Party, the ACU also stressed that the GOP was divided and leaderless like the Democratic Party had been during the late 1920s and early 1930s. The ACU founding members obviously aimed to turn the party rightward to fight against Democrats and liberals, declaring, "To reshape, to revitalize, to build and employ the GOP: that is ACU's role."[27]

From its beginning, the ACU was intimately connected with YAF. Young conservatives cut their teeth in YAF as they were engaged in conservative politics on campus. YAF members organized rallies for conservative candidates in election years and began to conflict with New Left students during the 1960s. Some of the young activists continued to participate in the conservative movement as they shifted to the ACU after graduating. When Bauman was assigned as a secretary in 1965, ACU directors indicated that the ACU would recruit promising YAF "graduates" so that young conservatives could be professional activists or politicians in the future.[28] Simultaneously, the ACU strengthened its grassroots activities in cooperation with YAF chapters throughout the nation. As an internal memorandum described, the ACU was designed to play a role as the "brainpower" of the conservative movement, while YAF "would furnish the manpower."[29]

As a public relations activist, Liebman stressed the role of the ACU in shaping public opinion as one of the goals of the new conservative organization. In his memo, Liebman asserted that conservatives needed to build up a movement "willing to speak and act in terms easily understood and generally acceptable to the public."[30] The ACU began to publish its monthly newsletter, *Battle Line*, informing members of what was going on at the White House, in Congress, in party organizations, and in state politics. *Battle Line* looked more formal than newsletters of other right-wing groups, such as the John Birch Society's *Bulletin*, helping to project an image of respectability for the ACU in the conservative movement.[31]

A fundamental problem that the ACU faced from its establishment was how to gain respectability in American politics. In order to make conservatism an alternative to liberalism, conservatives needed to avoid the image of the extreme right and become a movement acceptable to more Americans. This issue of being perceived as a respectable conservative organization inevitably forced ACU directors to distinguish themselves from the JBS. During and immediately after the 1964 presidential election, the JBS was the largest grassroots anticommunist group. Birchers were active at the precinct level and played a central role in contacting millions of people throughout the campaign. Therefore, the JBS attracted popular and academic attention, casting a public image of American conservatism. Most national media coverage deemed the JBS "extremists" whose ideology was replete with conspiracy theories, and intellectuals such as Daniel Bell, Richard Hofstadter, and other "consensus" scholars scrutinized the rise of the "radical right" by focusing on the JBS.[32] Scholars, liberal media, and the public usually linked the image of the JBS to the modern American conservative movement as a whole. This indictment of conservatism annoyed right-wing groups in the post-Goldwater years.

At the founding meeting in Washington, Buckley proposed nobody in the JBS's leadership be permitted to join the board of directors and the advisory assembly of the ACU. "The question inevitably arises, What is the relationship between the American Conservative Union and the John Birch Society?" A public statement issued by the ACU declared, "the answer is: There is no relation between the two organizations."[33] Similarly, Liebman proposed that the ACU aim for a "'leadership cadre' rather than a mass group," believing that the respectable conservative movement needed to engage in top-down operations rather than grassroots activism.[34] Rusher also suggested that the ACU direct the conservative movement and support itself in a different way from the JBS:

> I most emphatically do not encourage you to assume that we can (or that we should) best Robert Welch at his own game. The ACU will probably not amass a membership as large as that of the John Birch Society; certainly it won't command anything like the same financial resources. . . . But, provided you do not set your sights impossibly high, I think the ACU may reasonably hope to serve as a substitute medium of effective action of the salvageable members of the John Birch Society.[35]

If the ACU was to be a "leadership cadre" rather than a "mass group," as Rusher mentioned, they were required to construct a new financial model. The JBS was well-financed as it depended on the membership fees collected from the rank and file around the nation. Alternatively, without tens of thousands of members, the ACU had to search for new financial resources immediately after its foundation. The founding members of the ACU understood the problem caused by their deviance from the JBS model. "As had been anticipated, our primary problem is a question of finance," ACU Chairman Bruce said to Liebman in late January. "A study of our financial situation would almost incline one to a feeling of despair. There is no question but what the next few weeks may well be the most critical period for the ACU."[36]

The conservative business community was among the first contributors to the ACU. Liebman sent letters to wealthy conservatives to invite them to join the Advisory Assembly and to appeal for "seed" money. Henry Salvatori of Los Angeles donated $5,000, and Jeremiah Milbank of New York gave $1,000 in December 1964. In February 1965, Walter Knott of Orange County, Eli Lilly of Indianapolis, and Roger Milliken of Spartanburg, South Carolina, contributed over $500 to the ACU.[37] Furthermore, these conservative magnates helped raise funds by soliciting other businesspeople and philanthropists in areas such as Los Angeles, New York, Chicago, Texas, Milwaukee, and Georgia.[38] Yet the ACU was not able to rely exclusively on such business conservatives because "the big-money boys seem to be in a mood to wait and see before putting really heavy support behind the ACU."[39] The big money interests did not offer enough money to sustain the ACU; instead, the organization had to demonstrate its ability to collect substantial funds from other sources.

As the ACU was confronted with a financial crisis in the first months, the Marin Liebman Associates took the responsibility for "all facets of all direct mail fundraising campaigns" on behalf of the organization.[40] Liebman and his colleague Richard Viguerie began to raise funds for the ACU. However, despite the two political consultants' experience and expertise, ACU leaders were skeptical about their ability to raise funds from direct mail. It was not because they doubted the effectiveness of the medium but because they recognized the market of political direct mail was highly competitive within the conservative movement. "Over 2,700 autonomous organizations are currently competing for the 'conservative dollar' to finance their operations," the ACU's report of fundraising program indicated in 1965. "It appears that most of these organizations use the direct mail technique."[41] Concerned over "the truly alarming proliferation of conservative fund appeals," Rusher accurately observed that the Goldwater campaign accelerated the competition for political funds as lists of contributors grew during the election.[42] Viguerie was one of the first, but not the only operative who astutely realized the significance of contributor lists in direct mail politics. James M. Day, a former staff member of the National Citizens for Goldwater and Miller, Neil McCaffrey of the Conservative Book Club, and many other conservative activists successfully employed direct mail by targeting those who had contributed to Goldwater. Buckley, who had worked with Liebman since the mid-1950s, felt that their privileged position in direct mail politics was being undermined. "[I]t is very disturbing that people are discovering how to raise money by mail. I think we probably pioneered that route—we and Marvin."[43]

Liebman attempted to overcome the ACU's financial predicament with several additional fundraising projects. He planned to decentralize the financial burden by naming chairmen in fifty states and asking them to fill annual quotas.

Setting the goal of collecting $10,000 each month, Liebman's fundraising plan also included $100-a-place fundraising dinners, programs to increase ACU membership, and "special projects" for producing rental films on conservatism.[44]

Still, the ACU proved that direct mail was the most profitable way of fundraising. Direct mailings by Liebman and Viguerie for the ACU stood out in the conservative movement of the mid-1960s in part because Viguerie obtained Goldwater's contributor lists, which enabled the fundraisers to reach many prospective donors. More important, as he described it himself, Viguerie elaborately turned political direct mail into "ideological" direct mail by stressing partisanship and highlighting emotion most effectively. Liebman and Viguerie differentiated their appeals from many other political solicitations by aggressively asserting that the ACU was the authentic conservative organization that took over the Goldwater movement and that it was a respectable "grassroots" organization that fought with both the Republican establishment and right-wing extremists in the conservative movement.[45]

The ACU launched a series of fundraising campaigns against the request of RNC Chairman Bliss to refrain from independent solicitation. In late June 1965, Bliss called on conservative splinter organizations, including the ACU, for a moratorium on fundraising. Bliss said, "We will never have a strong, united party until our fund-raising efforts are also united and coordinated." Nevertheless, in August, Liebman and Viguerie initiated a direct mail fundraising program for the ACU, which was in effect an effort by conservatives to challenge mainstream Republicans in the wake of the 1964 campaign. ACU Vice Chairman Ashbrook declared, "The battle for control of the Republican party is underway."[46]

The direct mailing of August 14 indicated how the ACU carved out its position in the Republican Party. The ACU sent thousands of solicitation letters to conservatives who had donated money to the Goldwater campaign in 1964. While applauding Goldwater's nomination as the achievement of conservatives, the appeal partook of a conspiratorial denunciation as it claimed Goldwater lost the general election because liberals in the GOP were more interested in maintaining control of the party than in electing the Republican nominee to the presidency: "Despite the clear mandate of the convention, the liberal minority took its revenge for our delegate victory." Similarly, the appeal implicitly criticized the Bliss group in the RNC, saying that "the liberal minority has become reestablished in a position of political control of the National Committee" since the presidential election.[47]

The direct mailing was characterized by populist rhetoric manipulation that contrasted the "majority of grassroots Republicans" with the "liberal minority."

Goldwater's nomination at the national convention was proof, in the words of the appeal, that "it is still possible for the grassroots to be heard in a national political convention, and that the vast majority of grass roots Republicans are still devoted to the traditional principles of conservatism." If the conservative movement was properly coordinated and inspired, the ACU's fundraising letter went on, conservatives "can achieve control of the Party's national machinery."[48] Another direct mailing similarly demonstrated the ACU was dedicated to taking over the Republican Party rather than forming a third party. In the spring of 1966, Liebman mailed out an appeal that maintained that the GOP was not over. "The opportunity remains," the direct mailing contended, "to make the Republican Party not only an effective opposition force, but also truly reflective of conservative political philosophy."[49] The direct mail drive aimed at prospective supporters with antielitism, accelerating ideological partisanship not merely against liberals but also against moderates of the Republican Party.

Whereas the ACU challenged the Republican establishment, ACU leaders criticized the John Birch Society to emphasize that they represented a respectable conservative movement. The ACU directors, as well as many other conservatives, were aware of the major and negative impact of the JBS on their movement. As the ACU's document mentioned, "The public . . . equate [the JBS] with all conservative groups and our effectiveness is damaged."[50] For as long as the public image of the JBS as extremists was applied to the whole conservative movement, Republicans would continue to purge conservatives from the party and the ACU would remain unable to generate wide support in American politics.

Under the leadership of Buckley, *National Review* and the ACU launched the campaign against the JBS through direct mail and publication. In August 1965, Buckley made statements to condemn Robert Welch's leadership by describing the JBS founder as "paranoid and unpatriotic," and Buckley also criticized the JBS membership for staying in the extreme anticommunist organization. In October, moreover, *National Review* published more denunciations by several prominent conservatives.[51] The ACU sent nearly fifty thousand letters from January 15 to February 14, 1966, based on multiple mailing lists of organizations, including conservative magazine *Human Event* and the Conservative Action Party. While 29 percent of all mail was about the ACU's programs, 30 percent of all mail dealt with the JBS, mentioning the *National Review* article criticizing the JBS and the fact that ACU board of directors and the advisory assembly were opposed to the JBS.[52]

National Review's criticism of Welch immediately received reactions from the JBS membership. "I do not want to write lengthily but basically I cannot support *NR* so long as you so vehemently disagree with Robert Welch and the

JBS," a Birch member wrote to *National Review*. This was part of "the flood" of letters from the JBS.[53] Because many Birchers also subscribed to *National Review*, they received direct mailings from the magazine and predictably reacted to the appeals with anger. Another Birch member said it was "a very unfortunate approach to raising money," and many JBS members stopped contributing to *National Review* or sent a storm of protest letters.[54]

Although the influence of the JBS remained strong in the mid-1960s, the ACU directors expected that the radical right group would shortly lose its centripetal force. In addition to the *National Review*'s article, national media, academics, and politicians accused the JBS of promoting extreme ideology. This avalanche of attack took a toll on the JBS, and the Birch membership declined over the latter part of the 1960s.[55] Emphasizing "leadership cadre" rather than "mass movement," the ACU never attempted to fill the void left by the JBS. The ACU managed to support itself by amassing funds through direct mail solicitation instead of membership fees, and in election years, the ACU rallied support for conservative candidates by sending out mails from the ACU headquarters to prospective contributors throughout the country. In 1969, the ACU created its political action committee, Conservative Victory Fund, which provided politicians with funds collected from the conservative ranks. The ACU also sponsored several programs to strengthen the conservative leadership in education, journalism, and state legislatures by establishing the ACU Education and Research Foundation, the National Journalism Center, and the American Legislative Exchange Council.[56]

However, discontent smoldered within the ACU over its grassroots mobilization. William J. Gill in Pennsylvania sent ACU Chairman Donald Bruce a letter, which mentioned that he and his friends were disappointed that the ACU was hesitant to form local chapters. "My own feeling is that you have to build from the grass roots up," Gill said. He made his case that the ACU needed to construct closer relationships with the grassroots by organizing more conservatives through means other than just direct mail, stressing, "They must have something to do, besides write checks."[57] Likewise, Leo Synnestvedt of the Philadelphia area was critical of the ACU activities based primarily in Washington, DC. The "ACU *must organize locally*," Synnestvedt urged, arguing that local conservatives lived in a local world and therefore the ACU was not able to maintain their interests by the operations from Washington that seemed so often "out of our hands."[58]

Responding to the calls for more local activities, the ACU made some efforts to mobilize grassroots conservatives. The anti-John Birch Society campaign carefully distinguished the JBS rank and file from their leader. The *National Review* article blamed Welch for his conspiracy theory without attacking his followers. Simultaneously, the ACU attempted to attract grassroots conservatives from the right-wing organization. Before *National Review* issued the anti-JBS article, Rusher was assigned to organize a division of the ACU to "receive JBS members and others who desire a JBS-type relationship."[59] Rusher's political action programs were an important step in making the ACU a broadly based organization. An example of such attempts to broaden the ACU's membership base was the organization's political action handbook, which instructed its members on "how to get active in the affairs of their local party organizations; how to work upward toward real influence in them; etc."[60] Although the ACU sought to develop an echelon of conservative leaders at its foundation, it also tried to reach rank-and-file conservatives by offering local programs and establishing chapters around nation as the JBS did.

Yet, as Rusher acknowledged in his memoir, the ACU did "not always successfully" organize local conservatives.[61] In his reply to Synnestvedt who insisted the ACU build local chapters, Rusher agreed that the ACU had an important function in the field of political action but noted that "the Board [of Directors of the ACU], for reasons it has deemed sufficient, has chosen to go slowly in this matter."[62] Rusher and other ACU leaders were afraid that local chapters frequently drifted away from national programs into other "more immediately rewarding forms of political activity," such as local campaigns.[63] Despite the increasing number of requests for authorization to establish ACU local organizations over the course of the late 1960s, Rusher continued to disappoint many local activists by letting them know that "we are prepared to continue along the same line of inaction locally," or "we do not feel that time is ripe for the organization of a chapter of the ACU in Oregon."[64]

The ACU maintained its top-down structure to direct the conservative movement. Instead of organizing the conservative ranks through local and state chapters, ACU directors defined "political action" as working on national politics. In consultation with other members, Rusher set forth his proposals for political actions that included "research on issues" for use by incumbent conservative congressmen and candidates for offices, or a program to put the RNC "under surveillance."[65] For this purpose, the ACU disseminated research materials to conservative politicians so that they could choose and develop their issues, while attacking the moderate policies under the RNC.[66] Eventually, the ACU settled into the position of a membership organization. But unlike the JBS, which kept its members active in neighborhoods and precincts, the ACU made its members pay their dues to Washington. In 1969, the ACU founded a Conservative

Victory Fund that made contributions to candidates who deserved conservative support. In Rusher's view, the fund was "a very useful device for conservatives who may not have the time or facilities to research such matters themselves but who don't want to make contributions through party channels." Additionally, the ACU created institutions such as the ACU Education and Research Foundation, which in turn financed the National Journalism Center that trained conservative journalists, and the American Legislative Exchange Council, which specialized in activities of the state legislatures.[67]

The Development of Political Direct Mail

Like Viguerie, a new generation of direct mail operatives contributed to the expansion of conservative politics, competing sometimes with older right-wingers over financial sources. Neil McCaffrey was among the ambitious and entrepreneurial conservative activists. Born to a Catholic family in the Bronx, McCaffrey began his professional career in publishing. He worked for Doubleday as an editor and direct mail copywriter for six years before Macmillan hired him to set up a mail order department in 1961. McCaffrey expressed interest in nascent conservatism during the 1950s. In 1957, he wrote to Buckley's *National Review*, saying that he could increase the magazine's readership through his expertise in advertising. He promoted *National Review* with a direct mail program that he believed helped increase the circulation of the political magazine from 17,000 to 142,000 during the Goldwater campaign.[68] McCaffrey comprehended how to reach out to new consumers by means of extensive but selective direct mail advertising, saying, "This simple device will speak more loudly than a dozen salesmen."[69]

McCaffrey was dedicated particularly to promoting conservative bookstores in the post-Goldwater years as the president of the Conservative Book Club that he founded in April 1964. Using the list of active subscribers to *National Review*, the book club shortly gained about thirty thousand members, to whom McCaffrey mailed a selection of right-wing books at discounted prices each month. In its turn, the Conservative Book Club provided its mailing lists to Liebman when the political consultant launched direct mail solicitation in 1965. McCaffrey's direct mail promoting broke through the publishing wall that conservative writers and publishers faced in the 1960s. Conservative publishing companies, such as Regnery Publishing and Devin Garrity of Devin-Adair Publishing, signed contracts with the club to sell their books directly with potential conservative readers. By 1967 the Conservative Book Club had average sales of fifteen to twenty thousand conservative books a month.[70]

But at the same time, McCaffrey began to menace older right-wing publishers. In late 1964 McCaffrey founded his own publishing company, Arlington House, to explore the market for works written by "responsible conservatives." "Most houses barely scratch the surface of this market," McCaffrey claimed, contrasting conventional publishers with his direct mail operations. While average publishers used one-third of a page in a magazine for advertising a book, he asserted, the direct mail was more effective in "selling directly to consumers." Although publishers traditionally asked bookstores to order a sufficient stock of a book before the publication, McCaffrey's new publishing company attempted to generate demand by direct mail promotion.[71] Henry Regnery, the founder of Regnery Publishing that had contributed to conservatism by publishing books including Buckley's *God and Man at Yale* and Russel Kirk's *The Conservative Mind*, faced the new competition. To meet the threat posed by the newly emerging publishing company, Regnery teamed with other conservative publishers to organize their own book club to rival McCaffrey's business. Regnery shortly abolished his plan to found the joint book club, but he remained concerned about the competition from the direct mail promoter.[72]

The older generation of conservatives thought that the new wave of conservative activism decreased their revenues within a small pie of the conservative movement. However, Viguerie argued that direct mail helped enlarge the market of conservatism. He developed political direct mail during the 1960s, learning how to carve out niches in American politics. Viguerie especially stressed the importance of branding. In the early 1960s when he raised funds for Young Americans for Freedom, he discovered that solicitation did not work well if his appeals only explained YAF's programs for the Goldwater campaign; instead, his direct mail was more successful in collecting money if his letters detailed the group's activities on campus. Recognizing that fighting against the New Left in universities was what the "Republican campaign groups weren't going to do," direct mail of Viguerie and other conservatives highlighted brand identity in their direct mail to make their clients stand out in the conservative movement.[73]

Over the course of the 1960s, the conservative student organization maintained its policy of sticking to its brand by sending direct mailings that stressed its fight against young left-wingers. In the early 1960s, the main target of YAF was left-wing students in the National Student Association (NSA). Founded in 1947, the NSA was a national student organization intended to promote the interests of university students, but conservative students were concerned over the liberal orientation of the group. In 1961, YAF created the Committee for a Responsible National Student Organization, headquartered in YAF's New

York offices, to advance their opposition to the NSA. Viguerie's direct mail high-lighted the fight against the NSA as one of YAF's main campus issues in the early 1960s. Naming the NSA "the far left-wing," Viguerie announced that YAF had initiated a nationwide campaign to drive the NSA off college campuses when his direct mailings solicited funds for the activities of young conservatives.[74]

As the Vietnam War sparked a series of antiwar protests and the New Left movement, the late 1960s witnessed the rise of student uprisings on campuses from coast to coast. Facing the emergence of the New Left and Students for a Democratic Society (SDS), YAF branded themselves as the student organization that resisted left-wing "radicals." A letter in 1969 aggressively remarked that the "Student Revolution . . . is a growing menace to our educational institutions and to the whole structure of our society."[75] YAF direct mail fundraising at the end of the decade frequently stressed patriotism. While American soldiers were mak-ing "the supreme sacrifice for Flag and Country," a letter said, protesters were "making mockery of the patriotic sacrifice of our beloved sons with anti-war, peace at any price demonstrations and electioneering."[76] Another appeal, appar-ently designed for adults who had children, emphasized violence on campus to stir up fear and antipathy for SDS. "If you had a son or daughter who was beaten up or had their life threatened by SDS hooligans," the direct mailing noted, "I'm sure you would be fighting mad and want to take immediate action." With an enclosed memo that listed reports of "SDS terror tactics," the letter was designed to stress the New Left's "radicals," the term that had been applied to the conser-vative movement just a few years before.[77]

By 1968, direct mail solicitation brought increased sums of funds to many con-servative groups. The American Conservative Union (ACU) was still struggling financially as the organization began the year with a deficit of $10,641.[78] After the debt grew to $20,826 in April, the ACU launched a direct mail fundrais-ing campaign. With a return rate of over 18 percent and an average contribution of $8, this solicitation drive successfully reduced the ACU's debt to $6,053 by July.[79] This improved ACU financial picture resulted from its efforts to increase the effectiveness of direct mail fundraising. For instance, the ACU kept their fundraising cost down by using YAF's offset machines to print their letters and promotion inserts.[80] The ACU also tried to amass funds at minimal costs by em-ploying selective lists, instead of bigger lists including unlikely donors, to gain a higher percentage of return.[81] Joint appeal was another method used to maximize the profit of direct mail. In 1969, the ACU, *Human Events*, and the Conservative Book Club joined together in a cooperative direct mailing so that they "cut our costs by nearly two-thirds."[82] As a consequence, the ACU's improved finances remained so stable that a report mentioned, "ACU's financial base is such that we can continue to meet our monthly budget without difficulty."[83]

Democratic organizations and politicians, too, became aware that political direct mail was immensely beneficial by the time they entered the electoral cycle in 1968. Among liberal groups that began to deploy direct mail was the Democratic Study Group (DSG). Organized as a contender to the conservative Republican-Dixiecrat coalition in 1959, the DSG engaged in research and analysis of political agendas, legislative proposals, and policy issues for Democratic policy makers. The organization promoted information exchange among Democrats by circulating *Legislative Report*, as a weekly summary of bills; *Fact Sheet*, a report with comprehensive analysis of major legislation; and other periodicals. Simultaneously, the DSG offered its support to candidates for office in key congressional elections. For these activities, the Democratic group collected money for liberal politicians during the 1960s, but its methodology transformed over the years.[84]

During the election year of 1968, the DSG implemented its first direct mail fundraising campaign, discovering that the medium brought about a great amount of financial benefit. The DSG collected campaign funds of approximately $15,000 in 1968, "the largest in its history," raising more than $90,000 through direct mail in the year. As a result of the appeals, the DSG also gained a mailing list of nearly ten thousand contributors, whose names were recorded on computer and would be used in ensuing campaigns.[85] The success of direct mail dramatically altered the DSG's view of fundraising. In 1964, the DSG and the Democratic National Committee had shared the conventional wisdom that the best way of fundraising was to ask people, whether they were a few wealthy millionaires or a mass of small donors. A memo of the DNC strongly recommended that candidates rely on direct solicitation by asking for funds in person, while saying that direct mail was not "as effective as face-to-face confrontation or even a telephone campaign."[86] However, by the early 1970s, a guideline entitled "How to Shake the Money Tree" emphasized that direct mail "can be quite successful if your lists are selective and your appeal is well written," and it recommended personal visits be limited to "potential big donors."[87]

Democratic politicians and candidates were also intrigued by direct mail by the end of the 1960s. Probably the most unusual anecdote about political direct mail in those years was George McGovern's contact with Viguerie. According to Viguerie's autobiography, the Democratic senator telephoned the conservative political consultant in 1967, requesting his direct mail fundraising services for the 1968 senatorial campaign. After a long chat, Viguerie declined McGovern's request due to their ideological distinctiveness. But Viguerie was pleased by the liberal senator's appreciation of direct mail when most politicians did not understand its effectiveness. McGovern found another direct mail fundraiser who was politically closer to him and successfully raised campaign funds in 1968. After his reelection, McGovern advised his liberal colleagues to employ direct mail, and more Democrats acknowledged the efficacy of the political device in raking in money.[88] Antiwar liberal Eugene McCarthy also contacted Steven Winchell, vice president of the Ricard A. Viguerie Company (RAVCO), to ask for direct mail solicitation in the 1972 campaign. But again, the RAVCO did not assist the liberal politician, confining its fundraising efforts solely to conservative politics.[89] Although the RAVCO did not work with liberals in their campaigning, these episodes indicated that conservatives and liberals alike considered Viguerie the godfather of direct mail, even just a few years after the foundation of his consulting firm.

Compared with conservative direct mail, the language of liberal fundraising letters was designed to appeal to ideals rather than stirring up anxieties. Harold Oram, a New York liberal consultant who had engaged in direct mail fundraising from the 1940s and briefly mentored Liebman, was involved with educational programs for peace when the antiwar movement was in its heyday. "It is a crime against nature for the young to die first," stated a direct mailing with the signature of Martin Luther King Sr., which pointed to the casualties in the Vietnam War. This contrasted with conservative direct mailings that gave weight to the patriotism of American soldiers. Soliciting funds for the Fund for Peace that established a Peace Fellowship Program to financially support students of peace and international affairs, the letter made rather lofty remarks: "We must stop the arms race. We must develop new systems to resolve conflict, systems to match the new world in which we live."[90] Similarly, another appeal signed by J. William Fulbright called for financial support by stressing idealism. "Against the concrete, dramatic face of war," a writer of the letter stated, "peace seems a remote ideal, but the building of peace requires commitment to this idea." The appeal went on that there was no ready answer to the question of how to build peace, but there was "hope" that consisted primarily in "the creative power of education."[91] Unlike Liebman's and Viguerie's fundraising letters, these direct mailings by liberal Oram did not bring partisanship to the fore in the late 1960s.

However, sharing several characteristics with conservatives' direct mail, the rhetoric of liberals' solicitation letters sometimes highlighted ideology. When the Oram, Inc. mailed out fundraising letters for a peace educational program, an appeal with the signature of David Riesman noted that he had been concerned over peace since he had left his position as war contract termination director at

Sperry Gyroscope Company in 1946. But the letter's writer said that the public did not take the issue seriously, and pointed to the "injection of right-wing chauvinism into our national life," including not only McCarthyism but also 1960s conservatism, which had discouraged many liberals from devoting themselves to problems of international politics.[92]

The DSG launched direct mailings with rather harsh language characterized by a sense of urgency and partisanship. In the solicitation letter during the 1968 election, the liberal group asserted that an "ugly tide of racial backlash" had swept through the political landscape, threatening liberal social programs. The direct mailing mentioned that, with the "backlash coalition" comprised of traditional Republicans, southern conservatives, and the racially fearful lower middle class, the Nixon and Wallace campaigns caused "the repressive forces" that created "political and social disaster."[93] Whereas some liberal direct mail attempted to raise funds without partisan rhetoric, many consultants relied on the common wisdom that contests, fears, and menaces effectively urged individual donors to send checks. This iron law was slowly but surely becoming more common among direct mail consultants beyond political tendencies over the years.

***

With the benefit of hindsight, the year of 1968 was the turning point of American politics in several senses. In this year, the Democratic Party was breaking asunder over the Vietnam War and urban unrest. Running as an antiwar candidate, Senator Eugene McCarthy of Minnesota stunned Americans by winning a 41 percent against President Lyndon B. Johnson in the New Hampshire primary on March 12. At the end of the vote, LBJ announced his withdrawal from the race. Senator Robert Kennedy was assassinated immediately after winning the California primary on June 5. To make matters worse, George Wallace ran as a third-party candidate and pulled up southern votes from the Democratic Party.[94]

Richard Nixon triumphantly returned to the national stage of the Republican National Convention in August 1968, whereas a violent and gloomy atmosphere hung in the air at the Democratic National Convention in Chicago, where the Chicago police responded to street protests. The war in Vietnam also cast a shadow on the Republican Party, as George Romney had ruined his campaign by claiming that he had supported the war due to "brainwashing" by American generals and diplomats. Nelson Rockefeller, the standard-bearer for moderate Republicans, participated in the presidential race too late to place his name on state ballots. Ronald Reagan, whose 1964 speech "A Time for Choosing" had propelled him into prominence among conservatives, was not ready for the presidential election just two years after he was elected governor of California in 1966. Alternatively, Nixon had gained the endorsement of Barry Goldwater in early 1965 and William Buckley in 1967, followed by many conservative politicians and activists.[95]

However, conservatives were not as zealous in 1968 as they had been four years earlier. William Rusher, Buckley's comrade in *National Review* and the American Conservative Union, supported Nixon because he was "conservative enough," though not as conservative as Reagan. F. Clifton White, another veteran of the 1964 Goldwater campaign, similarly calculated that conservatives' support was only "skin-deep." Richard Viguerie also mentioned that conservatives upheld Nixon because of "who his opponents were, but he was not one of us."[96] Anticipating Reagan could hardly be nominated at the convention, conservatives had few other choices than to back Nixon as a candidate against moderates like Rockefeller.

Despite the lack of enthusiasm among many conservatives, the Nixon campaign keenly realized that the future Republican Party hinged on their support. Kevin Phillips, a young New Yorker hired as an assistant by the Nixon campaign, designed the "southern strategy" during the 1968 election. In his 1969 monograph, *Emerging Republican Majority*, Phillips argued that "the revolt against established political interest has to be 'conservative,'" observing that the votes in the South, the West, and middle-class suburbia were increasingly the keys to winning elections. He considered 1968 a turning point that represented these shifts in ideology, population movement, and regionalism, pointing to the post–World War II migration of many White Americans to suburbs across the Sunbelt and the "Negro problem" that was transformed to a national issue as the result of the northern movement of African Americans since the 1920s.[97]

Coupled with the southern strategy, public relations consulting played a key role in the 1968 Nixon campaign. In 1969 Joe McGinniss published his book, *The Selling of the President*, which revealed how advertising agencies were engaged in image making on behalf of Nixon. Echoing political scientist Stanley Kelley who had warned the impacts of the advertising business on American politics in the 1950s, McGinniss stressed how "television men" and "TV politicians" altered truth in politics. Drawing from Daniel Boorstin's 1962 work, *The Image*, McGinniss outlined "a reshaping of our concept of truth" in the political use of television: "Television seems particularly useful to the politicians who can be charming but lacks idea. Print is for ideas. . . . On television it matters less that he does not have ideas. His personality is what the viewers want to share." In his book, McGinniss recounted how politicians and advertising agencies, such as Harry Treleaven, Frank Shakespeare, and others, worked together to sell Nixon to voters.[98]

The Selling of the Presidency called public attention to the cooperation of advertising agencies with political candidates, which had taken firm root in the national elections in 1952. However, McGinniss simultaneously demonstrated the divide among political operatives. The campaign manager John Mitchell and White House Chief of Staff H. R. Haldeman doubted the value of television. Nixon never trusted television either. He disliked looking at himself on the display and refused to use a teleprompter, no matter how long his speech was. Advertising agencies in the Nixon campaign were frequently interrupted by politicians. "The perfect campaign, the computer campaign, the technicians' campaign, the television campaign . . . had collapsed beneath the weight of Nixon's grayness," Treleaven was quoted as saying. "The total split between the advertising and political people was very bad."[99]

As McGinniss indicated the significance and tension in political television ads, the late 1960s witnessed a sea change in the relationship between Capitol Hill and Madison Avenue. As advertising agencies worked for candidates during the 1950s and 1960s, political consultants gradually shifted from general to specialized consulting. Back in the 1952 presidential election, press editor Robert Humphreys had comprehensively directed the Dwight Eisenhower campaign, crafting his basic plans for public relations, fundraising, volunteer mobilization, and so on. By the end of the 1960s, however, candidates for office turned to political consultants with a specialized expertise in one area of electioneering such as polling, television advertising, filmmaking, direct mail fundraising, and computer campaigning, among others. The specialized consultants were involved with political campaigns as full-time professionals, focusing solely on political activities. In tandem with this professionalization, the advertising industry on Madison Avenue was gradually distancing itself from the political arena, partly because it did not fit into the heightened partisanship. Filling the void in the political consulting industry, professional political consultants, including Viguerie, moved from New York to Washington to work more closely with candidates and political organizations. The professionalization of consultancy and the separation of political consulting from the advertising business accelerated ideological partisanship in American elections.[100]

The formation of the November Group, Nixon's in-house advertising agency in 1972, evinced the geographical shift of political consulting from New York to Washington. This shift occurred in part because an in-house agency was less expensive as the Nixon campaign staff expected that they could save as much as $1,200,000 by forming an agency in Washington. But the main reason was political. A memorandum of the Nixon campaign team indicated that they decided to set up an independent agency in Washington because the White House could directly control its campaign advertising. Jeb S. Magruder, who managed the Committee for the Re-Election of the President (CRP), assumed that quite a few ad agencies in New York and Chicago were left-leaning and that "all agencies would have difficulty putting their best people on our account because of their political affiliations." As an advertising magazine article similarly pointed out, the Nixon campaign created its own agency in DC because "it's being argued so many young people in ad agencies were anti-Nixon."[101]

Gathering ad agents from several cities, the November Group produced campaign advertisements during the 1972 election. Peter H. Dailey, president of Dailey and Associates of Los Angeles, presided over the in-house agency. Other members were Phil Joanou from Doyle Dane Bernbach's Los Angeles office, William Taylor from Ogilvy & Mather in New York, and others. The general advertising strategy and its implementation were overseen by an advisory board that included prominent ad agencies such as Richard O'Reilly, executive vice president of Wells, Rich, Greene, and Henry Schachte, who was president of J. Walter Thompson. The staff produced ads, including print, film, radio, and television spins, for the CRP and Democrats for Nixon throughout the campaign.[102]

In addition to mass media advertising under the November Group, the Nixon campaign launched direct mail drives. In April 1971, Viguerie's firm tried to contact Nixon's campaign. Stephen Winchell, vice president of the RAVCO, sent a letter to Robert C. Odle, who was a friend since college days and later served as staff assistant to the president from 1969 to 1971, explaining that direct mail was effective in raising funds and reaching out to voters. The RAVCO offered their expertise to raise money, solicit votes, enlist volunteers, and increase the percentage of Nixon votes in primary states, while suggesting that its direct mail would raise $14,500,000 net to the Nixon campaign and develop a list of 950,000 contributors as well as 1,800,000 Nixon supporters. Although the Nixon campaign did not sign a contract with the RAVCO, Nixon's staff paid attention to the function of the personalized medium to reach individuals, especially Independents and swing voters.[103]

Unlike the RAVCO's direct mail fundraising, Nixon's direct mail operations were intended mainly to solicit votes and recruit volunteers. There were three objectives of the direct mail campaign: "1) To provide a highly personalized mass medium to communicate with and influence the voter to support the President, 2) To increase the voter turnout of those supporting the President, and 3) To motivate a large number of people to involve themselves in the campaign as volunteers."[104] The Nixon campaign staff deployed direct mail on two levels. The "mega-level" operation aimed at politicizing tens of millions of independent and swing voters by Election Day. These voters had no particular relationship to Nixon and the Republican Party, and Nixon's direct mail operatives attempted to acquire the names through a public vendor. The other level of mail operation focused on voters who supported Nixon or the GOP, calling on them to engage in the campaign effort. The mailing lists for these voters came from the White House and the RNC. "There is reason to believe that direct mail can be highly effective in striking narrow yet highly responsive cords among fertile voters," an operative stressed; thus, "direct mail [should] be viewed as a major campaign thrust."[105]

Robert Morgan participated in massive direct mail campaigns on behalf of Nixon. He was a professional direct mailer and was employed by the CRP during the 1972 election. Issues that Morgan emphasized in direct mail were unemployment, Vietnam, environment, health care, the economy, drugs, crime, and foreign policy. Understanding the importance of selectivity for direct mail, Morgan disseminated effective messages targeted at specific groups. For example, in California, he identified diverse voters such as high-income and low-income citizens, Italian, Jewish, Los Angeles Spanish, San Diego Spanish, other Spanish, and other ethnic groups. The Nixon campaign sent out appeals stressing "Social Security, e.g., Humanitarian, Israel, Education, Environment, Defense, Peace" for Jewish Americans, while emphasizing "Drugs, Defense, Inflation & Taxes, Busing" for middle-income voters.[106] Direct mailings in each state had local prominent Republicans' signatures. When Californians received a solicitation letter, they discovered Ronald Reagan's signature. And direct mailings in New York usually contained the signatures of well-known figures: James L. Buckley, William F. Buckley's brother and conservative New York senator; Jacob K. Javits, a towering liberal Republican senator; and Harold Jacobs, a leader of the American Jewish community in New York.[107] Morgan and his staff organized their mailing operations so that direct mail's function of personalization worked well to gain as much support as possible.

Like the Nixon campaign, George McGovern's campaign carried out direct mail drives in 1972. McGovern was no match for Nixon, who raked in a record amount of campaign money during the presidential election. But in the sense that the McGovern insurgency was a combination of centralized program and grassroots fervor, the Democratic presidential candidate was more successful than Nixon in marshaling direct mail in populist ways. Morris Dees was a central figure in the direct mail campaigns for McGovern. Based in Montgomery, Alabama, Dees had developed one of the largest direct mail businesses outside

New York and Chicago by 1969 when he sold his company and became a public interest lawyer. When the McGovern campaign was continually confronted with financial crises in 1971, Dees became an unpaid consultant to the campaign and assumed a role in raising funds. The direct mail operations under Dees built on a centralized model. Transferring donors' names from cards, lists, and tapes to computer tapes, the campaign managed the information of hundreds of thousands of supporters and efficiently sent deliberate appeals to them.[108]

The McGovern campaign was financed largely by people with modest incomes. Observing the 1972 presidential election, journalist Theodore H. White wrote that McGovern was the most successful candidate in gaining "grass-roots money," by which he meant funds raised by direct mail or televised solicitation.[109] McGovernites estimated the total of contributions that the campaign received throughout the presidential election reached between $20 and $25 million, most of which came from small contributors. Dees conceived a direct mail program through the McGovern for President Club, which McGovern supporters joined and contributed $10 each month throughout the campaign. Club members received monthly "insider's newsletters" and coupon books, which enclosed payment slips. The McGovern for President Club took shape after Dees sent invitations to twenty-two thousand individuals who had contributed to the McGovern campaign. The membership started at roughly four thousand in March 1971 and grew to almost ten thousand by January 1972, with over 90 percent of the participants paying their monthly dues. In early 1972, the club generated nearly $100, each month, keeping the McGovern campaign afloat. Pointing to the tradition of associational democracy in the United States, Dees said that the ardent engagement indicated that "Alexis de Tocqueville was right when he observed almost 150 years ago that America was a nation of joiners."[110]

McGovern also applauded the financing of his campaign, contrasting his small donations from ordinary Americans and Nixon's campaign cash donated by the few. In his acceptance speech at the Democratic National Convention in July, McGovern highlighted the difference of the two campaigns by saying, "Let the opposition collect their $10 million in secret money from the privileged. And let us find one million ordinary Americans who will contribute $25 each to this campaign."[111] White, too, emphasized in his book that the McGovern campaign's direct mail collected an "altruistic kind of money," adding that "its success may have begun a hopeful revolution for the future."[112] As liberals implemented direct mail fundraising campaigns, they optimistically regarded the computerized medium as drawing clean money in an open way, spurring political activism among the grassroots and providing opportunities for American democracy.

However, unlike Dees's remarks on Tocqueville, individual contributions to the McGovern campaign were not necessarily rooted in American tradition of grassroots participation. The small contributors were grassroots in the sense that they were the gathering of small involvements, but they were selected and targeted by the campaign's computer database, instead of being mobilized through organizations and communities from the bottom up. In fact, the McGovern campaign's centralized mobilization through data analysis at times conflicted grassroots fieldworkers. For instance, Miles Rubin, a California entrepreneur, helped the McGovern campaign in the state with his expertise on marketing and computers. When Rubin organized county registration data and crafted canvassing plans for the volunteers in the field, many organizers in the campaign felt antipathy to the centralized computer system because, they claimed, it undermined the autonomy of McGovern's grassroots army.[113]

Besides, when McGovern appraised his small funds by making a contrast with Nixon's big money, he ironically shared the antiestablishment tenets with Viguerie. Direct mail's "grassroots" mobilization frequently worked with a sort of populism that drew out contrasts with the elite, as antithesis to the establishment, summoning up great enthusiasm on both the left and right beginning in the late 1960s. Alternatively, computerized direct mail was predicated on a centralized system, which was pursued by RNC Chair Ray Bliss but occasionally incompatible with grassroots liberals. As the new political technology was accompanied with antielite populism and sometimes at odds with a conventional fashion of the grassroots, direct mail gradually transformed political participation among many Americans.

***

The post-Goldwater years saw the expansion of direct mail politics. Richard Viguerie has been considered the pioneer of political direct mail. However, by the time he founded his direct mail firm in 1965, the political use of computerized direct mail was already popular among right-wing activists, conservative Christians, moderate Republicans, and liberals. As many candidates and political organizations launched fundraising campaigns, there were several methodologies of direct mail operation. Bliss employed direct mail fundraising to gloss over ideological conflicts within the Republican Party by focusing on the practical issue of political money. When Democrats and liberal organizations used direct mail, they attempted to raise funds by illustrating hopes and progressive changes. Yet conservatives capitalized on negative emotions, such as fear, anxiety, and frustration, to call for political contributions and immediate actions.

Among diverse direct mailings, Viguerie's appeals proved that his alchemy to turn fear into money was most successful in collecting money.

Money and corruption riveted public attention as one of the key issues by the end of the 1960s. Because television ads in political races had skyrocketed from the early 1950s on, several political scientists and lawmakers warned that swelling campaign finance caused ethical problems in American politics. During the 1972 race, McGovern made fundraising efforts that appealed to the "little people" who were confronted with the "rich cat," including the Nixon administration, with intimate relationships with big business. Democrats condemned President Nixon's acceptance of tremendous amounts of contributions from giant corporations in the early 1970s, and immediately after the Watergate scandal, the Democratic-controlled Congress passed Amendments to the Federal Election Campaign Act in 1974. This campaign finance reform championed by Democrats, however, would accelerate the ascendancy of Viguerie's ideological direct mail in the 1970s.

CHAPTER 5

Debates over Campaign Finance Reform

"RAISING CAMPAIGN FUNDS HAS been a pressing difficulty for generations, but it assumed new dimensions," said Alexander Heard, a political scientist who served as chairman of the President's Commission on Campaign Costs in 1963. Both major political parties spent larger amounts of money than ever for political campaigns in the early 1960s, and the budgets continuously grew throughout the decade. In the 1960 presidential election, for instance, expenditures reported by Democratic and Republican national campaign committees increased 55 percent from the 1956 race.[1] One of the reasons for the mounting political costs was obviously television advertising in the postwar years when a half hour of prime-time TV was estimated to be more expensive than Lincoln's total campaign in 1860. In 1964 when "the admen came in here with a saturation television campaign," a veteran of the 1960 and 1964 Democratic presidential campaigns mentioned, party operatives had "never seen that much money around Washington." The increasing war chest resulted in political parties' dependence on "fat cat money" provided by certain wealthy individuals and organizations. According to a report, 60 percent of the funds received by the Democratic and Republican national committees came from four thousand people.[2] As Democrats and Republicans attempted to rake in big money through various methods, the intimate connections between political parties and money interests shortly attracted public criticism in the 1960s. "The burden of raising such sums weighs heavily on the political parties and the methods they use are often open to serious objections," Heard added.[3]

Democrats and Republicans faced the same issue of campaign costs, but they dealt with the problem in different ways. While political consultants for Republicans employed new technologies, including direct mail and television for raising funds, during the 1960s, John F. Kennedy and Lyndon B. Johnson poured money into the Democratic Party by taking advantage of their national prominence as incumbent presidents. These Democratic presidents collected big contributions from magnates and corporations by organizing galas, dinner parties, and special interest groups. In this sense, the issue of money in politics was more serious to the Democratic Party over the years. As Democrats secured large contributions through several schemes, mass media covered scandals regarding Democratic solicitations.

As a result, the 1960s witnessed a series of proposed campaign finance reform bills. In response to several fundraising scandals, legislators and experts made efforts to transform campaign finance laws, believing that big money would decay American democracy. While a coalition of public interest reformers tried to ease the danger of money corruption in electoral politics, however, their election reforms encountered partisan opposition throughout the 1960s. Republicans sought to decrease Democrats' ability to collect political funds from wealthy donors. Liberal Democrats pursued new campaign reforms without undermining the political activities of labor unions. Southern Democrats were warm to campaign reform unless the change would increase the growing influence of the federal government in primary elections and state organizations. Indeed, public support for campaign finance reform was not high enough to transform elections in the 1960s, but the congressional debates over money and politics laid the groundwork for the campaign finance reforms in the 1970s.[4]

If diverse interests revolved around the debates on campaign finance reform during the 1960s, election reform in the 1970s was the product of partisan struggles primarily between liberals and conservatives. When big money turned away from the Democratic Party after Richard Nixon seized control of the White House in 1969, Democrats called for more electoral regulations. At the same time, conservatives argued against liberal reforms, claiming that regulations on individual contributions would violate the First Amendment and freedom of expression. The Federal Election Campaign Act (FECA) of 1971 and the Amendment to the FECA of 1974 were the major achievements of Democrats. Ironically, however, the liberal reforms led to the ascendancy of conservatives who utilized direct mail fundraising more effectively than liberals in the 1970s. Campaign finance reform of the 1960s and 1970s demonstrated how liberals and conservatives intertwined with each other in an unexpected way.

Controversies over Democratic Fundraising Dinners

In the early 1960s, John F. Kennedy played a starring role in raising funds for the Democratic Party, which incurred an unprecedented debt of $3 million during the 1960 campaign. Beginning with the inauguration eve gala in Washington, DC, President Kennedy organized many events to contribute to his party's coffers. Most of the events were $100-a-plate dinners, a solicitation method that began back in the New Deal years. Through organizing the traditional fundraising parties, Kennedy helped pour approximately $10 million into the party's treasury, which easily wiped out the $4 million debt by the summer of 1963.[5]

Such remarkable fundraising campaigns sometimes came under attack. One of Kennedy's controversial solicitations was an invitation to the second inaugural anniversary on January 18, 1963. In the winter of 1962, federal government career employees received formal invitations to purchase $100-a-plate tickets for a second inaugural salute dinner, which was sponsored by the Democratic National Committee. In honor of President and Mrs. Kennedy and Vice President and Mrs. Johnson, the gala would be attended by stars of the stage and screen, including Carol Channing, Gene Kelly, and Kirk Douglas, to name only the most notable celebrities. In this invitation, the DNC asked government employees for "the pleasure of your company," while making it clear that the money raised by the event would go to the campaign coffers of the DNC.[6]

This sort of solicitation lay in the gray zone of campaign finance laws. The 1939 Hatch Act prohibited federal employees from participating in any partisan activities, and the civil service system assured that the employees would be compensated and promoted on the basis of merit.[7] Civil Service Commission officials noted that the invitation to the gala did not violate the Hatch Act so long as the letters were mailed to the employees' homes, not to government buildings nor at government expense. However, some government personnel officials questioned the ethics in such a practice to raise funds from government employees. According to an anonymous personnel director of one of the biggest government agencies, some Democratic officeholders actually mentioned to their career subordinates that "it might be nice if they could see their way clear to attending" the event.[8] When they got the letters from the DNC, some career employees complained that the invitations were "not-too-subtle pressure" on them to buy the $100 tickets if they wanted to remain in the good graces of their bosses and hang on to their jobs or receive promotions.[9]

The DNC invitation ignited partisan debates between Democrats and Republicans. Shortly after newspapers had reported the fundraising event for the Democratic Party, Republican Senator John L. Williams, a prominent watchdog of Civil Service operations, directed the Senate's attention to the DNC solicitation. Claiming that federal government employees were being solicited in government buildings to buy the tickets, Williams pointed out that such a solicitation was "morally and legally wrong." On their part, Democrats asserted that the solicitation never breached campaign finance laws. Senator Hubert H.

Humphrey refuted Williams by making his case that solicitation of political funds from federal government employees was nothing new and "there is no evidence of coercion."[10] A spokesperson for the DNC also said that the committee did not pressure any government employee to purchase the tickets for the gala celebration. When a newspaper reporter asked White House Press Secretary Pierre Salinger if President Kennedy had approved of the invitation, Salinger denied Kennedy's responsibility, saying, "I have not discussed it with the President."[11]

Even a few Democrats expressed concern over the invitation sent to federal employees. Representative Richard E. Lankford of Maryland sent a telegram to John W. Macy, head of the Civil Service Commission. Lankford mentioned in his message that the nonpartisan federal civil service was essential to the proper functioning of the executive branch, adding, "It would be most unfortunate if this tradition were jeopardized as the result of over-zealous activity of a few individuals." The gala invitation could be regarded as putting pressure or threats on government workers, which was unethical and undemocratic behavior, thus provoking some dissents in Democratic circles.[12]

Government employees themselves also spoke out against the invitation to the Democratic celebration. John E. Durrett, an electronic engineer who had worked for the Veterans Administration for fourteen years, sent a letter to the DNC in which he rejected the invitation to the $100 gala to protest what he considered a "politically inspired infringement on the career service" that was not conducive to confidence in the national leadership.[13]

Despite these criticisms and protests, the second inaugural anniversary was held at the Washington National Guard Armory on January 18, 1963. It successfully raised enormous funds for the Democratic Party. This event alone collected $1 million overnight, enough to wipe out the Democratic Party's deficit of $800,000, making the party solvent for the first time since 1952. The income flowed into the Democratic Party coffers from two events: a foodless gala at the Armory in which four or five thousand guests paid $100 to attend; and a dinner at the International Inn attended by six hundred guests who paid $1,000 each to join "the President's Club." At the dinner, President and Mrs. Kennedy showed up in the center of the large ballroom with Vice President and Mrs. Johnson and other prominent Democrats. President Kennedy moved from table to table, visiting with such guests as New York Yankees center fielder Mickey Mantle and Charles Clark who lobbied for the Francisco Franco government of Spain. Using his dazzling personality in the spectacular fundraising events for the Democratic Party, Kennedy helped the DNC attract big money during his presidency.[14]

Bipartisan Direct Mail Campaign in 1964

As political parties were suffering from increasing television costs and astronomical debt by the early 1960s, a nonprofit group of experts, including scholars, politicians, and philanthropists, began to investigate campaign finance. In January 1958, William H. Vanderbilt, former Republican governor of Rhode Island, initiated the Committee on Campaign Contributions and Expenditures, which would be renamed the Citizens' Research Foundation. The organization was dedicated to studying political campaign costs and informing the public of campaign finance. When the foundation was established, there was no reliable information available about contributions and expenditures in political campaigns. With a special emphasis on disclosure, Vanderbilt appointed Herbert Alexander, who taught political science at Princeton University, to direct a research division of the foundation. Known as the "dean" of political finance and election reform studies, Alexander would direct the Citizens' Research Foundation for forty years, constructing a framework of campaign finance reform throughout the 1960s.[15]

At the White House, while collecting money through galas and dinner parties, JFK appointed a bipartisan commission to discuss measures for improving campaign finance. In 1961, Kennedy invited Alexander Heard into the executive branch to lead the President's Commission on Campaign Costs, and also assigned Herbert Alexander as executive director of the commission in December. The political scientists in the commission crafted a unanimous report concerning the financing of the presidential election campaigns in April 1962. As a bipartisan project, the report was endorsed by DNC Chairman John M. Bailey, RNC Chairman William E. Miller, Harry S. Truman, Dwight D. Eisenhower, Adlai Stevenson, Thomas E. Dewey, and Richard Nixon.[16] Heard's proposals included several matters on campaign finance. Although Kennedy supported a public funding program, the commission suggested small individual contributions as an alternative solution. Heard emphasized that presidential initiatives were essential to achieve several programs and changes, especially bipartisan fundraising activities and legislative reforms, to encourage more citizens to contribute to the party of their choice.[17]

The projects of the commission went through twists and turns. After Kennedy's assassination in November 1963, Lyndon Johnson took over the President's Commission on Campaign Costs. Yet President Johnson was initially uninterested in campaign finance reform. He cancelled a White House conference on political contribution and declined to resubmit Kennedy's reform proposals to Congress. Alexander left the administration to work again in the Citizens' Research Foundation, and efforts for campaign finance reform stagnated in the

Johnson administration.[18] However, by the time that the 1964 general election was about to begin, Johnson became more positive about dealing with campaign finance issues. "As I understand it, the basic point made by your Commission is that the broadest possible participation in fund-raising should be encouraged," Johnson said in his reply to Heard. Johnson considered swelling campaign finance a serious problem, saying that contributing money to politics was also "contributing to the health of our democracy."[19]

Johnson's words were not just lip service to campaign finance reformers. Based on the proposals by the Commission on Campaign Costs, Democrats and Republicans implemented a bipartisan fundraising campaign for the 1964 presidential election. The commission sponsored a White House Conference on Campaign Finance in the spring of that year. Alexander stated that the conference had three purposes: to alert the public by assembling representatives of the major parties, to focus attention on the responsibility of citizens to participate in the political system through contribution, and to encourage private groups, associations, unions, and corporations to undertake bipartisan campaign activities.[20] As both parties shouldered the burden of mounting campaign finance, the president's commission announced a bipartisan fundraising drive in New York in June 1964. This was the latest effort in a series of attempts to help both the Democratic and Republican parties raise more money through small contributions from "average voters." Although many candidates for governor and senator had already made similar efforts, it was the first initiative beyond party lines. By enlarging the base of financial support for Democrats and Republicans alike, the bipartisan solicitation campaign aimed at making candidates more independent of large contributors.[21]

It was direct mail that, as in the 1964 Goldwater campaign, the president's commission deployed for the purpose of promoting small funds from a larger number of contributors. Walter N. Thayer and Dan A. Kimball were the planners of the bipartisan fundraising drive. Both men were members of the President's Commission on Campaign Costs. Thayer was a Republican and president of the *New York Herald Tribune*, and Kimball was a Democrat and chairman of the Aero-Jet General Corp., and also former secretary of the navy under President Harry Truman. While each of them recruited five Democrats and Republicans, respectively, Thayer and Kimball employed R. L. Polk & Co,. a Detroit political consulting firm, which specialized in direct mail advertising, to handle the bipartisan solicitation campaign.[22] Julian Haydon, vice president and assistant general manager of the Polk firm's marketing service division, suggested the direct mail appeal to the president's commission Chairman Heard. Haydon remarked, "This is a noble effort to solve a problem that has nagged this country for decades—how to get the 'little man' to do his share in national campaigns," estimating that the revenue from the direct mail solicitation could amount to $45 million.[23] The commission accepted the scheme. Former presidents Truman and Eisenhower signed the joint bipartisan mail appeal for contributions to finance the 1964 campaign. Plans called for direct mailings to be sent to forty-five million voters beginning in September, asking the voters not only to give money to the party of their choice, but also to get out the vote.[24]

However, the joint direct mail fundraising failed in 1964. "The bipartisan Dwight Eisenhower–Adlai Stevenson direct mail pitch for political campaign funds from average citizens has flopped," a newspaper article reported in late September. Although the Polk firm did not reveal how much cash they collected through the direct mail drive, the advertising firm discontinued the fundraising campaign probably because the revenue fell short of their expectations.[25] There were several reasons why the bipartisan direct mail drive was less successful than the Goldwater campaign's solicitation. In a sense, many "average voters" were fed up with a torrent of direct mailings to their mailboxes throughout the general election. When emphasizing the importance of direct mail solicitation, a letter in a newspaper implied how people felt in the campaign: "So look for that 'dunning' letter some time before November. Junk mail? No indeed!"[26]

However, what truly distinguished the joint direct mail fundraising from Goldwater's solicitation was partisanship. Several experts indicated the nature of direct mail politics, blaming the bipartisan concept for the failure of the commission's solicitation. "People are just too partisan, at least in this election," a spokesperson commented.[27] Advertising operatives recognized the significance of partisanship and emotion in direct mail politics. As the political consultant Robert Humphreys demonstrated in the 1952 Eisenhower campaign, aggressive messages were likely to attract public attention and encourage unconcerned voters to go to the polls. As the personalized medium, direct mail was suitable for provoking emotional reactions from individual voters and became immensely profitable when consultants used it to highlight ideological differences rather than common problems shared by Democrats and Republicans. More importantly, the failure of the joint bipartisan fundraising suggested that successful direct mail campaigns might promote the schism between Democrats and Republicans, and liberals and conservatives, in American politics.

Post-1964 Controversies over Political Funds

The efforts in constructing a large bipartisan financial base collapsed in the 1964 presidential campaign, and the dependence on large contributions remained unsolved in years to follow. "Many ideas have been proposed, but the experts haven't yet hit upon a system for financing elections that will broaden the base of participation," lamented a journalist during the 1964 election.[28] The issue of campaign finance was evident, but nobody had yet to discover a panacea for a series of problems—swelling campaign costs, debt after election, and the danger of fat cat money.

The issue of campaign financing remained more crucial to the Democratic Party well into the mid-1960s. Notable journalists Rowland Evans and Robert Novak reported the fragile financial situation of the Democratic Party after the 1964 race. "The best-kept secret in Washington," Evans and Novak mentioned, "is that despite President Johnson's landslide election, the Democratic National Committee is nursing a gargantuan deficit." Although the DNC did not publicize the amount of their debt, Evans and Novak estimated it was close to $2 million.[29] President Johnson then resorted to conventional ways to raise campaign funds. Democrats tackled the mounting costs and debt by raking in large donations during and after the campaign. Partly due to Goldwater's unpopularity among big business, executives did not give cash to the conservative candidate. Henry Ford II, who had donated $7,000 to Republicans in 1960, gave $40,000 to Democrats and $4,100 to non-Goldwater Republican committees in 1964.[30] As the financial reports were issued by the DNC and RNC in 1965, mass media found out that a historic switch took place in party financing in the 1964 election campaign. The "Democrats became the party of the 'fat cats' and the Republicans the party of the small contributors," the press, including *Fortune* magazine, the *New York Times*, and the *Washington Post*, reported in October 1965.[31]

The President's Club was a central organization to draw big contributions during the Johnson administration. The club was another legacy of JFK, who had founded the group to wipe out the party's deficit of $4 million in 1960. Johnson expanded the club and proved more adept than his predecessor in attracting big money. The membership fee of the club was a $1,000 contribution. Members of the club had privileges such as dinners with the president during the Kennedy years, and Johnson added other benefits, including briefings from government officials and invitations to the national convention and to the White House.[32] The club was estimated to have four thousand members across the nation.[33] The President's Club raised more than $600,000 by August 1964,[34] and pulled in over $1 million from the members based in New York, Illinois, and other populous states, for one year from July 1966 to June 1967. The club raised much of the cash at events attended by Johnson, and most of the money was intended to be used in his reelection campaign in 1968.[35]

Democrats continued to search for big contributions in another way. In the winter of 1965, the Democratic Party planned to solicit advertisements from national corporations for a program book. Titled "Toward an Age of Greatness," this full-color book included tributes to Johnson's Great Society, and its copies were distributed at a series of fundraising film premieres. The DNC asked the business establishment to purchase full-page ads at $15,000 a page. Among the 168 giant corporations that purchased ads in the book were General Motors, Ford, Chrysler, General Tire, and Xerox. Defense contractors, including Lockheed, Sperry Rand, Hughes Aircraft, Martin-Marietta, and Ling-Temco Vought, also bought the ad spaces. The ad book was a technique that the DNC had employed to successfully raise $1.5 million during the 1964 election, and Democratic National Treasurer Richard Maguire directed the ad book project in 1965, expecting that the revenue would be spent for the 1966 congressional election.[36]

The Republican Party, which groped for new sources of political funds after Goldwater's fiasco, imitated the DNC's advertising book.[37] The RNC similarly planned a 1966 congressional campaign book, whose advertisements were sold to corporations at $15,000 a page. "If it is legitimate for one party to tap corporate funds through advertisements in a partisan publication," the *Washington Post* suggested, "all parties will be doing it."[38] Furthermore, the scheme of collecting campaign funds through book advertisements trickled down from the national to the state level. "Political publishing ventures, with advertising for sale at up to $2,500 a page, are booming as Democrats and Republicans hunt money to finance the coming state campaigns," journalist Walter Mears observed in early 1966. Following Johnson's examples, Democrats in California, Louisiana, and a half-dozen other states were planning publications of their own.[39]

However, like the invitation to Kennedy's gala in 1963, the ad book plan to tap corporations for campaign funds was legally and ethically troublesome. Federal laws on campaign contributions, such as the Federal Corrupt Practices Act of 1925, prohibited corporations from making political contributions, making illegal the purchase of goods or commodities from political parties if the money benefited any candidate for elected federal office. The lucrative but ethically questionable practice soon faced public attack. "Whatever else is new about the Great Society, obviously its politics are financed in the same old way," an editorial in the *New York Times* criticized the Democratic Party's ad book.[40] When many pundits indicated that the ad book might circumvent campaign finance laws, some Democrats rejected the dissemination of "Toward an Age of Greatness." Representative Charles Weltner, Democrat from Georgia, remarked that he would not distribute the ad book at his fundraising movie premiere in

Atlanta.[41] Responding to the complaints from the public and within the party, the Democratic Party finally dropped the ad book plan and gave away the $600,000 gained through the advertisements to a nonpartisan foundation in March 1966. Simultaneously, the Republican Party also quietly and reluctantly abandoned their plan to distribute their ad book.[42]

Facing a major financial crisis during the 1960s, Democratic and Republican party organizations were desperately looking for new channels of political contribution. Those years witnessed two general trends in campaign finance. In a traditional fashion, the Democratic and Republican national committees actively conducted solicitation campaigns, such as fundraising dinners and magazine advertisements, to obtain large contributions. At the other end of the fundraising scale was fundraising from small contributors. Republican Finance Chairman James Middleton said, "We found out in the last campaign, quite by accident, that you can tap the small donor. The Goldwater campaign proved this," and added, "This develops more interest in the party because the donors feel they are part of it. This is grass roots politics."[43] The conventional fundraising reliant on big money went hand in hand with the Goldwater model of small contributions in the post-1964 election years. Demonstrating that big money interests were tenacious and small fundraising was possible, solicitation scandals promoted reform debates in the late 1960s.

Campaign Finance Reforms under Johnson

However, with the public uproar over fat cat money, the mood grew in favor of campaign finance reforms in 1966 and 1967. Campaign finance reform became a bipartisan agenda in Congress over the years. While a coalition of public interests including nonprofit groups and campaign finance experts formed the framework of the debates, the Democrats and Republicans were actively engaged with making new laws on campaign finance. But at the same time, the congressional debates were colored by partisanship and intraparty factionalism. Liberal Democrats, southern Democrats, and moderate Republicans pursued reform for their own purposes, suggesting new approaches such as ceilings on contributions and spending, improving publicity of campaign finance, and direct public subsidies to political parties.

In his State of the Union address in January 1966, President Johnson called on Congress to reform laws governing campaign contributions and spending. The statement was a special surprise and delight for advocates of campaign finance reform because Johnson had never shown official interest in this issue since he assumed the presidency in 1963. For the purpose of enlarging the base of financial support to national parties, President Johnson specifically stressed the necessity of tax incentives to stimulate small contributions, and of closing loopholes of campaign finance laws. As Johnson stated again later in 1967, the Corrupt Practices Act, which had been created and revised in the Progressive Era, was "more loophole than law." The Democratic Party and the Republican Party alike endorsed his stand. Johnson achieved the bipartisan support partly because both parties shared similar financial problems, and also because the Republicans were deeply concerned that the Democrats had made some big strides in securing large contributions.[44]

In March 1966, immediately after the Democratic Party announced that they canceled their plan for the "Toward an Age of Greatness" ad book, Senator John J. Williams (R–DE) drew up an amendment that forbade corporations from claiming tax deductions for advertisements in political handbooks. The chief purpose of Williams's ad law was evidently to regulate big contributions through political ad books. Calling the Democratic ad book "blackmail," the Republican senator criticized Democrats' gimmick for raising political funds from big corporations. President Johnson signed the tax bill. There was general agreement that the regulation would choke off revenue from all the political ad books both on the national and state levels, and therefore that Democratic and Republican parties would face a more serious financial crisis. As Senate Minority Leader Everett McKinley Dirksen (R–IL) mentioned, the Williams amendment was "a sword that cuts both ways," harming Republicans as well as Democrats. Senator Williams, too, admitted that "there weren't too many people very happy about it." Nevertheless, the Williams amendment enabled the Republicans to claim chief credit for ending a practice of attracting large corporate contributions, although a Democratic-dominated Congress would eliminate the amendment just a year later.[45]

Moreover, in May, President Johnson demanded that Congress extend disclosure laws into primary and general elections, and also establish a tax deduction for small contributions up to $100. Senator Joseph Clark (D–PA) offered a bill based on Johnson's proposals. Herbert Alexander drafted a more ambitious measure. In the House of Representatives, Democrat Robert Ashmore (D–SC) and Republican Charles Goodell (R–NY) introduced the measure drafted by Alexander, which included disclosure, an independent commission, ending spending limits, and preventing unions and corporations from spending voluntary contributions for political expenditures. However, the legalization did not go into effect when it was confronted with fierce opposition in Congress and lukewarm support from LBJ, who did not endorse the establishment of an independent commission to monitor elections.[46]

In June Senator Russell Long (D–LA), President Johnson's old Senate friend, attempted to improve campaign finance with a direct subsidy to the national parties. In tandem with Senators Gaylord Nelson (D–WI), Lee Metcalf (D–MT), and Paul Douglas (D–IL), Senator Long proposed the amendment that for the first time introduced public finance into presidential elections without any regulations of contribution or spending. In order to evade criticism that a direct subsidy was too expensive, Long proposed an income tax checkoff. When a taxpayer filed a federal income tax return, one could designate that one dollar of the taxes could be voluntarily paid into the Presidential Election Campaign Fund. Contributions would be allocated to the major parties, and could go to minor parties if they gained more than four million votes. The Long amendment encountered criticism from both Republicans and Democrats. Republicans such as Senator Williams rejected the plan for public funding, charging that the amendment was still too costly. Senator Robert Kennedy (D–NY), who led an anti-Johnson group in the Democratic Party, also opposed the bill. Another Senate liberal, Albert Gore Sr. (D–TN), advocated public funding and disagreed with how the funds would be disbursed in the bill, warning that third parties would be crippled. However, after weeks of deadlock and a series of compromises, Congress passed the bill and Johnson signed the "Christmas Tree" bill into law in November.[47]

At this point, nobody could precisely understand the effects of Long's Presidential Campaign Fund Act of 1966. "This is an important building block on which we can build a proper system for controlling political campaign contributions," Long noted, but the senator himself conceded that he did not know exactly what would follow his legislation. Yet several politicians were afraid that the Long amendment would increase the power of the federal government over campaigns and national parties. A Democratic Party official speculated that Long's introduction of subsidies would alter party organizations, saying that it would "change the whole function of the national committees." An official of the RNC, too, interpreted the amendment as a "major step toward government control of both parties."[48] Likewise, Senator Kennedy noted that direct subsidies accelerated the centralization of power, raising constitutional issues such as freedom of speech when the 1966 Campaign Fund Act required limits on contribution and spending.[49] Regarding the new legislation as only "a beginning," President Johnson appointed a bipartisan study group headed by Harvard Professor Richard Neustadt to study improvements of campaign finance.[50]

Other attempts at campaign finance reform went on in 1967. After investigations revealed that Senator Thomas Dodd (D–CT) and Representative Thaddeus J. Dulski (D–NY) embezzled testimonial dinner funds, Democrat Robert Ashmore and Republican Charles Goodell authored a bill that made it a crime for a representative or congressional candidate to use testimonial dinner funds for personal purposes. According to their announcement, Ashmore and Goodell received bipartisan support for the regulation. When the House Subcommittee on Elections, which was chaired by Ashmore, unanimously approved the proposal, the Republicans strongly endorsed it, while House Democratic leaders did not take any position.[51]

While several scandals convinced some legislators to support campaign finance reforms, partisan opposition also emerged when Representatives Ashmore and Goodell attempted to accomplish a more thorough reform in June 1967. Their proposal expanded disclosure to primary elections and to all political committees, established a bipartisan commission to monitor financial activity, regulated political action committees, and abandoned limits on campaign spending. This far-reaching legislation faced oppositions from southern conservatives, liberal Democrats, and Republicans for different reasons. Southerners rejected primary regulations, which was what they considered an expansion of federal power. Liberal Democrats opposed the regulation imposed on political action committees. Their opposition came from the AFL-CIO's announcement that the definition of "committee" was so broad that the provision could be menacing to their Committee on Political Education (COPE) and other labor union PACs. (The first PAC in American politics was established by the Congress of Industrial Organization in 1943, and PACs were primarily political organizations for labor unions in the 1960s.) Alternatively, Republicans did not support the Ashmore–Goodell bill, calling for a harsh provision against PACs. In October, Goodell charged that their bill was blocked by an "unholy coalition" including conservative southerners, liberal Democrats, and some Republicans.[52]

The 1960s reforms did not have a major impact on the American campaign system as legislation that did pass was not effective. Indeed, the coalition of campaign experts and policy makers attempted to elevate campaign financing into the forefront of the political agenda. But the majority of legislators showed little interest in the issue through most of the 1960s. The Citizens' Research Foundation made efforts to inform the public of campaign financing by publishing the series starting *Financing the 1960 Election* in every presidential race starting in 1960. But many Americans did not yet consider campaign reform an urgent issue. In public opinion polls, the public showed contradictory attitudes toward reform when most of those polled supported spending limits in elections but rarely favored alternative forms of campaign finance.[53] Nevertheless, the 1960s became the incubation period for campaign finance reforms in the following decade when partisan struggle sped up congressional debates after the Watergate scandal shook the Nixon White House.

Watergate and the 1970s Campaign Finance Reforms

The 1968 presidential election witnessed another campaign that cast light on the significance of political consultants and television in American politics. Richard Nixon, who had played poorly in the televised debates with John F. Kennedy eight years before, actively employed advertising agencies to sell himself in 1968. Ad agencies on Madison Avenue worked with Nixon in remaking his images. They made him an excellent "TV politician" to engage in intimate conversation with voters through televised speeches and spins, trying to construct the illusion that the candidate was communicating with the people as "one of the great joys of seeking the Presidency."[54] Critically examining how the advertising industry worked to package politicians in elections, writer Joe McGinniss vividly described the behind-the-scenes activities of political consultants in American election campaigns. McGinniss's work increasingly popularized the discussion of "selling the president" after the 1968 campaign.[55]

The 1968 election also exposed the essential role of money accompanied with political consulting. Broadcasting campaigns directed by consultants proved that electronic political advertisement was extremely expensive. The expenditure on television increased from $3 million in 1952 to $27.1 million in 1968, while spending on radio grew from $3.1 million to $13.3 million over the years. With candidates spending more funds for broadcasting, campaign expenditures skyrocketed throughout the 1950s and 1960s. When Adlai Stevenson and Dwight Eisenhower contested in 1952, Democrats and Republicans spent $6.1 million in their campaigns; in 1968, the figure amounted to $40.4 million.[56] The dramatically swollen campaign budgets ended up highlighting the importance of fundraising in political elections. In this field, too, the Nixon campaign broke records. Nixon took $2.2 million from more than 150,000 donors who responded to direct mail solicitation with $14 on average. But the main source of Nixon's political funds was the Richard Nixon Association (RNA), whose members contributed over $1,000. With approximately 1,200 members who had special privileges at the national convention and a promised postelection advisory role, the RNA upheld the Nixon campaign by providing more than half of the $8.5 million total.[57]

Democrats noticed that they had financial disadvantages in competing with Republicans in the late 1960s. As the party was deeply divided over the civil rights movement and the Vietnam War, Democrats lagged behind Republicans in raising political money during the 1968 election. Furthermore, after Nixon won the presidential election, the Democratic Party lost the presidency and large contributions steered away from Democrats. Democrats were no longer able to rely on any organization of big contributors, such as the President's Club, and thus they called for campaign finance reform more ardently than ever before.

As a consequence, Nixon's victory in 1968 accelerated partisan struggles over campaign finance reform, what some researchers have dubbed "Democratic reforms," in the early 1970s. Democrats and Republicans had already discussed campaign reform during the 1960s. However, whereas both Democrats and Republicans promoted reforms to undermine the financial strengths of the opposite party in the 1960s, Democrats primarily advocated campaign reform with Republicans opposing the changes to the electoral system in the 1970s. As public trust in government fell in the 1960s and more Americans paid attention to the issue of political elections, the Democratic-controlled Congress passed the Federal Election Campaign Act of 1971, improving publicity and creating a public funding system for presidential elections. Moreover, after the Watergate scandal helped push public opinion against political corruption, reformers successfully passed the Federal Election Campaign Act Amendments of 1974, which limited individual contributions and established the Federal Election Commission to monitor elections. The campaign finance reforms in the early 1970s were seemingly a victory for Democrats. Drawing from legislative debates in the previous decade, reformers closed loopholes in campaign finance laws, and Democrats were convinced that they succeeded in undermining Republicans' financial abilities to attract big money. However, the "Democratic reforms" ironically resulted in unintended consequences of direct mail fundraising and conservatism increasingly emerging in electoral politics during the 1970s.[58]

As in the 1960s, a coalition of reformers in and outside Congress worked for campaign reform during the early 1970s. A liberal organization added new momentum to the calls for reform. John W. Gardner, former secretary of health, education, and welfare in the Johnson administration, founded Common Cause in 1970. Believing that monied interests, such as the military–industrial complex, exercised disproportionate power in policy making, Gardner and other Common Cause founders were dedicated to promoting campaign finance reform while also lobbying legislators on other reform issues such as ending the seniority system in Congress. Gardner said before the House Administration Committee that "the root of campaign financing [abuse] can never be eliminated until candidates are assured of adequate funds to run a credible and competitive campaign without having to rely on big-money contributors."[59] With an educated, middle-class, liberal-minded membership growing from one hundred thousand in 1971 to more than three hundred thousand by 1973, Common Cause served as the main interest group for campaign reformers.[60]

In 1971, Common Cause led a movement arousing public interest in campaign finance to pressure lawmakers to pass new legislation. On January 11, the organization filed a lawsuit in a US district court against the New York Conservative Party, the RNC, and the DNC, claiming that these parties had violated the 1925 campaign laws. Joined by other groups such as the Americans for Democratic Action, the Twentieth Century Fund, and the National Committee for an Effective Congress, Common Cause pointed to loopholes of the existing campaign legislature, especially the absence of a public commission to enforce campaign laws. As the result of this lawsuit, interest groups obtained the "right of private enforcement" of campaign finance laws, which enabled those groups to bring "class action lawsuits" against the political parties on behalf of voters. Common Cause and the Citizens' Research Foundation also offered campaign financing data to the mass media. The press and television covered sensationalized stories, reporting how candidates for office received contributions from monied interests. The public gradually regarded campaign finance as an urgent issue in American politics.[61]

In the same year, Democrats on Capitol Hill took the campaign reform movement one step further by introducing a new bill. Democrats aggressively called for new regulations, including spending limits for presidential candidates in return for public funds of $20 million, limited expenditures on media, and strengthened disclosure of campaign finance information. Although these campaign finance proposals had been raised in the 1960s, Democratic leaders carefully chose the provisions to curtail Republicans' financial strengths without reducing labor unions' support for the Democratic Party. The bill prescribed that presidential candidates accept a $20 million limitation if they receive public funds in elections, but it did not curtail Democrats' reliance on contributions from unions. The limitations on presidential campaigns and media spending prohibited an arms race in campaign financing, where Republicans prevailed over Democrats during the late 1960s and early 1970s. The improved disclosure, which demanded candidates for national office report financial information on all contributions of over $100, would also help liberal organizations like Common Cause provide more information about political financing in order to stir up public debates on reform. Democrats vigorously pursued campaign reform primarily due to partisan politics, not purely in favor of public interests, in the early 1970s.[62]

Despite Republicans' resistance, Democratic majorities in Congress successfully passed the Federal Election Campaign Act (FECA) of 1971. The FECA, which Nixon signed into law on February 7, 1972, was a product of partisan struggles that Democrats largely won. However, the Watergate burglary enormously accelerated public distrust of the Nixon administration as well as conventional fundraising practices and the election system per se. For instance, the American Conservative Action (ACA) was forced to change its fundraising strategy. As one of the older types of organization, the ACA had been involved with "boiler room work," which referred to sponsoring luncheons, cocktail parties, and dinners for political candidates. However, "Cocktail circuit fund-raising is much more difficult now because of Watergate," ACA Director Charles McManus lamented, because lobbyists and businesses were "much less prone to participate."[63] Republicans understood that more Democratic campaign reforms would harm the Republican Party, and conservatives claimed that campaign reform violated constitutional rights such as freedom of expression. But they were unable to stem the tide of the reform movement on Capitol Hill.

As the Watergate scandal consumed national attention by 1973, Senator Sam Ervin (D–NC), chairman of the Select Committee on Presidential Campaign Activities, held televised hearings on the 1972 presidential election, inspecting how the Nixon reelection campaign had violated campaign laws. The investigations revealed the corrupt relationship between the Nixon campaign and big money interests by proving that Nixon had secretly received big contributions from the corporate sector. The campaign received $5.4 million from 100 defense contractors and another $5 million from 178 oil company officials, who sought access to the administration. The Ervin committee also uncovered that the Nixon administration had decided to give milk price support immediately after the Milk Producers Association donated $2 million to his reelection campaign in 1972. Furthermore, in 1974, Nixon's recorded conversations proved that the White House had spent campaign contributions on concealing the break-in of the DNC at the Watergate.[64] Public opinion immediately came to consider campaign finance reform one of the most important issues. Pollsters found out that the public support for public financing of presidential elections skyrocketed from 11 percent in 1964 to 67 percent in 1974.[65]

Enacted in October 1974, two months after Nixon's resignation, the Amendments to the FECA furthered campaign finance reform with limits on contributions and spending, establishing the Federal Election Commission (FEC) as an independent organization to monitor federal campaigns. The 1974 amendments set a limit of $1,000 contributions to a candidate's committee in each election, and an aggregate limitation of $25,000. The amendments also limited individual donations up to $5,000 to a political action committee, and $20,000 to a national committee. Candidates were not allowed to use more than $50,000 from their personal funds. The FEC was able to carry out investigations, take civil actions, and refer criminal violations to the attorney general.[66]

Conservatives outside of Congress aggressively opposed the 1974 campaign finance reform. The American Conservative Union (ACU) sent out a direct mailing to criticize the liberal campaign legislation, especially public funds for presidential candidates. The ACU's letter said, "Liberals say private contributions are a corrupting influence and that we can remove this evil through taxpayer subsidy." However, the mailing asserted that a public financing of presidential election would not eliminate political corruption. Rather, the ACU claimed, the public subsidies would "create many new ills" by violating "your First Amendment right of freedom of expression—by using your tax funds to support political candidates with whom you disagree." The ACU's mailing criticized the growing influence of the federal government in elections, too. The message opposed the liberal campaign reform measures, such as the creation of the FEC, and the ACU instead maintained that "citizens ought to be allowed to give money to candidates or parties of their own choosing, and not have that decision made for them by federal planners."[67] Conservatives never endorsed the 1970s campaign finance reform on ideological grounds, claiming that the liberal reforms would breach constitutional rights.

Political consultants, who were directly affected by the campaign reforms, officially criticized the new campaign laws for more practical reasons. Overviewing the 1971 FECA and the 1974 Amendments, John Quincy Adams of the American Association of Political Consultants (AAPC) crafted a discussion paper concerning the effects of the campaign laws. Adams encouraged other political consultants to discuss campaign finance reform and to "take more direct action, both individually and as an Association," to alter campaign financing, while pointing out several "deficiencies" of the laws.[68]

Adams made his case that the campaign laws in 1971 and 1974 were problematic because they hindered the free flow of information between candidates and voters. In political consultants' view, the limits on individual contribution and expenditure set by the laws were too low. Fundraisers knew that most contributions ordinarily came from a few large donors, and if the campaign finance laws imposed a low maximum, fundraisers would need to spend more time, effort,

and money on obtaining small contributions. Thus, Adams was worried, political consultants were required to allocate additional funds from the limited
regular campaign budget for fundraising, and that would cause fewer dollars to
be available for television, radio, and other media messages. As a result, "communications with the voters are reduced, thereby thwarting another election law
goal," Adams noted.[69]

The consultant's discussion paper also demonstrated concerns over the shift
in communication abilities from candidates to the mass media. Like other
conservatives who were hostile to the mainstream media, Adams claimed, "Bi-
ased newspapers and disinterested TV and radio stations are not uncommon
in America, and to the extent that candidates are statutorily inhibited in communication with the voters, the opportunity to dominate or ignore this communication falls to these minority of the fourth estate." Political consultants
interpreted the transformation of the electoral system as reducing the power
of political candidates—and of political consultants—to send messages to the
electorate. Adams argued that the campaign finance reforms were threatening
to American democracy by saying, "Democracy thrives on the market place
of ideas."[70]

Finally, the AAPC issued recommendations to the Federal Election Commission on campaign financing. On the basis of Adams's argument, the AAPC
contended that the 1974 Amendments to the Federal Election Campaign Act
reduced communication between candidates and voters, and that the law discouraged individuals from entering the political process, especially as new candidates. The AAPC also suggested that the campaign finance law discriminated
among candidates in favor of incumbents because the limited budgets for media
communication handicapped political newcomers. Announcing that they believed there were "serious flaws in the present law," political consultants were not
happy with the campaign reform provided by liberals.[71]

***

The federal campaign finance laws in the 1970s were a product of partisan
struggles between Democrats and Republicans. Democrats used the issue of
money in politics to attack the Nixon administration and to curtail big money
to the GOP, while conservatives opposed the reforms because they believed that
the limits on individual contribution violated the right of expression. Many realized that the new campaign laws were not unflawed. Some people were afraid
that the change might lead to another growth of the federal government in the
electoral process, and others were concerned over the development of political

action committees in political campaigns. However, few forecasted how the campaign finance reform would recast the contours of money in politics. When the new campaign laws went into effect, all of a sudden, campaigners had to build a base of contributors. Although they relied partly on telemarketing, political direct mail emerged as the best way to amass small money in the post–Federal Election Campaign Act years. It turned out that the progressive reform, which was designed to reduce the influence of fat cat money, accelerated direct mail fundraising of conservatives, particularly Richard Viguerie's ideological direct mail. As a conservative said, the "real effect of the Watergate campaign reforms has been to increase the power of one man—Viguerie."[72]

CHAPTER 6

The Formation of the New Right

"THE AMERICAN RIGHT WING is addicted to letter-writing." In 1977, the AFL-CIO issued two special reports on the emergence of conservatism in US politics with particular emphasis on Richard Viguerie's direct mail fundraising. Pointing to the impact of the 1974 Amendments to the Federal Election Campaign Act (FECA), the report noted that the "master fundraiser" was parlaying the legal limitation on individual campaign contributions into "a big boom for New Right fund-raising efforts." The labor union's reports spelled out how Viguerie and other conservatives elaborately amassed funds with direct mail, which was premised on big data, ideological conflict, and offensive rhetoric. Conservative political consultants identified supporters from their computerized mailing lists of approximately ten million potential contributors. The right-wing messengers dispatched solicitation letters under the guise of an official congressional mailing, instead of using the names of generally unknown organizations or activists, so that voters took the message more seriously. The rhetoric of conservative appeals was usually threatening, stirring up emotions of receivers. "Their language is always extreme, literally shrieking: Doomsday is imminent, right around the corner," the AFL-CIO report mentioned.[1]

By the middle of the 1970s, liberals became aware that a key reason for the success of conservative politics was the "ability of the right to establish control over the nation's intellectual agenda" through not only "writing and research" but also "advertising and direct mail."[2] A new generation of conservative activists were able to sell their ideology and political candidates by means of computerized direct mail more effectively than their counterparts. As right-wing mail campaigns vehemently attacked Democrats and labor unions throughout the 1970s, liberals realized that they faced conservatives distinctive from right-wingers of a decade earlier. AFL-CIO President George Meany pointed out the "hate merchants of the '70s" who were "not little old ladies in tennis shoes." The 1970s conservative activists were instead "Madison Avenue types, trained in mass psychology and propaganda techniques, who have a computerized mailing list, a printing press and a government-subsidized mailing permit."[3] Conservative direct mail was unpleasant even to many Republicans. Several Republican leaders bitterly complained that newly emergent conservative political action groups were "draining money from the GOP" and giving the funds to right-wingers who were ideologically pure with little chance of winning.[4] Conservative direct mail carved out political niches and raised vast amounts of money from small contributors, which was threatening to both liberal Democrats and moderate Republicans.

This chapter concerns the "New Right," which created networks of conservative politicians and organizations during the 1970s.[5] The new conservatism built up a coalition of diverse political forces to turn American politics rightward, and ideological direct mail defined the movement. They relied on direct mail for fundraising and advertising, which incited negative emotions such as fear, anger, and anxiety by inflaming hostilities toward liberals and labor unions. At the same time, the New Right was a pragmatic movement as it made gains in new constituencies over the years. Viguerie's direct mail successfully courted conservative Democrats and blue-collar Americans, who were discontented with political, economic, and cultural changes from the 1960s. During the 1970s when antielite populism rippled around the nation, the New Right movement carried out campaigns to defeat liberal Democrats and moderate Republicans in elections, assisting to bring about the Reagan Revolution in 1980.[6]

The basic strategy of the New Right was to capitalize on people's discontent in the wake of the sixties by stirring up offensive emotions through social issues. "The 1950s-style conservatives," a New Right figure called Paul Weyrich noted, did not "understand the politics of the average person." He emphasized that the New Right movement was "more concerned with family, right-to-life, schools, neighborhoods."[7] Instead of cohesive political issues, such as anticommunism in the early Cold War era, New Right activists narrowed in on single issues because computerized direct mail could identify those concerned with each issue. However, as a journalist succinctly observed, the New Right dealt with not only social issues, including abortion, gun control, and the Equal Rights Amendment, but also "emotional issues" that were not relevant with daily lives but generated fierce emotion, such as vehement patriotism and fears, among conservative Americans.[8] As Viguerie and other conservatives well understood that emphasizing emotional issues effectively raised funds, "emotionalism" characterized the New Right movement. "[E]motionalism, not facts, sway the Hill votes," Weyrich said.[9] Likewise, Senator George McGovern stressed the characteristics when he debated the New Right with *National Review* publisher William A. Rusher at

Purdue University. McGovern described the New Right as "extremist," "radical,"
and "negative," charging it with "substituting emotionalism for common sense."
Like Madison Avenue advertising agents who waged emotional and offensive
campaigns, New Right activists utilized resentments for raising funds.[10]

A typical example of such emotional issues for the 1970s New Right was the
Panama Canal. After a series of negotiations between the United States and
Panama, the Panama Canal treaties put an end to US control of the Canal Zone.
Whereas the ratification of the treaties never mattered to most of Americans in
the late 1970s, the New Right implemented massive antitreaties drives by claiming that the withdrawal of the United States from the Panama Canal would
bring a serious threat to American pride and national security. This chapter
closely scrutinizes the process by which the New Right attempted to place the
Panama Canal in the foreground of politics because it evidently demonstrates
how the New Right movement used narrowly focused, narrowly minded single
issues for appealing to public opinion. Despite the failure to block the ratification, the antitreaties campaign highlighted the New Right's strategic use of
irrationality as the movement increasingly emerged with their direct mailings
that included misinformation, emotionalism, and populism.

The road to the conservative ascendancy was accompanied by political conflicts within the American right-wing movement. The New Right was frequently
at odds not only with the Republican establishment, but also with conservative
organizations that had been active since the 1950s and 1960s. Even prominent
conservative politicians such as Ronald Reagan were not the perfect allies for the
New Right. While many liberals and conservatives criticized the New Right for
its extreme ideology and inconsistent arguments, over the course of the 1970s
the New Right marshaled direct mail and modern technologies to grow and
prosper. Yet by the end of the decade, many Americans, including AFL-CIO
leader Meany, realized that a once laughable farce had become the driving force
behind the transformation of American politics.

The Birth of the New Right

One morning in August 1974, Richard Viguerie turned on his television to find
out that the new president, Gerald Ford, had named Nelson Rockefeller as his
vice president. For conservatives, Rockefeller was their last choice. In Viguerie's words, the moderate Republican represented "the Eastern Liberal Establishment" of the Republican Party. Rockefeller had persuaded Richard Nixon
to agree on the Pact of Fifth Avenue placing a liberal stamp on the Republican

platform in 1960, and furthermore, he had strongly challenged Barry Goldwater during the GOP primaries in the 1964 election.[11] Viguerie believed that Rockefeller was the leader of the liberal bloc of the Republican Party who had stymied conservatives' agenda for years. In *The Right Report*, the newsletter issued by the Richard A. Viguerie Co. (RAVCO), a writer mentioned that Rockefeller's nomination outraged many conservatives. "Most 'responsible' conservatives, especially William F. Buckley, Jr. . . . have rejected the conspiracy theory. . . . However, the nomination of Nelson Rockefeller as Vice President by President Gerald Ford has shocked some conservatives and even liberals into reexamining the conspiracy theory."[12]

The announcement of the new vice president marked the formation of the New Right in 1974. Viguerie immediately made calls to invite fourteen conservative friends to dinner the next night to discuss how to prevent Rockefeller's nomination. Although they failed to stop Rockefeller from becoming vice president, these conservatives, including political activists, Capitol Hill aides, journalists, and attorneys, became the core members of the new right-wing network.[13] Viguerie raised funds for several organizations established by his colleagues such as Paul Weyrich, Howard Phillips, and Terry Dolan, while also connecting with allies in Congress including Republican Representative Phil Crane and Senators Jesse Helms and Strom Thurmond. New Right activists and politicians on Capitol Hill reorganized conservatism from the top down by reaching out to the "grassroots" via media.

A central figure of the New Right was Paul Weyrich. Born in Racine, Wisconsin, in 1942, he grew up in a blue-collar neighborhood. His father had migrated from Germany in the 1920s, firing the boilers at St. Mary's Catholic Hospital where he met and married a nurse of Norwegian descent. Paul was originally a Roman Catholic, but he switched to the Byzantine Rite Roman Catholic Church in response to liturgical reforms enacted by the Second Vatican Council. Influenced by his parents and by the ideal of Senator Robert Taft, young Weyrich was leaning to a conservatism that stressed religion and tradition. When the US Supreme Court ruled that it was unconstitutional for state officials to sponsor prayer in public schools in 1962, Weyrich attempted to protest the decision. He called on Claude Jasper, the Republican state chairman in Wisconsin, to make a statement on the issue of school prayer, but Jasper refused. Despite his failure to foster widespread protest, the case had a great impact on the political life of Weyrich, directing him toward social conservatism.[14]

Weyrich began his career in journalism. While attending the University of Wisconsin, Racine, Weyrich worked part-time at the radio station WLIP and also for the *Milwaukee Sentinel* from 1963 to 1964. When he was working as a news reporter, Weyrich confirmed his political identity as a conservative. He was a fervent supporter of Goldwater during the 1964 presidential election. After moving to Denver, Colorado, to work as a news director for the radio station KQXI, Weyrich encountered Senator Gordon Allott who invited the young journalist to Capitol Hill. During the six years he worked for Senator Allott, Weyrich gained access to political sources in Washington, socializing with other conservatives such as syndicated columnist George F. Will and Democratic Congressman William M. Colmer.[15]

Weyrich emerged as a prominent conservative organizer in the Washington Beltway during the 1970s. For example, in 1973 when he was special assistant to Republican Senator Carl Curtis of Nebraska, Weyrich along with Edward Feulner and conservative Representative Phil Crane established the Republican Study Committee. As the counterpart to the liberal Wednesday Group, the committee analyzed bills and issues, formulated electoral strategy, and refined political ideas. The Republican Study Committee of Weyrich organized about seventy members, including thirty of forty-four Republicans first elected in the 1972 elections. Observing that several conservatives entered national politics, but were more poorly connected with colleagues than liberal politicians, Weyrich played a role in supporting conservative lawmakers in DC.[16]

Weyrich's activities in Washington accelerated with financial aid from Joseph Coors, the beer magnate and conservative stalwart in Colorado. In 1966, Coors won a statewide election for regent at the University of Colorado, where he cracked down on student protesters on the campus and financed a conservative student newspaper. Some regarded Coors as a fanatical anticommunist because he supported the John Birch Society and circulated an article from the *American Opinion*, the JBS's magazine, to other regents. Weyrich met Coors at the 1968 Republican National Convention, which Coors attended as a Colorado delegate endorsing the candidacy of Ronald Reagan.[17]

As an ally in the business community, Coors established the centers of his activism in Washington, particularly the Heritage Foundation and the Committee for the Survival of a Free Congress (CSFC). Coors envisioned the Heritage Foundation, a tax-exempt think tank, to serve as the conservative equivalent to the Brookings Institution. With Coors offering the seed money to the foundation in 1973, and Weyrich as the first president, the Heritage Foundation began to assemble conservative intellectuals. The Heritage Foundation would later grow into a model for other conservative research institutions, influencing Reagan and other presidential administrations' policies by the 1980s.

The CSFC was a conservative political action committee established in southeast Washington. Funded by several wealthy conservative businesspeople, including $1,000 from Colonel Harland Sanders of Kentucky Fried Chicken and $5,000 from Coors and his relatives, the CSFC was created, in the words of Weyrich, "to elect conservatives."[18] Under the direction of Weyrich, the CSFC raised funds and contributed to conservative candidates across the nation to turn American politics to the right. Coors also poured his money into several other conservative groups, such as Television News, Inc. in New York, Midwestern Industries, the National Association of Manufacturers, the Committee of Nine, the National Federation of Independent Businesses, and the House Republican Study Committee.[19]

Howard Phillips was another leading New Right activist. A Jewish Bostonian, he was a Harvard graduate and one of the founding members of Young Americans for Freedom (YAF). Like congressional staffer Weyrich, Phillips began his political career on Capitol Hill, serving as an assistant to the chairman of the Republican National Committee, and later worked for the Nixon administration. As Phillips was frustrated with the Office of Economic Opportunity, established as part of Lyndon Johnson's war on poverty, he left the Nixon administration and joined Viguerie in organizing the Conservatives for the Resignation of the President. In 1974, with the assistance of conservative Republican Senator Jesse Helms of North Carolina, Phillips founded the Conservative Caucus that aimed to create "a conservative establishment" in the United States by supporting the election of conservative candidates. The founding statement of the caucus stressed social issues such as the "right to life," the "right of parents to define the conditions and content of their children's education," and the "freedom of individuals to pray to God."[20]

Morton Blackwell was a young conservative activist closely working with Viguerie. Raised in the countryside of Louisiana, he studied chemical engineering at Louisiana State University in the early 1960s. After he read a *Newsweek* article about Goldwater in October 1958, he began to devote himself to conservative politics and became a Republican. Blackwell cofounded a college Republican organization at LSU when the overwhelming majority of the student body were Democrats. He attended the 1964 Republican National Convention as the youngest delegate, and Blackwell's activism elevated him to the executive directorship of the College Republican National Committee in Washington, DC, in 1965. Blackwell was hired by Viguerie in 1972 and worked for him for seven years. While working as an editor of Viguerie's publication, he was well-known as a youth organizer in the New Right circle after 1979 when he established the

Leadership Institute to train young conservative journalists, policy makers, and political strategists.[21]

Terry Dolan, twenty-three in 1974, also played a key role in New Right politics. A YAF lawyer, Dolan formed the National Conservative Political Action Committee (NCPAC), which followed the model of the American Medical Association. Using Viguerie's computerized lists, Dolan's NCPAC raised millions over the course of the 1970s. While Dolan was enormously dedicated to the election of conservative candidates in many congressional districts, he was the most controversial leader of the New Right movement. He devoted the NCPAC to defeating liberals in any possible way, ranging from slander and blackmail, to attacks on their private life.[22] Even when Dolan campaigned to defeat a liberal candidate in the 1977 Virginia gubernatorial election, John Dalton, the Republican candidate, denounced Dolan for his campaign and disassociated himself with the New Right. Dolan symbolized the keys to the success of the New Right: fear and anger. A conservative journalist recalled Dolan's methodology of direct mail fundraising:

> As Terry Dolan of the National Conservative Political Action Committee told me, his organization's fund-raising letters try to "make them angry" and "stir up hostilities." The "shriller you are," he said, the easier it is to raise funds. "That's the nature of our beast," he explained. The fund-raising letters of the New Right groups depict a world gone haywire, with liberal villains poised to destroy the American Way of Life.[23]

The rise of new right-wing groups was nothing new by the 1970s. But the newness of the 1970s New Right lay in their efficiency in attracting funds from small contributors. Prominent journalist Alan Ehrenhalt pointed out that the "important factor in the current 'new conservatism' is money."[24] In this sense, the New Right groups revolved around Viguerie's consulting firm, then many journalists and pundits paid attention to his direct mail, inquiring into the core of the newly emerging conservative movement. "In the rapidly evolving and growing nether world of conservative politics," another journalist observed, "a 'New Right' is emerging and Richard A. Viguerie is its godfather," adding that it was "difficult for other candidates to match."[25] Wyatt Stewart, a fundraiser for the Republican Party and former RAVCO executive, noted that Viguerie "established his own ball game" by wielding financial influence over the New Right organizations. "Without him, they don't exist," Stewart said. The NCPAC of Dolan, for example, was so dependent on the RAVCO that the organization gained approximately 90 percent of its funds from Viguerie.[26]

With his mailing lists and sophisticated computerized direct mail technique, Viguerie's fundraising was unrivaled in the 1970s. Conservative journalist Alan Crawford explained in detail how Viguerie's empire worked in the mid-1970s. Crawford was the first assistant editor of *Conservative Digest*, the magazine published by Richard Viguerie, while working on the editorial staffs of *Human Events* and YAF's *New Guard*, and as a speechwriter for Senate James Buckley of New York. The former associate described how the "virtuoso in the advertising medium" played a crucial role in the conservative movement. From his company with a staff of 250 nonunion employees in Falls Church, Virginia, Viguerie mailed out 50 million appeals every year from 250 mailing lists including the information of 10 million Americans. The RAVCO's client list was also growing. He raised $6 million for George Wallace from 1974 to 1976. Other clients were political and religious right-wing organizations such as the National Rifle Association, Conservative Books for Christian Leaders, and No Amnesty for Deserters.[27]

Viguerie's direct mail financially supported and delineated those New Right groups, drawing a line from the old style of conservative activism. The ideology of the New Right was actually almost identical with the Old Right, both of which challenged the growth of federal government, interference with the personal enterprise system, and liberal permissiveness. Old Right groups, including *National Review*, YAF, and the American Conservative Union (ACU), and the New Right had the nearly complete overlap in their lists of candidates to support in elections. However, there were clear differences between the two conservative factions in tactics and strategy. M. Stanton Evans, a founding member of YAF and chairman of the ACU in 1977, compared the Old and New Right by saying that the "real difference between the two elements is fund raising."[28] Viguerie's capacity to amass large amounts of small contributions was obvious. When the Conservative Victory Fund, an affiliate of the ACU, played a central role in fundraising in the 1974 congressional elections, national conservative organizations raised about $250,000. However, in 1976 when Viguerie and the New Right actively raised funds, conservatives collected about $3.5 million.[29] The emergence of the New Right's fundraising caused some troubles with Old Right groups in the 1976 elections. "It's tougher to raise money this year," said Becky Norton, executive director of the Conservative Victory Fund in 1976. As the RAVCO and its associates raised and spent overwhelming amounts of money, conventional right-wing organizations attracted limited funds and felt that they were "taking a back seat to these other groups."[30]

The issue of party loyalty also contrasted the Old and New Right. While conservatives since the 1950s had been close to the Republican Party and worked

with Republicans, New Right activists frequently endorsed conservative Democrats. "The old right does not like to associate themselves with Democrats,"
Viguerie noted. "They just can't identify themselves with Democrats, which I
think is important for conservatives," he added.[31] After he raised funds for the
Wallace campaign in the 1972 presidential campaign, Viguerie's mailing lists
increasingly grew with many Democrats filling his computers. Tom Winter, editor of *Human Events* and a vice chairman of the ACU, believed that "most of
the people on Viguerie's lists . . . are Democrats."[32] The New Right placed the
top priority more on conservative causes, supporting and financing candidates
whether they were Republicans or Democrats. As the Trends Analyses Division
of the American Jewish Committee stated, "[loyalty] to issues take precedence
over loyalty of political parties" for the New Right.[33]

The ability to raise money, the importance of social issues, and the lack of party
loyalty led the New Right to new relationships with business and blue-collar
workers. Whereas several Old Right organizations had been financed by large
contributors and built a close relationship with big business, most of the New
Right organizations did not work so intimately with the business and industrial
political action committees. It was partly because the New Right was able to
draw money for themselves, but also because antielitism distanced New Right
activists from business magnates with the notable exception of Joseph Coors.
In his book *The Establishment vs. The People*, Viguerie demonstrated his hatred
against something big including big government, big labor unions, big media, as
well as big business. Viguerie claimed that business magnates, such as Rockefeller, Ford, and Carnegie, constructed a "system of government monopolies that
would prevent the untimely rise of the 'little guy,'" and also blamed big banks
for making "big profits for the insiders at the expense of everyone else." Viguerie
criticized the intimate relationship between the government and big businesses
in favor of a capitalism for ordinary Americans. Although the New Right movement endorsed business's agenda, including low taxes, reduced regulations, and
antiunionism, it used the language against business giants.[34]

Meanwhile, the New Right approached the working class to form a new political coalition. New Right activists were never hesitant to reach out to Democrats if the voters could be interested in conservative causes. They even supported an activist federal government in terms of economic issues so that the
New Right activists could construct a constituency that contained blue-collar
workers and ethnic groups who shared conservative values. Although Viguerie
emphasized that he believed in economic conservatism, such as laissez-fair and
minimum government interference, he mentioned that Americans needed to use

the federal government to stimulate the economy. Viguerie stated that he was able to be friendly to federal government in order to seize power in election. "I'm willing to compromise to come to power," he said.[35]

There have been controversies among pundits and researchers over the nature of the New Right. Kevin Phillips, a former 1968 Nixon campaign staffer credited with the "southern strategy" and unofficial theorist of the New Right, highlighted the populism of the new conservative activists. "It's inaccurate to call the New Right truly 'conservative,'" Phillips said. "On the contrary, it represents traditionally populist constituencies, espouses anti-establishment politics, focuses on lower-middle-class social, cultural and nationalist themes, and utilizes organizational tactics of the sort associated with past populist-radical movements here and abroad."[36] Placing the New Right in the tradition of American populism, Phillips also wrote that "the 'New Right' descends not from Hamilton and Taft but from Andrew Jackson, William Jennings Bryan, Franklin Roosevelt, Truman and Wallace!"[37] The populist impulses created the protean and contradictory characteristics of the New Right, extending to southern Democrats and blue-collar workers.[38]

Similarly, conservative journalist Alan Crawford stressed that the New Right was radical populism. Drawing on Richard Hofstadter's concept of "entrepreneurial radicalism," Crawford held that American populism was not that of the peasants because North American had no European-style class structure. But American populism, he went on, generated from a class of commercial farmers who lived in a world where a bustling capitalist life was coupled with a small-town way of life. According to Crawford, the New Right of the 1970s was a neopopulist movement in the American tradition. Raising millions of dollars in small donations from housewives and blue-collar workers, the newly emerging conservatives fanned class hostility among lower-middle-class Americans. Lacking the intellectual backbone and philosophical discipline, the 1970s conservatives fed on insecurity, discontent, and backlash politics of the "average" Americans. The New Right was "anything but conservative," Crawford concluded.[39]

If the New Right was analyzed as populism, it was not surprising that the New Right activists and other observers regarded the New Right as a "grassroots" movement. Weyrich, for instance, asserted that while the Old Right had been engaged in political education, New Right activists aimed at developing political action. He claimed that the New Right pursued "building a grass roots base of activists and contributors who would constitute a participatory majority to achieve the election of conservative leaders and the implementation of conservative policy."[40] Direct mail, a medium collecting small contributions from many citizens, also colored the New Right as a grassroots movement. When many observers understood that the power of the New Right lay in "grass-roots mailings" in the 1970s, they saw the New Right force as a movement building on the large base of grassroots discontents.[41]

Despite their grassroots aspiration, the grassroots nature of the New Right was dubious. As historian Allan Lichtman maintained, most New Right figures were active inside the Beltway, forming study groups and political action committees for an echelon of conservative activists and legislators. The New Right attempted to make an alliance with blue-collar workers, but they did not socialize with them at union halls. The conservative activists rallied conservative movements in electoral campaigns yet organized few local chapters or voluntary associations on the local level. Weyrich, Phillips, and Dolan established organizations for political action without large membership. If the John Birch Society and antifeminist activist Phyllis Schlafly believed in American associational democracy when they actively organized grassroots conservatives beginning in the 1960s, the New Right of the 1970s was a mass movement that had few rank and file.[42]

The fundraising activities provoked controversy when the New Right juggernaut loomed large in the 1970s, bringing to the fore the moral issue of money in politics. Several activists and pundits complained that the New Right fundraising operation was extraordinarily expensive. Journalist Alan Ehrenhalt mentioned that New Right groups such as the CSFC, NCPAC, and Gun Owners spent much money for their fundraising campaigns and the expenses far exceeded contributions sent to candidates. Ehrenhalt reported Old Right critics charged that these New Right organizations were "wasting the contributors' money."[43] Tom Winter of the ACU claimed that Viguerie's direct mail was too costly, adding that there was also an ethical question about Viguerie's fundraising as his direct mail firm leased its mailing lists to clients, which other direct mail companies usually did not.[44] Herbert E. Alexander, director of the Citizen's Research Foundation and the political scientist who had played a crucial role in campaign finance reforms, also held, "Much of the money is literally being wasted—and is making Viguerie a millionaire."[45]

New Right activists and their allies made their case that money was used for building up the conservative base. William Rusher, publisher of *National Review*, claimed that the New Right's political action committees required seed money for their various activities, including distributing research materials, direct or indirect lobbying on key issues, and formulating the strategies in legislative battles.[46] However, when asked if the contributors comprehended that most of the funds would not be sent to the candidates, Weyrich answered no. "I don't think they did." Weyrich asserted that his CSFC spent money not merely on political campaigns but many other tasks. "We spent money to recruit candidates to train campaign managers, to analyze every vote cast in the House and the Senate, to publish newspaper and weekly reports, and none of this is reflected in the financial reports."[47]

Other reasons for the criticism of the New Right's direct mail was ideology or its absence. As New Right activists launched miscellaneous programs, rather than principled issues, several conservative critics considered the tendency "apparent indifference to ideology." Daniel Joy, legal counsel to Republican Senator James Buckley of New York, said, "The Viguerie people address only those issues which tend to stir up hostilities among lower-middle-class whites," focusing on busing, abortion, and gun control. Joy argued that New Right activists dismissed more important problems to the majority of Americans, such as a stagnant economy, turning public attention to sensational but narrower single issues.[48] William Brock, chairman of the Republican National Committee, similarly remarked that the New Right emphasized the wrong issues and menaced the GOP: "You can't build a party around those emotional social issues. . . . The New Right groups are competitive not only in that they draw away money from us but they draw away attention in Congress from the broad issues of tax reduction, job creation, health care, housing—the American Dream issues."[49]

Alternatively, some critics analyzed the effect of direct mail in turning the New Right more ideological. David Keane, a former aide to Senator Buckley and to California Governor Reagan, noted that "direct mail has made conservative organizations both more ideological and more accountable." In Keane's view, the New Right became more ideological because ideological direct mail was the best way to generate responses from constituents, and the movement became more accountable because it needed to answer to thousands of contributors who sent money in exchange for the achievement of campaign promises.[50] An article in the *Wall Street Journal* quoted Viguerie as saying that he was willing to help candidates in both major parties, but adding, "I don't take on candidates I don't agree with."[51] Because he institutionalized ideological direct mail that highlighted partisanship and conservative causes during the 1960s, Viguerie recognized that ideology was the key to effective fundraising and financed philosophically pure candidates regardless of political parties. If he was to be successful in the direct mail business, Viguerie was required to go to the extreme on the political spectrum.

Along with the moral issue revolving around raising money, as several others pointed out, a fundamental problem lurked in the direct mail market. If an American citizen answered Viguerie's solicitation letter, the recipient's name would be recorded on Viguerie's master list, then would receive appeals for other causes. Furthermore, as Viguerie leased his lists to other organizations and candidates, the contributor would face a torrent of direct mailings from these groups. Bruce W. Eberle, another leading fundraiser in conservative politics, was seriously concerned over the future of political direct mail. As duplication among the mailing lists of right-wing organizations ran at "about 30 per cent," Eberle said that conservative fundraisers needed to reach out beyond the closed circle.[52] Republican fundraiser Wyatt Stewart suggested the market was being saturated, supposing that "probably the same names get mailed 35 to 40 times a year." He added that "this system won't work forever"[53]

The 1976 Elections

In 1976, the New Right poured its energy into electing conservatives in congressional elections, which demonstrated both the impacts and limitations of Viguerie's direct mail. New Right groups successfully raised and spent a large amount of money for conservative candidates in order to change Congress. But the result of the congressional elections proved that money did not directly lead to political power that year.

Despite the fact that the New Right was formed just two years earlier, the groups most successfully amassed funds via direct mail during the campaign period. The Committee for the Survival of a Free Congress (CSFC) of Paul Weyrich spent $2,034,156 in 1975 and 1976, while Terry Dolan's National Conservative Political Action Committee (NCPAC) spent $2,334,426 over the years, and the Gun Owners of America (GOA) spent $2,015,632. Yet, as a newspaper article reported, most of the funds did not go to candidates. If the CSFC spent 11.5 percent of its expenditures for candidates, the NCPAC sent 9.6 percent and the GOA gave 6.7 percent to conservative candidates. As many criticized, the New Right drew funds away from the GOP and other conservative groups. But the money obviously influenced several congressional elections that year.[54]

Viguerie's direct mail brought about several surprising victories, such as the election of Stan Burger in the Montana state primary in 1976. When Senate Majority Leader Mike Mansfield announced his retirement, Viguerie and other conservatives persuaded Henry Hibbard to run for the Senate. But Hibbard, who had lost a close election to Montana Senator Lee Metcalf in 1972, declined. Instead, Burger visited Viguerie's office in Falls Church to raise funds for his campaign. Burger was a complete novice in politics as he had been executive secretary of the Montana Farm Bureau. Viguerie took the first step by collecting money. Within a few days, he obtained more than $20,000 from his political allies: $5,000 from the CSFC, another $5,000 from GOA, $3,500 from the Committee for Responsible Youth Politics, $1,500 from the Conservative Victory Fund of the ACU, and other funds from conservative PACs and business magnates such as Joseph Coors. Viguerie's next step was a massive direct mail campaign. He targeted 110,000 potential contributors with a fundraising letter signed by North Carolina Republican Senator Jesse Helms, which stressed that "your contribution in a sparsely populated state such as Montana goes a lot further . . . a budget of $20,000 can elect a Senator in Montana." The solicitation generated $40,000 that was immediately used for another direct mail drive. By the primary on June 1, Burger received contributions from 4,500 individuals who lived in every state; 550 conservatives in California contributed more funds than Burger received from Montana itself. The Burger campaign spent $128,000, an extraordinary sum for a Montana primary, winning a close election by five thousand votes.[55]

More significantly, Viguerie raised funds for the 1976 George Wallace campaign, which was a breakthrough for Viguerie's direct mail business as well. Wallace, who had lost the 1968 presidential election, sought to run again in the 1976 election. Although the Wallace campaign already had contributor lists from prior elections, the campaign attempted to widen the supporter base in order to win the race. The campaign committee planned to develop the name lists in search of a consulting firm adequate for this task. Charles S. Snider, manager of the Wallace campaign, said that he approached Viguerie because religious conservative Billy James Hargis recommended the political consultant. Snider explained that "we found that Viguerie was involved with conservative individuals and organizations and involved with religious groups like Rev. Billy James Hargis' Christian Crusade. We got good reference on Viguerie from Rev. Hargis."[56] Viguerie agreed to finance Wallace. The cooperation indicated a difference between the Old and New Right because several writers of *National Review* did not accept the Alabama governor as a respectable conservative. In the May 1967 issue, for example, Frank Mayer described Wallace as "the radical opposite of conservatism," being worried that his candidacy in 1968 would "poison the moral source of its strength."[57]

In June 1973, the Wallace campaign committee employed Viguerie for direct mail solicitation, bringing benefits to both the candidate and the conservative consultant. Viguerie began with Wallace's mailing lists of one million contributors, which he trimmed to 750,000. Then, he obtained other mailing lists possessed by the RAVCO, other conservative groups, subscribers to the *Saturday Evening Post*, and police and firefighters to build the list of "salable supporters." Viguerie's computers organized these names by zip code, occupation, and income. By September 1974, Viguerie dispatched three mailings for Wallace, including a presidential preference poll, a general solicitation, and a commemorative coin solicitation. Snider proudly remarked, "In 1976, if the governor runs, we'll have the largest, most sophisticated mailing list in the business." Indeed, Viguerie's work was satisfactory to the Wallace campaign as the RAVCO amassed $6 million for the Wallace campaign from 1974 to 1976. On Viguerie's side, the engagement with the Wallace campaign provided a great opportunity to expand his mailing lists. After gaining Wallace contributor lists and involving with direct mail operations, the RAVCO gained access to more conservative Democrats in the South. Armed with lists containing many conservative southern Democrats, Viguerie accelerated his strategy of reaching out beyond the Republican Party.[58] Yet the marriage of Viguerie with Wallace concluded unhappily because of the expensive direct mail operation. The Wallace campaign committee paid nearly $800,000 to the RAVCO between August 1973 and September 1974. Snider noted Viguerie's fundraising was "totally satisfactory," but also complained that "he made a hell of a lot of money off us."[59]

While the Democratic governor of Alabama signed the contract with Viguerie, Ronald Reagan, the Republican governor of California in 1976, did not want to use Viguerie's ideological direct mail when he ran for president in 1976. John Sears, the campaign manager for Reagan, said he swore off direct mail because, as a great orator, Reagan was able to raise funds on national television. "The first time we did it we raised $1.3 million at a cost of $100,000. It was cheaper, and easier." Viguerie later said, "If they'd used me, they wouldn't have run out of money when they needed it most."[60] Although Sears rejected Viguerie's expertise, the manager of the Reagan campaign understood direct mail was essential for fundraising in the post-Watergate period. He stressed the necessity to tap many people for political contributions via direct mail, saying that "in earlier times relatively few wealthy men could provide the finances for this kind of effort. Under the federal election laws, however, no person can give more than $1,000 before the primary elections. This means we must turn to many persons for their help."[61]

The Citizens for Reagan, a citizen committee to support Reagan, actively employed direct mail. With Senator Paul Laxalt as chairman, the Citizens for Reagan was formed to nominate Reagan as the Republican presidential candidate in 1976 and set out a fundraising drive to conduct the electoral campaign.

The organization chose Bruce W. Eberle, instead of Viguerie, to handle direct mail solicitation for Reagan. Since the early 1960s, he had been active in Young Americans for Freedom, first as president of the Missouri YAF and elected to the national board of YAF in 1967. Eberle founded his direct mail firm, Bruce W. Eberle & Associates, Inc., in a Washington suburb in May 1974. The young consultant shortly became among the most successful direct mail fundraisers in conservatism. Conservative political consultant Marvin Liebman wrote, "Bruce Eberle . . . seems to be the 'new' Richard Viguerie, who used to be known as the 'new' Marvin Liebman."[62]

The Citizens for Reagan launched a series of solicitation letters as it signed a contract with Eberle to use his mailing list six times a year. According to a staff member of the Citizens, fundraising, both by direct mail and personal solicitation, passed the half-million-dollar mark by October 1975 before Reagan's announcement of his bid for president boosted the campaign effort.[63] The Reagan campaign sent out several direct mail packages with each appeal stressing a specific issue. A direct mailing emphasizing gun control, for example, began with, "The time has come when a price must be paid if you want to keep your right to own a firearm." Pointing to the rise of crimes, such as "murders, rapes, and robberies," in the United States, the letter concluded, "The dues—the prices—can be paid with a check in support of Ronald Reagan's presidential election. For there is no doubt where Ronald Reagan stands on the issue of gun control."[64] Many farmers also received Reagan's fundraising letters. The appeal highlighted American farmers' "economic and social freedom is in serious danger," while it put forward antielitist populism when it described the farmer as "a victim of Washington bureaucrats."[65] Still another fundraising letter targeted Americans who were concerned over foreign affairs. The letter mentioned the threat of communism looming large on the globe, including Angola and Panama. The appeal simultaneously combined anticommunism with the growth of the federal government in the United States, noting, "Some of this growth has been brought about by temporary catastrophic events: wars, depressions, and extraordinary problems. While this was at times unavoidable, there is *no reason why it should be permanent.*"[66]

Many conservatives replied to the direct mail drive by sending checks and letters. Wilbert Hallock of Elmwood Park, New Jersey, recommended that Reagan lay stress on social issues and foreign policy rather than economic issues. Hallock thought that the two Republicans in the race sounded similar in their economic policy, and wondered whether Reagan's emphasis on economic matters would undercut his position. "But you are drastically different," he continued. "You are in favor of the restoration of the inalienable right to life for all human beings regardless of age, as solemnly guaranteed by the heart of our Declaration of Independence. . . . Mr. Ford is in favor of death for the youngest, most innocent, and most defenseless of our fellow human beings." Hallock also suggested that Reagan emphasize foreign policy, which was Ford's "particular disaster area." He enumerated several problems, such as "the Communist movement toward world domination" and "the loss of South Vietnam and Cambodia." After he was disappointed by the results of the first three primaries Reagan lost, Hallock still strongly supported the conservative candidate.[67]

Some Republicans did not endorse the nomination of Reagan. Frank Gard Jameson of Beverly Hills, California, received a solicitation letter from the Reagan campaign, but he did not support Reagan's candidacy. Though he said that he admired the California governor, he was worried about the division of the GOP. "To me the worst thing we can do today is to divide ourselves when we have a Republican President whom all the polls indicate will be a winner." Instead, Jameson wrote that he would support Reagan if he became the vice presidential candidate in place of Nelson Rockefeller, suggesting that he was a conservative Republican rather than moderate.[68]

The efforts to nominate Reagan as the Republican presidential candidate evinced the tensions of the New Right with the Old Right and Republican conservatives. Reagan had emerged among conservatives since giving his speech "Time for Choosing" on behalf of Barry Goldwater in the 1964 presidential campaign, and many right-wing activists expected him to be a leading politician of conservatism. Older conservative groups, such as the ACU and *Human Events*, were supportive of Reagan in the Republican primary, while the New Right looked askance at him.[69] In a confidential memo, Weyrich showed his distrust in the California governor: "Reagan may abandon us at the crucial moment when we need him most. I am convinced that some of the leadership we are looking for comes not from traditional Republican sources but from Democrats and Independent ranks."[70] Viguerie similarly remarked, "I don't think you can come to power in America with the Republican Party."[71] Viguerie was searching for another candidate as a truly conservative president. "I, along with most conservatives, want Ronald Reagan to win the Republican nomination and to be elected president this November," Viguerie mentioned in his magazine *Conservative Digest*. "But," he went on, "if this does not happen we must have an alternative plan."[72]

After winning the nomination at the Republican National Convention on August 18, Ford marshaled direct mail for fundraising. Because the new election laws provided federal funds for presidential candidates, Ford did not collect money for his own campaign. But he gave his signature to many solicitation letters for Republican congressional candidates. For instance, Republicans in states such as Tennessee, New Jersey, Oklahoma, and Connecticut received an appeal that highlighted Ford's achievements by saying, "Something wonderful happened to this country of ours over the past two years." This letter simultaneously charged the Democrat-controlled Congress with cutting down the defense budget that Ford requested, and with passing a succession of bills that would lead to "bigger government, increased inflation, more taxes, larger deficits, higher unemployment." Ascribing many challenges that the United States faced in the mid-1970s to Democrats, Ford's letters called on voters to support Republican candidates.[73]

Direct mailings over the signature of Ford reflected his fiscal conservative philosophy. As a proponent of small government, Ford approved solicitation letters stressing "a limited government and unlimited opportunity." One letter pointed to several goals that the Ford administration attempted to attain, including "the line of government spending to reduce inflation, a strong national defense, less government regulation, and a national energy program to prevent us from being at the mercy of foreign energy suppliers." Another appeal also claimed that Congress promoted the growth of the government by giving up important authority to "faceless bureaucrats who have become an unresponsive and unchecked fourth branch of government."[74]

However, Ford's direct mail could not summon up enthusiasm when anti-establishment populism swept through the nation. As *Newsweek* called 1976 the "Year of the Outsider," the election witnessed the rise of candidates, such as Reagan and Carter, who challenged the authority of Washington, DC. In the post-Watergate years, many Americans were suspicious of politicians boasting their Washington experience, seeking a new leader who emerged outside of Capitol Hill. The populist atmosphere undermined the Republican Party and Ford as the incumbent president in favor of Carter. During the campaign, Carter criticized Ford, arguing that he preferred a slow economic recovery with low inflation and vetoed bills that would have increased federal funding to decrease unemployment. Such remarks by the Georgian peanut farmer struck a chord with many working-class and middle-class Americans, while southern evangelicals endorsed Carter as a born-again Christian.[75]

Viguerie and other New Right activists pursued the realignment of the American political system by establishing a third party of populism. Conservative political analyst Kevin Phillips described the new constituency as the "New

Majority," including blue-collar workers, urban ethnics, and disgruntled Republicans, in favor of policies such as defending American tradition, middle-class welfare, and further government intervention in the economy.[76] At first, Wallace was the first option for the leadership of the conservative party. Viguerie attempted to run himself for vice president on the American Independent Party ticket, but he bowed out when the party nominated Lester Maddox in the primary. Disappointed by the Republican Party and the American Independent Party, Viguerie announced that he was planning to establish a new political party called the Independent Party, inviting conservatives to a national meeting in Chicago in December 1976. "We should make plans at the December 1976 meeting to run candidates for Congress in all 435 congressional districts. And for all 34 U.S. Senate seats in 1978. . . . Then in 1980 we will be one of the two major political parties and will be in position to elect a conservative Congress."[77]

Looking back at the 1976 election, the New Right fell short of their grander ambitions. Indeed, New Right organizations with which Viguerie was associated indicated they had the ability to amass vast funds, but they had just a slight impact on the results of the congressional elections. The CSFC tallied only 30 winners out of 143 candidates it supported; the NCPAC did a better job with 130 winners out of 208 because the organization contributed to statewide races along with congressional campaigns. And most of the conservative candidates whom Viguerie wanted to elect lost on election day. Titled "Why the 'New Right' Isn't Doing Well at the Polls," a *Business Week* article analyzed the reasons of the New Right's failure. It ascribed the fiasco to the ideological rigidity of the 1970s conservatives. Steven F. Stockmeyer, executive director of the National Republican Congressional Committee, charged that the New Right political action committees caused party leaders to support candidates with slim prospects for victory. "In 1976, these PACs picked 20 target districts and tried to get a hard-line conservative nominated in all of them," Stockmeyer explained. "They got only two nominated—and we lost both." The New Right also dedicated their energy to "purifying" politics through their efforts in ousting Republican moderates, rather than developing new candidates.[78]

In this sense, direct mail proved both lucrative and problematic as a political device in the 1976 elections. The individualized medium enabled the New Right to move beyond the Republican Party, carving out political niches and gaining financial support from individuals such as Democrats and working-class White people, a political field older conservatives had not explored. However, if direct mail solicitation worked well when it was emotional and ideological, the New Right had little space to make compromise with nonconservative forces. As a result, Viguerie and his associates needed to be purely conservative and launch offensive mailings, speeding up partisan conflicts in American politics.

The Panama Canal Treaties

Immediately after the 1976 election, the New Right focused on several single issues to gain public support. One of the central affairs was the ratification of the Panama Canal treaties in 1977. In actuality, the Panama Canal was not a major issue among Americans. Nevertheless, New Right activists vehemently opposed the US withdrawal from the Canal Zone. Their purpose was not to keep economic and military interests, but rather made use of emotional patriotism to garner support through such a narrowly minded issue. The antitreaties movement indicated again the nature of the New Right's emotional direct mail, and simultaneously widened the schism between Old and New Right activists.

The Panama Canal was not a new item on the agenda in US diplomacy. America's negotiations with Panama had begun with the Dwight Eisenhower administration and continued throughout six presidencies. The treaty talks took long as riots and military coups in Panama and public objections in the United States affected the negotiations. Following an anti-American riot that killed four Americans and twenty-four Panamanians on January 9, 1964, the Lyndon Johnson administration started to take into consideration an idea of withdrawing from the Panama Canal. Panama's President Roberto Chiari asked President Johnson for a revision of the 1903 treaty, and on March 21, Johnson stated that he wanted talks regarding "every issue which now divides us, and every problem which the Panamanian Government wishes to raise." New treaties were agreed on, under which US control would end no later than 2009 and a new canal would be built at sea level. However, because of opposition in both Panama and the United States among Republicans, Johnson did not submit the treaties to the Senate. On the Panamanian side, the 1968 presidential election in Panama selected Arnulfo Arias who criticized the new treaties. The negotiation was thrown into greater confusion as a military coup that year drove out Arias and put Lieutenant Colonel Omar Torrijos Herrera in power. Torrijos survived another coup, and he rejected new negotiations with the United States because he thought that American government backed the countercoup.[79]

The Nixon and Ford administrations both faced the Panama issue. Considering issues such as Vietnam, Russia, and China more seriously, Nixon gave little attention to Panama during his administration. His first secretary of state, William P. Rogers, and national security adviser Henry A. Kissinger were concerned that the tensions between the United States and Panama might foster wider anti-American sentiments throughout Latin America. They resumed negotiations with Panama in April 1971. Signed on February 7, 1974, the delegates promised to replace the 1903 treaty with one that would provide a prompt end to US control of the Canal Zone, a greater share of Canal profits to Panama, and commitment that Panama would participate in the administration and defense of the Canal. It guaranteed the US use of lands, water, and airspace necessary to operate and defend the Canal.[80] But these treaties provoked vehement oppositions by both Democrats and Republicans. Democratic Representative John Murphy of New York told the House that Kissinger was undertaking "a course of action which borders on insanity." Senator Strom Thurmond told his colleagues the principles "invite disaster," and he introduced a resolution "in support of continued undiluted United States sovereignty over the United States-owned Canal Zone on the Isthmus of Panama." Although Ford faced many important issues, such as inflation, the tensions with the Soviet Union, and fallout from his predecessor's resignation, Thurmond demanded the Ford administration address the Panama issue.[81]

During the 1976 election, several conservative candidates attacked the negotiation with Panama. Samuel I. Hayakawa, Republican senator from California, claimed that the United States deserved to keep the canal since "we stole it fair and square."[82] While Ronald Reagan focused closely on foreign affairs, especially the relationship with the Soviet Union, he also touched on the Panama issue by calling Panamanian President Torrijos a communist dictator. "Apparently everyone knows about this except the rightful owners of the Canal Zone, you, the people of the United States. General Omar Torrijos, the dictator of Panama, seized power right years ago by ousting the duly elected government.... Torrijos is a friend and ally of Castro and like him is pro-communist."[83]

Conservative citizens were worried over the Panama Canal as one of the critical foreign issues the United States faced. In reply to the Reagan campaign's solicitation letter, Frank McDonald wrote to Paul Laxalt, chair of the Citizens for Reagan. McDonald was a motion picture and television director. Although he had few opportunities to work with Reagan, McDonald was an admirer of the conservative politician and complained that his conservative words and actions had been "shunned" by liberal colleagues. In his letter, McDonald criticized foreign affairs such as SALT I and Henry Kissinger's strategies, then put heavy emphasis on the Panama Canal issue by writing, "The Panama Canal Belongs to the United States. Let's keep it that way!!!!"[84]

Even Jimmy Carter opposed the new treaties during the presidential election. In an interview with *Newsweek*, Carter commented, "I am not in favor of relinquishing actual control of the Panama Canal or its use to any other nation, including Panama," although he was sympathetic to Panamanians.[85] However, after he assumed the presidency, Carter reversed course. Prior to his inauguration, Carter read the report of Sol Linowitz's Commission on United States–Latin-American Relations, which stressed the importance of creating a new, equitable treaty and argued that the Panama Canal was the most urgent issue in the Western Hemisphere. Carter gave top priority to the Panama issue, saying, "I think the Panama treaty ought to be resolved quite rapidly. That's almost uniquely our responsibility."[86] Carter's national security adviser Zbigniew Brzezinski hired political scientist Robert Pastor as a member of the National Security Council Staff on January 8 and asked him to prepare a memorandum on Panama by January 21, the first working day of the new administration.[87]

Carter and Torrijos agreed on two new treaties on September 7, 1977. The first was the Treaty Concerning the Permanent Neutrality and Operation of the Panama Canal, or the Neutrality Treaty, which guaranteed that the United States could use its armed forces to defend the Panama Canal against any threats to its neutrality, and allowed American perpetual usage of the Panama Canal. The other agreement, the Panama Canal Treaty, stated that the Canal Zone would cease to exist on October 1, 1979, and that Panama's sovereignty over this territory would be fully restored on December 31, 1999. It was a conclusion of the negotiations between the United States and Panama, and a beginning of heated debates over the ratification of the treaties in the Senate.[88]

The Torrijos–Carter Treaties of 1977 immediately sparked a wave of protests among conservatives. Phyllis Schlafly, a conservative activist and founder of the Eagle Forum, had paid attention to the Panama issue in the 1950s, warning that Alger Hiss in his opening address to the United Nations in 1945 had called for the internationalization of the Panama Canal. And the first issue of her political newsletter, *Phyllis Schlafly Report*, in 1967 vehemently criticized Lyndon Johnson's treaty to turn over the canal to the Republic of Panama. In the campaign against the 1977 treaties, Schlafly used the anticommunism theme when she claimed, "Torrijos is part of a Marxist military junta operating in close collaboration with Communist Cuba and the Soviet Union." This anticommunist message was a typical strategy among conservatives. Furthermore, Schlafly took the Panama issue beyond communism by accusing the Carter administration of being in bed with multinational corporate interests. In the October 1977 issue of the *Phyllis Schlafly Report*, she charged that "ten of the largest banks in the United States joined with several foreign banks in lending $135 million to Panama." She pointed out that Linowitz was a director and member of the executive committee of Marine Midland Bank in New York, which had loaned money to Torrijos. Schlafly's rhetoric of anticommunism and distrust of eastern financial elites showed a conventional right-wing ideology that had existed since the 1950s.[89]

A coterie of conservative intellectuals in *National Review* looked at the Panama issue differently. Immediately before the treaties were signed, an article in *National Review* pointed to the significance of the Panama issue for conservatives. "Clearly, the Panama Canal is an object of national pride and rightly so. It is a part of our historical patrimony as much as it is of Panama's. For those ashamed of our past, the treaty poses an easy downhill decision—one that can even be worn as a penitential hair shirt. For conservatives, it presents a personal spiritual crisis." But at the same time, this article maintained that the new Panama treaties revised no national security concerns. "In fact, given the state of warfare in 1977, our own military men support the treaty on the ground that the Canal can be better defended with the treaty than without it. In case of external attack, it can be defended only by air and sea and, in the treaty, Panama agrees that we should continue to defend it."[90]

Similarly, James Burnham argued in *National Review* that the Panama Canal was no longer important militarily and that the debates over the treaties were merely "nostalgia politics." He noted, "To view the Panama issue clearly, we must adjust our perspective to take account of the fact that in itself the Zone is a relatively minor matter, no longer of any great importance to our security or interest. The feelings many of our citizens have about the Canal are nostalgic; they reflect outmoded ideas of both its strategic and its economic importance."[91] Similarly, William F. Buckley asserted that "it was very difficult to criticize that treaty."[92] As a consequence, he distanced himself from other conservatives who adamantly opposed the new treaties.

Several politicians also changed their postures on the Panama Canal. In 1976, Senator Hayakawa from California criticized treaties that the United States would give up sovereignty over the Panama Canal. Yet in his statement in October 1977, he was in favor of the Torrijos–Carter Treaties. While admitting that "the treaties have become a highly emotional issue," Hayakawa simultaneously foresaw the impact of the new treaties, remarking that "it is all too clear that ratification will be interpreted in many quarters as 'America on the run.' We therefore ought to be prepared for new pressures to abandon Guantanamo,

Cuba, and to evacuate Clark Air Force Base and Subic Bay in the Philippines." But he was anxious about the results of failing to ratify the new treaties when he said, "An important byproduct of such action would be the warning to the rest of the world that the United States not only is unwilling to give up the canal, but also is prepared to defend its rights regardless of consequences." Unlike the senator in 1976 who had said "we stole [the canal] fair and square," he warned in 1977 that "[it] is our political leaders' task to alert the America people and to make it clear that, contrary to their expectations, the Senate's verdict will not dispose of the issue."[93]

Even if the Torrijos-Carter Treaties stirred up emotional reactions among the public, conservatives were not monolithic concerning the Panama Canal issue. Some conservatives considered the new treaties a serious threat to American national security and economic interest, while others did not think the Panama Canal was that important for the United States any longer. Nevertheless, the Panama treaties offered an opportunity for the New Right to gain momentum in the late 1970s. Reacting to the issue immediately after the Carter administration announced the terms of the treaties in August 1977, the New Right in tandem with conservative groups created a coalition of the antitreaties campaigns. The Committee for the Survival of a Free Congress (CSFC), the Conservative Caucus, the National Conservative Political Action Committee (NCPAC), the American Conservative Union (ACU), and Citizens for the Republic, which was founded by Reagan, cooperated to oppose the Panama Canal treaties.

For Richard Viguerie and his allies, the Panama Canal treaties were a critical issue through which the New Right could legitimate their "grassroots" activism. "This is a cutting issue," said Viguerie. "It's an issue the conservative can't lose on" because "it's a sexy issue. It's a populist issue." Viguerie raised the treaties as a significant issue not only because he believed the withdrawal from the Canal Zone undermined US national security, but also because he was able to connect the issue with his antiestablishment populism. "These treaties as much as anything else are a bailout for big New York bankers with loans in Panama," Viguerie remarked, adding that "here's a populist President who's going to bail out David Rockefeller." Gary Jarmin, legislative director of the ACU, also comprehended the significance of the issue for the conservative movement. "It's not just the issue itself we're fighting for. This is an excellent opportunity for conservatives to seize control of the Republican Party." Whereas the Carter administration stressed direct appeals to the Senate and to opinion leaders across the nation, conservatives attempted to stop the ratification of the treaties by approaching the public. Viguerie carried out direct mail drives, calling for funds and petitions, which highlighted the New Right's focus on populist persuasion. "We'd doing some direct lobbying, but not so much as the White House. Our strength is not in Washington. Our strength is in Peoria and Oshkosh and White River Falls."[94] Despite the fact that his operations were primarily based on the Washington area, Viguerie was able to arm the New Right with populist persuasion by gathering small contributions and petitions from the American public.

Other New Right activists indicated that the movement against the Panama treaties was a people's uprising so frequently that journalism took notice of the protest as "the groundswell of popular opposition." Howard Phillips of the Conservative Caucus stressed that the Panama issue was important not merely for conservatives and anticommunists but Americans in general, seeing the issue as "a symbol of their country's policy of appeasement." Paul Weyrich also asserted that the antitreaties campaign was a bipartisan movement, emphasizing, "We don't care how we do it, as Republicans and conservatives or whatever, but we have the American people on our side now and we will win in the end."[95]

For Reagan, the Panama Canal issue turned out to be a critical topic as he aimed at the 1980 presidential election. After he failed to be nominated in the 1976 Republican National Convention, Reagan was required to distinguish himself from Ford through his hardline foreign policy posture. The difference between Reagan and the Republican establishment was obvious over the canal issue. In October, the Republican National Committee mailed out five hundred thousand solicitation letters signed by Ford. The package enclosed a "critical issues survey" that asked for recipients' opinions on ten questions. Five of the questions concerned foreign and defense policy but did not mention the Panama Canal.[96] Moreover, RNC Chairman Bill Brock exasperated right-wing Republicans when he refused to invest $50,000 of party funds in a national congressional caravan against the ratification, which was proposed by Reagan and Senator Paul Laxalt of Nevada.[97] On this battle line, Reagan was willing to go hand in hand with the New Right activists.

Viguerie launched an immense direct mail campaign, which vividly demonstrated the New Right's populist and emotional aspects. In the fall of 1977, the RAVCO sent out five million copies of a fundraising letter with Reagan's signature. The letter was designed to appeal to patriotism. "I need your immediate help to prevent our country from making one of the most serious mistakes in its 200 year history," the fundraising letter began, emphasizing the treaties' negative impacts on American diplomacy. The letter introduced readers to the terms of the treaties, such as the duty of the United States to pay millions of dollars to Panama, while mentioning that the Panamanian government might raise prices on goods shipped through the canal. "This is not a partisan issue," the letter stressed, claiming that the overwhelming majority of Americans opposed the canal "giveaway."[98]

However, mixing true and false stories on the Panama Canal treaties, Viguerie's letter depicted the consequences of the ratification in his usual menacing language. The letter noted that "one of our most vital shipping and defense waterways will be in the complete control" of General Torrijos. This description was wrong because the Panama Canal Treaty granted the United States operating control of the waterway and the right to defend it until December 31, 1999, while granting Panama general territorial jurisdiction over the Canal Zone and the use of portions of the area not required for the canal operation and defense. Furthermore, this direct mailing charged both Panamanian and American leaders. It called General Torrijos an "anti-American, pro-Marxist dictator," and condemned Carter for not "consulting Congressional leaders." Actually, the Carter administration had lobbied senators and congressional committee staffs before they reached the final agreement. As many other direct mailings of Viguerie, this appeal was aimed to fan popular fury by demonizing political opponents and implying that political decisions were made behind the scenes.[99]

Direct mail was part of the New Right's multimedia campaign against the ratification of the treaties. The main goal of Viguerie's fundraising letter was to send the millions of signatures to US senators prior to the Senate vote in January 1978. For the purpose, the letter continued, they needed to raise a minimum of $2 million for the advertising to generate the petitions. At the same time, the ACU premiered a half-hour television film critical of the Panama Canal treaties in early November 1977. Conservatives expected that the film would provoke antitreaty sentiments and raise funds for the movement.[100]

The Carter administration received many letters from conservatives who protested against the treaties. A fifteen-year-old boy bitterly accused Carter, "You have made as many intelligent decisions so far as a frog has." Emphasizing that the building of the Panama Canal had been accompanied with American casualties and millions of money, the young conservative said that Carter's decision affected national security and hurt American citizens. "Before you make another decision," the letter concluded, "think about all the people and the kids that will be voting in the 1980 Presidential Election."[101]

Another conservative from Pasadena, California, sent a long letter to the White House, making a similar case as Viguerie's direct mailing. "Do you realize that [you] are giving away taxpayers' money and valuable property of the United States?" asked the eighty-five-year-old Californian, blaming the Carter administration for singing the treaty that required the United States to pay millions

to Panama. As many other conservatives, the writer of the letter opposed the
Panama Canal treaties partly because she considered the Panama leader a treach-
erous communist dictator. The Californian asserted, "It is a known fact that
communistic Russia of which both Castro and this Truijos [*sic*] are so-called
pals. It is also known that the commies have never kept faith with one treaty
except that it was all in their favor." Furthermore, like Viguerie, this letter took
on antielitist populism when it believed in the bankers' conspiracy. Pointing
to Panama's debt, the writer asserted, "This is money which the international
babkers [*sic*] have lent to this despot and so we, the taxpayers have to repay these
millionaire bankers, among them the Rockefellers, as well as Messers."[102]

The New Right targeted US senators who were undecided over the Panama
Canal treaties. Several public opinion polls indicated that the majority of southerners opposed America's retreat from the Canal Zone, but thirteen Democratic
senators from southern states remained uncommitted. Conservatives assumed
that these southern senators were undecided because, in Weyrich's words, "The
he-is-our-President argument is strong." The New Right attempted to pressure
senators with the petitions from Americans who did not want the new treaties,
suggesting that the senators would lose support in their next elections if they
were to vote for the ratification.[103]

However, the New Right's massive media campaigns against the treaties
failed to achieve its goal. The US Senate ratified the Neutrality Treaty on March
16, 1978, and the Panama Canal Treaty on April 18 by a vote of sixty-eight to
thirty-two. As the Senate was controlled by Democrats and sixteen Republicans
voted for the ratification, the New Right and their supporters lost their struggle
to stop the two treaties. But they were lost just by two votes, keeping Democrats
on guard in the years to come.

Nevertheless, liberals could not dismiss the threat of the New Right. According to conservative commentator Kevin Phillips, President Carter cited the
New Right as a political menace in a 1977 fundraising letter for the Democratic
Party.[104] DNC Chairman Kenneth M. Curtis also warned that "millions of dollars . . . will fund a vigorous nationwide effort against progressive Democratic
representatives and senators in 1978," strongly criticizing the New Right movement for their "shrillness, stridency and superficiality." Yet liberals simultaneously imitated the methods of intimidating direct mail. The National Committee for an Effective Congress (NCEC), the left-wing counterpart to Weyrich's
CSFC, oftentimes denounced the conservative organization in its appeals. An
NCEC solicitation pamphlet began with a bold headline, saying, "There's a new
'enemies list' and some of your best friends are on it." A *Congressional Quarterly*

article pointed out, "NCEC and CSFC frequently use each other's claims to stir up concern among their own supporters over the threat from the other side."[105] Efficient but gloomy direct mail fundraising was contagious and swept through American politics in the late 1970s.

Over the course of the antitreaty campaigns in 1977, the New Right showed its presence in the conservative movement. As Viguerie received funds from conservatives in response to his direct mail, he collected names and addresses of more conservatives across the nation. Enlarging the naming lists of possible supporters and evolving his direct mail techniques, Viguerie and other New Right activists were ready for another midterm election in 1978 and the 1980 presidential election in pursuit of a conservative revolution in American politics.

The 1978 Elections

As the New Right geared up for the 1978 congressional elections, Viguerie prepared for an enormous assault on liberal and moderate incumbents. The New Right's objective in the year was to defeat "the Watergate babies," liberals who had been elected in the wake of Nixon's resignation in 1974, while also attacking Republican moderates, including Senators Clifford P. Case of New Jersey and Edward W. Brooke of Massachusetts. Viguerie was so convinced that he said his direct mail campaign would be "many, many times more effective" in 1978 than it had been two years earlier.[106]

The campaigns against Representative John Anderson and Senator Thomas McIntyre indicated how strong and effective the New Right's blitz was. Anderson was a representative from Illinois and a moderate Republican. When the Illinois primaries were held in March 1978, the New Right targeted him as an early test. Paul Weyrich's Committee for the Survival for a Free Congress (CSFC) encouraged a fundamentalist minister, Rev. Don Lyon, to run for the House. Whereas Viguerie launched direct mail fundraising drives, Terry Dolan's National Conservative Political Action Committee (NCPAC) sent "coalition-builders" to work for Lyon, and the Gun Owners of America (GOA) also dispatched several staffers who "play[ed] on the fears of people," said Anderson. On the last weekend, the Conservative Victory Fund, a political arm of the American Conservative Union, ran newspaper ads against Anderson. "The Far Right resorts to primal passions," the Republican moderate later recalled. "There is real danger that they can so totally focus on relatively narrow issues and dominate the political dialogue." Despite his nomination in the primary, Anderson keenly realized the threat of the New Right movement.[107]

Senator Thomas McIntyre was another target of the New Right. A Democrat, McIntyre had been a New Hampshire senator since 1962, the first Democratic senator from the state since Fred H. Brown in 1932 as well as the first Democratic senator in the state's history to win a third term. In 1978 when he ran for reelection for a fourth term, New Hampshire was divided over the ratification of the Panama Canal treaties. New Hampshire Governor Meldrim Thomson, a conservative Republican, looked for a Democrat to run against Senator McIntyre. And if McIntyre would vote in favor of the Panama Canal treaties, Governor Thomson suggested running against the senator himself. The New Right instead supported Gordon Humphrey, a politically unknown airline pilot, in his bid for the Senate. Backed by the national wave of conservatism and with the help of the New Right, Humphrey surprised many political observers as he narrowly defeated the veteran senator.[108]

Immediately after he was defeated, McIntyre published his book *The Fear Brokers* (1979) to warn against the extremism of the New Right. Accusing the New Right of "the blandishments and fear-mongering," McIntyre wrote that New Right activists were "eager to prey upon the frustrations and anxieties" of the public, and the movement "would ease anxieties with absolutes and certainties, with the promise of decisive action and magic elixirs. And they would do all this in the name of 'real Americanism.'" McIntyre grasped the central role played by Viguerie and his direct mail in mobilizing conservative Americans. He made his case that the technique of computerized direct mail "changed not only the face but the very character of the American political process." As computer technologies developed and dominated American politics, McIntyre thought, direct mail solicitation swept through US politics. Republican national organizations and business political action committees actively utilized the medium for collecting money. But conservatives were the forerunners among political direct mail users. McIntyre wrote that the right could "carry its message to between six and seven million people," while the conservative movement diffused its messages exclusively via elitist publications such as *Human Events* and *National Review* only a decade earlier.[109]

But few right-wing politicians demonstrated the capacity to organize nationwide conservatives more clearly than North Carolina Senator Jesse Helms, whose 1978 campaign was regarded as "a textbook example of organizational and technical competence."[110] Helms's electoral campaign owed its success to his powerful political machine, the Congressional Club. After developing his career as a radio host, congressional aide, lobbyist, and television broadcaster, Helms won the US Senate race in 1972. To pay off a $150,000 debt of the campaign, the

Congressional Club was established in 1973 with Senator Helms as an honorary chair and Tom Ellis, a longtime Helms confidant and attorney, serving as a political adviser.[111] Shortly, combining conventional and modern methods, the Congressional Club came to play a major role in raising funds, broadcasting political messages, and mobilizing support for Helms and other conservative candidates. The Congressional Club sponsored a series of dinners and receptions as forums to which it invited many conservative speakers. The club also founded Jefferson Marketing, Inc., a production company to produce Helms's television ads. Helms used these vehicles to disseminate his messages against inflation, arms limitations, and liberal politics, bypassing the mainstream media. Ellis said, "I think we know how to get conservatives elected, how to put the nuts and bolts together to go over the heads of the liberal editors and TV commentators and get the conservative message out there to the people on TV."[112]

Helms built an intimate relationship with the New Right during the 1970s. When Charlie Black, a member of Young Americans for Freedom, introduced Viguerie to the club, Helms and Ellis doubted that direct mail worked to amass funds. But Viguerie proved the efficacy of his direct mail fundraising when the Congressional Club mailed out an appeal to the constituency in the summer of 1975. As letters with checks flooded his office, Ellis was astonished, and the Helms campaign was able to pay the remaining debt of the 1972 campaign. Ellis also realized that Viguerie's direct mail not merely brought political contributions to Helms's coffer, but also a database of a national constituency for ensuing campaigns. Now with mailing lists of conservatives, the Congressional Club constructed a national network of supporters across the country, transforming itself from North Carolina's local political group into a national PAC. Helms also helped found Washington-based organizations of the New Right such as Howard Phillips's Conservative Caucus and Terry Dolan's NCPAC in 1974. Riding the wave of the New Right movement, Helms emerged as one of the towering conservative senators in the 1970s.[113]

The Congressional Club was involved with the campaign to nominate Reagan as the Republican candidate in the 1976 presidential election. At the request of Helms and Ellis, Reagan withdrew his campaign staff from North Carolina so that the Congressional Club could take on the primary campaign in the state. Carter Wrenn, a twenty-seven-year-old executive director of the club, and Ellis focused on key foreign policy issues such as the Panama Canal treaties and a "one way" détente with the Soviet Union. Their strategy worked so well that Reagan upset President Ford by winning the North Carolina primary after three earlier defeats.[114]

In 1978, the Congressional Club waged an extensive campaign for Senator Helms's reelection race. When the club organized volunteers in every precinct across the state, the organization took the New Right's strategy by depending heavily on Democrats and Independents as well as Republicans. Several New Right activists were engaged in the Helms campaign. In the early stage, the Congressional Club held a series of lectures for over eight hundred young conservatives on a Raleigh college campus. The "crash campaign school" featured lectures by conservative political consultants, such as youth organizer Morton Blackwell, and speeches by conservative representatives, including Jack Kemp of New York and Phil Crane of Illinois.[115]

Simultaneously, Helms's political action committee carried out direct mail fundraising in and outside the state so successfully that a *Nation* journalist described the Congressional Club as "the very model of modern, high-technology politics." Supported by Viguerie, the club compiled a mailing list of approximately three hundred thousand names, gaining $7.5 million from a national constituency with the average contribution between $12 and $15. The Helms campaign used the funds for organizing all precincts of the North Carolina state as it opened campaign offices, installed telephones, and conducted public opinion polls.[116]

Sending ten to twenty million copies, the Congressional Club developed ideological direct mail in the 1978 campaign. As Ellis explained that the club aimed "to counterbalance the political activities of the union bosses, the ERA crowd and the other far-left political campaigns," Helms's fundraising letters were designed to rally support by condemning liberals, particularly labor unions and détente proponents. An appeal under Reagan's signature attacked union bosses as Helms's main political enemy, saying, "I am not exaggerating when I say that Big Labor and Radical pressure groups will pull out all the stops to defeat Jesse Helms. Jesse's State of North Carolina will be literally swamped with out of state money and Union organizers who are really political experts who specialize in voter registration." In another solicitation letter of September 15, Helms similarly noted, "[AFL-CIO President] George Meany and the other big union bosses have handpicked me as their #1 Target for defeat in 1978!" In the same letter, Helms also attacked "anti-defense activists," asserting that the administration defense advisers and liberal senators tried to shrink national defense by "scrapping the B-1 bomber . . . without getting any concessions from the Soviet Union."[117]

The 1978 elections indicated that the New Right's financial might grew through political direct mail and political action committees. Special interest groups spent $76.3 million during the 1978 campaign period, increasing from $74 million in the last off-year election in 1974. Conservative money was outstanding as six conservative PACs outspent all other special interest groups by a considerable margin. Reagan's Citizens for the Republic was the largest single PAC, raising $2.9 million over the period and sending money to 238 House candidates and 27 Senate candidates. Weyrich's CSFC ranked the third largest PAC as it spent $1.9 million, whereas the AFL-CIO's Committee for Political Education and its state affiliates spent the same amount. Yet a large sum of the political funds was absorbed in direct mail operations. Of $2.9 million raised by Reagan's PAC, only $1 million was actually sent to candidates. In the case of the Helms campaign, Viguerie controlled two-thirds of Helms's mailing list of three hundred thousand conservatives and received rental payment from the Congressional Club every time the names were used. Although several observers were critical of Viguerie's direct mail operation, his national network did not stop expanding. As Viguerie's influence extended to conservative Democrats and blue-collar Americans, the New Right movement assisted conservative candidates in congressional campaigns. Now they attempted to have a conservative president in the White House.[118]

The 1980 Reagan Campaign

The conservative waves, which gathered force throughout the 1970s, culminated in the election of Reagan. While television advertising continued to play a major role in selling candidates, direct mail and the New Right movement served to ferment the conservative mood by 1980. As political direct mail became a key device for solicitation, Viguerie rivetted public attention as the best direct mail operative in the political arena. But at the same time, Viguerie's approach of emotionalism for fundraising faced public criticism for fostering negativity. Furthermore, Viguerie's ideological direct mail kept the New Right movement away from the mainstream of conservatism. Although the 1980 election was the historic victory for American conservatives, the New Right's antielitist populism prevented it from being integrated into the conservative establishment.

As in 1976, the relationship between the New Right and Reagan was strained during the 1978 campaign due to their difference over political strategy. Despite his cooperation on the fight against the Panama Canal treaties, Reagan refused to support New Right challengers to moderate Republican incumbents because he wanted to distance himself from feverishly ideological conservatism. His hesitancy to work closely with the New Right irritated Viguerie and Weyrich.

Although Reagan was the most desirable option for many conservatives in the 1980 election, New Right activists kept a distrust of him as the authentic conservative during and after the race.[119]

Thus, it was not a surprise that the Reagan campaign did not select the Richard A. Viguerie Co. as its fundraising firm for his 1980 campaign. Bruce Eberle, who had been engaged with the 1976 Reagan campaign, eagerly proposed his assistance in fundraising. "I am very anxious to be of service to Governor Reagan again in 1979–1980," he wrote in a letter to the campaign. One of the advantages, Eberle said, was the access to his mailing list that he had organized in the previous campaign. As a coowner of the 1976 Reagan for President donor file, Bruce W. Eberle & Associates was the only agency that could guarantee the exclusive use of the list throughout the entire campaign. Eberle simultaneously submitted a fundraising proposal, whose goal was "to raise approximately $12 million at a cost of $2 million" over an eighteen-month period. He also emphasized the evolution of the computer in the proposal. "One of the most dramatic and practical advances in computer technology as applied to direct response fund raising is in the area of data entry.... Thanks to the advent of the so-called 'mini-computer' and advances in peripheral technology, direct response source information can now be entered on a 'real time' basis." Eberle's proposal indicated the development of computer technology and the sophistication of conservative fundraising by the end of the 1970s, assuring that his direct mail would be immensely helpful.[120]

The Reagan campaign, however, inherited political consultants from previous Republican presidential candidates, and assigned L. Robert Morgan to handle direct mail fundraising. Morgan had participated in the November Group, the team of advertising executives and political consultants for the 1972 Nixon campaign. In 1980, he was president of Integrated Communication Systems, Inc., which was the exclusive agency that directed all of the direct mail and telephone fundraising on behalf of the Reagan for President Committee. Several other former members of the November Group served in the Reagan campaign. For instance, Phil Joanou was vice president of Doyle, Dane, Bernbach, a prominent advertising agency on Madison Avenue, had been executive vice president of the November Group and served as a free advertising consultant to Reagan in 1980. "In my 20 years in the business world," Morgan mentioned, "I rate Phil Joanou as having the finest advertising and marketing mind I have met." The Reagan campaign also employed an advertising firm called SFM, which the 1972 Nixon and the 1976 Ford campaigns had used.[121]

The former November Group members crafted a marketing strategy that was markedly different from that of the New Right. They thought that it was not enough just to capitalize on the conservative mood for winning the presidential race. For the purpose of developing confidence in Reagan among moderate and conservative Democrats as well as independents, the consultants attempted to create the positive image of Reagan as "a reasonable, responsible and acceptable choice." The marketing plan of the 1980 Reagan campaign stressed, "We must give people a reason to vote *for* Governor Reagan, not just against President Carter." Unless they could build trust in Reagan, the consultants analyzed, moderate Democrats and independents would display their dissatisfaction with Carter either by voting for another Democrat or not voting whatsoever.[122]

The marketing strategy defined Reagan's direct mail fundraising. The Reagan campaign actively mailed out appeals partly to finance television advertising. When Reagan conducted a campaign for the Republican nomination in January 1980, his fundraising agency sent a fundraising letter to those who had contributed money. Intimacy characterized the direct mailings from Reagan. "Dear Ed: I hope you'll keep the special photograph I've enclosed for you," said the letter, which was sent to Ed Meese of La Masa, California, who had contributed $200 before. Enclosed was a photo taken during the filming of Reagan's announcement on television, and Reagan asked for more donations to reserve air time on television. "With the support of people like Paul Laxalt, Jack Kemp, Orrin Hatch and you, I know we can win—if we can raise enough money," the mail stressed.[123]

The New Right similarly implemented massive direct mail campaigns for the 1980 election, sharing many conservative names on their lists, but taking a negative approach. Ed Meese also received an appeal from Terry Dolan of the National Conservative Political Action Committee in January 1980. Attacking Ted Kennedy who sought the Democratic nomination, Dolan's letter asked "Mr. Meese" several questions: "Do you think he lied about Chappaquiddick? Do you think America can afford Kennedy as President? Do you think he is qualified to be President?" The appeal doubted Kennedy's leadership, criticizing his welfare policy and his voting record against national defense, gun control, and school prayer. This fundraising letter asked for money to develop two campaigns, the Kennedy Poll and the Emergency Stop Kennedy Squad, in order to launch negative ads that emphasized that Kennedy was a "Big-Spending, Anti-Defense, Pro-Big Labor superliberal." While condemning the Democrat, however, this direct mailing never mentioned any candidates whom Dolan endorsed as the next president. This was one of the typical fundraising letters of the New Right, which stressed what they were *against* rather than *in favor of*.[124]

Other conservative organizations involved themselves with the Reagan movement largely through attacking political enemies. The American Conservative

Union dispatched copies of a direct mailing in August, emphasizing the threats of liberals such as John Anderson who ran for president as an Independent in 1980. "You see, the Anderson and McGovern types are willing to do almost anything to keep Conservatives out of power," the letter noted. Simultaneously this appeal suggested that, if Democrats won the 1980 elections, a Democratic-ruled Congress would dismiss voters' choice, saying, "If Anderson . . . can win just a few states this fall he can throw the election into the Democratic controlled House of Representatives. And if that happens your vote won't count. The liberals who control Congress—rather than the voters—would select our next President." The ACU obviously supported Reagan as the Republican presidential candidate, but its appeal put heavy emphasis on the opponent campaign against Democrats.[125]

The strategy of constructing Reagan's positive images, rather than attacking his adversary, resulted partly from the public opinion against negative campaign in 1980. Both the Reagan and Carter campaigns were not able to evade the criticism. David A. Schwartz, president of Consumer Response Corporation, investigated New York voters' impressions of the two candidates' political advertisements. In his report in October, Schwartz found out that many voters in the New York area were quite dissatisfied with the advertising of both candidates, which displayed opponents negatively. He acknowledged that Reagan's attacks on the president were more acceptable than Carter's attacks, but he added that voters did not perceive Reagan's criticisms as a positive portrayal of the former California governor. Schwartz suggested, "There are other criticisms of course, but *intelligence* and *generalities* are two themes that work their way into every discussion."[126]

The Carter campaign, too, observed the backlash against a negative campaign. Because opposition campaigns had been effective in 1976, the media strategists for Carter devoted a great deal of time and money to negative campaigns by using facts sheets, print ads, columnists, and Ford's speeches. But Martin Franks, Carter's opposition research chief, opined that negative campaigns tended to backfire. Anthony R. Dolan, a staff member of the Reagan campaign, agreed with him, saying, "[H]e is right, guttersniping does tend to backfire." But at the same time, Dolan maintained that negative campaigns would be highly effective if they were truthful and not strident. "The point here," he stressed, "is that we should not get carried away with the latest from the experts—sure, opposition campaigns need to be handled very carefully—but they are essential in most campaigns, especially this one."[127]

Viguerie showed his support for Reagan in the 1980 presidential campaign, even though he did not wholeheartedly trust the politician. In his publication

Conservative Digest, Viguerie declared that he formally endorsed Reagan for president. But he added, "Which is not to say that he is perfect." Even when Regan ran for president, Viguerie wished a conservative politician close to the New Right, such as Jesse Helms, Jack Kemp, or Paul Laxalt, would be his running mate. "Our endorsement of Ronald Reagan does not extend to George Bush," Viguerie wrote. The remark indicated that the schism between the conservative candidate and the New Right still ran deep.[128]

Nevertheless, when Reagan won the race on November 4, 1980, Viguerie celebrated the victory, exulting that direct mail contributed to the conservative revolution. "Few people realize how much of this great conservative victory is due to direct mail," he emphasized. Viguerie claimed that over 75 percent of the funds Reagan raised in his 1976 and 1980 campaigns came from direct mail, and over 90 percent of the money collected by Reagan's PAC was the result of direct mail drives. These figures were probably exaggerated, but the enormous number of direct mailings surely played a part in raising funds and sending Reagan's messages to conservatives. Viguerie wrote that conservatives had sent out one billion pieces of advertising mail directly to voters after 1974. He stressed that the new technology enabled conservatives to bypass the liberal ascendancy in mass media including television, radio, newspapers, and magazines. "What is the new technology? It's computers, direct mail, telephone marketing, TV (including cable TV), and radio that asks for contributions, cassette tapes, and the use of toll-free phone numbers, among other things," he boasted.[129]

Indeed, the result of the 1980 presidential election came primarily from Carter's unpopularity, and Reagan might have won the race without new technologies. Yet direct mail of the New Right was doubtless an important factor of America's right turn by 1980. While neoconservatives offered the theoretical backbone of foreign policy and the new Christian right, including Jerry Falwell and Pat Robertson, sent conservative messages to many evangelicals across the nation, New Right activists provided conservative candidates with pragmatic expertise in organizing and fundraising. As an analyst mentioned, a good budget and a good system for controlling costs would not automatically win the election—"but without them we could lose it."[130]

Epilogue

"A PROVEN METHOD OF PROMOTING bookstore sales is by direct mail. A sound and methodical direct mail promotion will increase in-store sales and develop mail orders."[1] The John Birch Society (JBS) employed direct mail to advertise its American Opinion Bookstore beginning in the mid-1970s. The JBS mailed out a monthly direct mail promotion called "Book News," with which it attempted to reach new customers and to inform old members of their wares. The JBS, which had emerged as the largest grassroots anticommunist organization in the 1960s but declined by the end of the decade, sought all channels to connect with the public. The group had made efforts to tout anticommunism by organizing small chapters across the nation, while sustaining itself on a traditional associational model like contacting conservatives at members' home chapters, local service clubs, and civic organizations. However, like many other conservative organizations, the JBS found out direct mail was among the most effective media to reach out to conservative individuals. "This is without a doubt the best tool," a JBS staff member said.[2]

Richard Viguerie's direct mail reached its apex in the early 1980s. His ideological fundraising appeals, which capitalized on resentment and discontent, became a model for not only conservatives but also moderates and liberals. New Right activists believed that they had played a pivotal role in electing Ronald Reagan to the presidency. However, they soon discovered that Ronald Reagan was not their ideal president. Furthermore, with the rise of other rivals such as Bruce Eberle and televangelists, Viguerie's alchemy that turned emotion to money rapidly lost its power. One legacy of the Reagan Revolution resulted in the decline of the New Right as few donors responded to their missives.

The New Right considered Reagan's presidency their own achievement. "Many people believe that a great victory was won on November 4, 1980 when Ronald Reagan was elected President of the United States," a prominent New Right activist Howard Phillips remarked in his speech at the Freemen Institute Century Club Banquet in 1981.[3] As the New Right successfully conducted direct mail campaigns to amass funds for right-wing candidates and to mobilize conservative Americans across the nation, New Right operatives regarded themselves as a key factor of the conservative revolution in 1980. Viguerie denied the argument that Reagan had not been indebted to the conservatives for his election. "This, of course, is incorrect," he asserted. Viguerie proudly wrote that conservative groups, including Young Americans for Freedom and the American Conservative Union, had supported Reagan over years, whereas moderate Republicans had distrusted the conservative politician. Viguerie stressed the roles of the New Right particularly in supporting conservative candidates in the 1980 congressional races. "Without the New Right, President Reagan would have faced a Congress still dominated by liberal Democrats in both Houses."[4]

However, the Reagan administration soon frustrated New Right activists. In his speech, Phillips highlighted four issues that President Reagan needed to address. He emphasized that Reagan should discontinue arms control, eliminate the Soviet's power in Latin America, implement spending cuts, and stop federal subsidies for liberal organizations such as the National Endowments for the Arts and Humanities. Yet Phillips did not completely endorse Reagan's policies. For instance, he noted that at that point of 1981 Reagan's policy on arms control was almost the same as that of the Carter administration. The New Right had continuously opposed Strategic Arms Limitations Talks (SALT), but Phillips said, "Under Jimmy Carter we adhered to the provisions of SALT I which expired in 1977. Under President Reagan we are still adhering to SALT I."[5]

Similarly, Viguerie and his colleagues complained that the Reagan administration needed to assign more conservatives to its top positions. The February 1981 issue of *Conservative Digest* published an open letter to Reagan, in which the magazine's editor criticized the personnel operations at the White House. They took to task the work of Pendleton James, assistant for presidential personnel, and James Cavanaugh, special consultant to the president. The open letter contended that these White House aides were politically naive, and even worse, their backgrounds revealed a hostility to Reagan's conservatism. The *Conservative Digest* editor worried that President Reagan would not be able to attain major goals without any change in the personnel policy, writing, "There will be no Reaganism without Reaganites."[6]

Viguerie's criticism took aim at Reagan himself after the president announced that he would nominate Sandra Day O'Connor as an associate justice of the Supreme Court in July. The New Right opposed this appointment because O'Connor as an Arizona state senator had supported a bill legalizing abortion in the state in 1970. She had also cosponsored an act that made contraceptives and abortion available to minors without parental consent in 1973, and had voted against an amendment to prohibit the performance of abortion at tax-supported hospitals in 1974. Viguerie maintained that the choice of O'Connor ran counter to the Republican Party's platform for the appointment of judges at all levels of the judiciary "who respect traditional family values and the sanctity of innocent human life." Viguerie thought that, by nominating O'Connor, Reagan betrayed New Right activists who stressed social issues such as abortion.[7] Alternatively, Barry Goldwater, the conservative standard-bearer from Arizona, supported the nomination and warned that O'Connor's critics should "back off." As O'Connor was unanimously confirmed by the US Senate in September, it turned out that the New Right wielded limited influence on the government, although the movement had been a powerful driving force behind Reagan's electoral victory.[8]

In the second year of the administration, Viguerie became even more critical of Reagan. In February 1982, Viguerie groused about Reagan's personnel policies, saying, "You should immediately remove many of the people who do not share your deepest beliefs and philosophy from the senior positions." Likewise, although he assessed Reagan's efforts in slowing down the growth of the federal government, Viguerie suggested that the president take immediate action concerning social issues, including busing, school prayer, tuition tax credits, quotas and affirmative action, the right to life, and tough anticrime legislation, among others.[9]

New Right activists felt that the White House increasingly distanced itself from their movement. Viguerie mentioned in his column that several aides to Reagan told reporters off-the-record that "the administration was not worried about pleasing conservatives," and lamented, "That kind of attitude helped take the heart out of many of the President's 1980 grassroots supporters and voters and the soul out of his administration." Now Viguerie described Reagan's foreign policy as "Carterism without Carter," while blaming the president for his failure in federal spending cuts. Finally, Viguerie proclaimed that the New Right would not assist Reagan in his reelection campaign. "Except for isolated exceptions, the New Right was not as active this time around. Considering the attitude of the Reagan administration, there was no reason to be." In January 1983, Viguerie went so far as to say that "it is clear conservatives cannot, and should not, look to the Reagan administration for political leadership." Calling his movement the "New Populism," Viguerie attempted to mobilize a new political force to counter both Democrats and Republicans.[10]

At the same time, the rest of the conservative community was less critical of the Reagan administration. As *National Review* publisher William Rusher said, even though disagreements smoldered among many conservatives, relations between Reagan and conservatives remained warm. When *National Review* held a reception in Washington on February 21, 1983, President Reagan praised the leading conservative periodical as "my favorite magazine" and subscribed to the conservative periodical at the White House.[11] Likewise, Jerry Falwell, the leader of the Moral Majority, continued to have a close relationship with the White House even after many evangelicals realized that Reagan's policies did not live up to his conservative language. But Falwell understood that a rupture in the relation with Reagan would undermine his political influence in Washington. Thus he did not oppose the nomination of O'Connor and endorsed all of Reagan's initiatives.[12]

The New Right could not make the transition to mainstream politics in large measure because ideological direct mail defined the movement. Viguerie's direct mail was robust when he challenged formidable political opponents including liberal Democrats, labor unions, and moderate Republican leaders. He used emotionalism and extreme rhetoric as his political strategy in order to collect political contributions. But this strategy made the New Right movement inflexible. If Reagan was ideologically incompatible with the New Right, their leaders were not able to make a compromise with him. Howard Phillips believed that "loyalty to principle and policy objective" transcended any candidate or political party, and other New Right activists shared the attitude. Other conservatives, such as Lee Edwards, observed that Viguerie became "more sharply populist" in the 1980s.[13]

Because a conservative Republican was in the White House, however, conservatives' direct mail became less effective. Over the first half of the 1980s, Viguerie experienced the sharp decline of response rate and average contributions. As many critics had pointed out in the 1970s, the New Right poured tremendous amounts of funds to unsuccessful campaigns in order to support ideological candidates, which brought Viguerie's fundraising firm to the brink of bankruptcy. In 1985, Viguerie was forced to lay off most of his work force and sell his main publication *Conservative Digest*. After eight of Viguerie's creditors filed a suit for $2.3 million, Viguerie needed to dispose of his $9 million office building in Fairfax, Virginia. By early 1986, he returned to his direct mail business with a contract with Reverend Sun Myung Moon, the leader of the Unification Church, but Viguerie's business strategy was less optimistic than before. The breakdown of Viguerie's direct mail resulted in the decline of the New Right movement.[14]

***

The collapse of Viguerie's empire, however, did not mean the closing of direct mail politics. In fact, direct mail consulting remained imperative for diverse political organizations in the 1980s and beyond. Many political scientists observed that the direct mail industry flourished in US politics. Larry Sabato wrote that conservatives surpassed liberals in direct mail fundraising, yet he also pointed out that liberals actively deployed direct mail. For example, Craver, Mathews, Smith, and Company (CMS) was a preeminent left-wing direct mail firm in Arlington, Virginia, which financed liberal organizations including the National Organization for Women, the National Abortion Rights Action League, and the Sierra Club Legal Defense Fund.[15] Environmental groups also employed direct mail for raising funds and recruiting members in the late twentieth century. As environmentalism grew during the 1970s and 1980s, organizations such as the Defenders of Wildlife and the National Audubon Society sent out direct mail packages to generate revenue. Accordingly, the volume of direct mail delivered in America doubled from 1980 to the mid-1990s. The Direct Marketing Association, the umbrella organization of the direct mail industry, showed the statistical data that the US Postal Service delivered approximately seventy billion pieces of direct mail in 1995, and several experts anticipated that total annual revenues from direct mail would exceed $400 billion by the end of the 1990s.[16]

Furthermore, the direct mail industry set the stage for big data politics in the early twenty-first century. Nothing so clearly demonstrates the impacts of political marketing on our contemporary lives as Acxiom, one of the world's largest database marketing companies. Back in 1969, the corporation was established as Demographics Inc. to support the Democratic Party by compiling lists for direct mail campaigns. Acxiom continued to glean personal information from legal sources such as phone books, public records, and consumer surveys for decades, then it ended up emerging as a giant data broker in the United States. By the 2010s, Acxiom maintained its own database on approximately 190 million individuals and 126 million households in America. The company reportedly held about five hundred million active consumers around the world. As the corporation analyzed 1,500 data points for each person, it generated 50 trillion data transactions annually. With more than twenty-three thousand computer servers collating and mining such a huge body of individual data, Acxiom was trading the data basically for commercial purposes and the business was lucrative. As its customers ranged from big banks including Wells Fargo and HSBC and department stores such as Macy's, to manufacturers like Toyota and Ford, Acxiom announced sales of $1.13 billion and a profit of $77.26 million in the early 2010s.[17]

To be sure, the company has shifted its business from mailing list to digital information transaction. But Acxiom stresses that direct mailings are still effective today as a consultant senior director at Acxiom noted that direct mail could be important for such purposes as new credit card account acquisition.[18] Even if the amount of personal information and computer databases dramatically increased over the years, Viguerie's consulting firm in the 1970s and Acxiom in the 2010s similarly indicate the overwhelming influence of direct marketing on our daily life, demonstrating the close relationship between the commercial culture of advertising and American democracy. Out of the rubble of Viguerie's empire of direct mail, many new data marketers mushroomed and changed the US political landscape.

Cambridge Analytica is another consulting firm that suggests the New Right's data-driven grassroots strategy and emotionalism work in today's politics. Formed by a British data mining organization named Strategic Communications Laboratories (SCL) and funded by Robert Mercer, an American billionaire intimately connected with conservatives, Cambridge Analytica has helped Republican candidates who trailed Democrats in digitizing political campaigns since the 1990s.[19] After Mercer financed a $1.5 million pilot project in Virginia's gubernatorial election of 2013, Cambridge Analytica was involved with the presidential election of 2016, helping Ted Cruz at first. In December 2015, Cruz said that his funding and outreach apparatus were "very much the Obama model—a data-driven, grassroots-driven campaign—and it is a reason why our campaign is steadily gathering strength."[20] As Cruz gave in to Donald Trump in the Republican Party primaries, Cambridge Analytica became engaged in the Trump campaign. Steve Bannon, the vice president of Cambridge Analytica, joined the campaign as the chief executive, then was appointed the chief strategist of the White House after Trump won the presidential race.[21]

Cambridge Analytica came under attack two years later, sparking controversies over privacy, extremism, and emotionalism. In March 2018, media revealed a scandal that the political consulting firm had illegally harvested the private information of Facebook users for the Trump presidential campaign. The mainstream press, like the *Guardian* and the *New York Times*, covered detailed stories that Cambridge Analytica obtained the data on fifty million individuals from Facebook without their content, and how the firm marshaled the personal information for political advertising.[22] Yet even after Cambridge Analytica faced a backlash on both sides of the Atlantic, its relationship with Trump continued. Matt Oczkowski, the chief data scientist of Cambridge Analytica, established a new consulting firm called Data Propria to work with the Trump campaign of 2020. A news article showcased the campaign's contentious strategies: launching ads that featured Nazi symbols, spreading fake news on mail-in ballot fraud, implying violence against Black Lives Matter protesters, and so on.[23] As emotional and partisan conflicts frequently took place during the Trump years, many ascribed the emergence of political extremism to social media and partisan ads on the internet. But rather than novel developments, similar controversies already revolved around the rise of direct mail decades ago.

Many pundits emphasized that political direct mail was not only thriving but also dangerous to American democracy. As early as 1981, political scientist Sabato deemed direct mail "the poisoned pen of politics," quoting Robert Smith of CMS as saying, "The message has to be extreme, has to be overblown; it really has to be kind of rough." The New Right had been infamous for its emotionalism and extremism, but these characteristics were also common among left-wing groups by the 1980s.[24] Other intellectuals demonstrated how direct mail affected American civic culture. Kenneth Godwin argued in his book that the popularity of direct mail resulted in less political toleration and compromise because political messengers mailed out partisan letters to like-minded people, accelerating the echo chamber effect. Additionally, Kenneth contended that direct mail promoted passive membership as it functioned as a disincentive to political participation by discouraging any activity beyond writing a check. Other critics agreed on the transformation of participatory democracy. Marshall Ganz, who became a political consultant after working with the United Farm Workers for sixteen years, speculated that new campaign technologies were responsible for declining participation because "direct mail, databases of voters, polling, and targeted advertising also depress voter turnout and fragment the electorate."[25]

These discussions on direct mail were part of the bigger concern over declining American civil society. When Harvard Professor Robert Putnam published his article "Bowling Alone" in 1995 and a book with the same title in 2000, his research generated enthusiastic responses from the public. Putnam made his case that American associational democracy declined as Americans less frequently joined political activities, fraternal organizations, and even neighborhood groups at the end of the twentieth century. Although Putnam pointed to many reasons for the erosion of civic engagement, he stressed the deep-seated technological trends of "individualizing" American personal lives and thus disrupting many opportunities for social capital formation. Whereas several scholars disputed Putnam's argument, the public and many intellectuals shared the assumption that Americans were more socially isolated and politically indifferent than ever before.[26]

Despite these wider concerns over the crisis of American democracy, direct mail did not merely have negative impacts on political participation. As *Empire of Direct Mail* has excavated, the advance of direct mail politics created a new kind of "grassroots" activism. Today we take it for granted that American voters send money to political parties and candidates of their choosing.[27] This was not typical in the 1950s when political funds came mainly from big business and wealthy philanthropists. During the 1960s, direct mail revolutionized political fundraising by amassing great amounts of small money, such as one dollar or five. When civil rights advocates took to the streets and the New Left raised the ideal of participatory democracy, conservative direct mail redefined grassroots engagement as assisting political movements with small contributions. However, unlike many intellectuals' arguments that joiners became passive citizens, conservatives actively expressed their opinions by writing their messages in reply to fundraising appeals. While some conservatives fervently endorsed candidates by replying to solicitation letters they received, others sent criticism back to the candidates. By doing so, direct mail handlers and receivers built a public sphere in which they exchanged not merely money but also political ideas.

The story of political direct mail indicates that American political communication has experienced significant transformations since the 1950s. Indeed, many articles and books have emphasized the importance of direct mail in right-wing politics, because conservatives most effectively used the media technology by the 1980s. Yet *Empire of Direct Mail* demonstrates that the medium, which has been overshadowed more recently by telecommunications and the internet, affected American politics in more complicated and fundamental ways than imagined. The emergence of advertising agencies and political consultants influenced political campaigns over the course of the twentieth century, while both conservatives and liberals engaged with the development of political direct mail. Technological advances brought about by these actors evolved the ways to reach out to individual voters, transforming the contours of the major parties during the 1960s and 1970s. At the same time, direct mail consultants accelerated partisanship and emotionalism as their campaign strategy, which deepened political fissures in the United States. Data-driven hatred politics and misinformation did not begin with the advent of new media campaigning in the 2000s. It did not appear for the first time in the twenty-first century. It dates back to the mid-twentieth century when political advertisers altered the traditional act of writing letters toward a modern sophisticated communication device.

NOTES

Introduction

1. Nick Kotz, "King Midas of 'the New Right,'" *Atlantic*, November 1978, 52.

2. Rich Jaroslovsky, "New-Right Cashier: Mr. Viguerie Collects Funds, Gains Influence in Conservative Causes," *Wall Street Journal*, October 6, 1978, 1.

3. In her classic work, Kathleen Hall Jamieson analyzed presidential campaigns in the latter part of the twentieth century by narrating how presidential candidates from Dwight Eisenhower to Bill Clinton employed televised advertising. While investigating various "spins" in presidential races ranging from Theodore Roosevelt's publicity to Barack Obama's use of the internet, David Greenberg also looked closely at the role of television ads in US politics over the years. Jamieson, *Packaging the Presidency*; Greenberg, *Republic of Spin*, 276–436. For television in American politics, see Barnouw, *Tube of Plenty*; Bernhard, *U.S. Television News*; Greenberg, "A New Way of Campaigning."

4. Hendershot, *What's Fair on the Air?*; Hemmer, *Messengers of the Right*. See also Brinkley, *Voices of Protest*; Hendershot, "God's Angriest Man"; Hemmer, "The Dealers and the Darling"; Thrift, *Conservative Bias*; Jamieson and Cappella, *Echo Chamber*; White, *The Branding of Right-Wing Activism*; Peck, *Fox Populism*; Matzko, *The Radio Right*. While many scholars have paid attention to right-wing broadcasting, others have looked at the role of the press and print in conservative politics. See Nadler and Bauer, *News on the Right*; McPherson, *The Conservative Resurgence*; Gifford, "The Education of a Cold War Conservative"; Witwer, "Pattern for Partnership"; Hart, *The Making of the American Conservative Mind*.

5. Kenneth Godwin analyzed how direct marketing affected American politics during the 1970s and 1980s. Surveying the development of voter contacts from the 1920s to the early twenty-first century, journalist Sasha Issenberg explored "microtargeting technology" to assemble database and target prospective supporters. See Godwin, *One Billion Dollars of Influence*; Issenberg, *The Victory Lab*. See also Marshall Ganz, "Voters in the Crosshairs: How Technology and the Market Are Destroying Politics," *American Prospect* 16 (Winter 1994): 100–109; Bosso, "The Color of Money"; Berry, *The Interest Group Society*; Johnson, "Interest Group Recruitment"; Green and Gerber, *Get Out the Vote*, 55–73; Shea and Burton, *Campaign Craft*, 144–46; Johnson, *No Place for Amateurs*, 150–56.

6. Kreiss, *Taking Our Country Back*; Karpf, *The MoveOn Effect*.

7. Matthew Rosenberg, Nicholas Confessore, and Carole Cadwalladr, "How Trump Consultants Exploited the Facebook Data of Millions," *New York Times*, March 17, 2018, https://www.nytimes.com/2018/03/17/us/politics/cambridge-analytica-trump-campaign.html; "Revealed: 50 Million Facebook Profiles Harvested for Cambridge Analytica in Major Data Breach," *Guardian*, March 17, 2018, https://www.theguardian.com/news/2018/mar/17/cambridge-analytica-facebook-influence-us-election.

8. For the scholarship on conservatism in Southern California, see for example McGirr, *Suburban Warriors*; Nickerson, *Mothers of Conservatism*; Dochuk, *From Bible Belt to Sunbelt*.

9. Bell, "The Dispossessed," 31–32; Hofstadter, "The Pseudo-Conservative Revolt," 68–69, 77–78.

10. Daniel Bell, "The End of American Exceptionalism," *Public Interest*, Fall 1975, 193–224.

11. Kevin Phillips was among the first political analysts who coined the term Sunbelt when he observed a conservative realignment in national politics in the late 1960s. See Phillips, *The Emerging Republican Majority*. For the literature of Sunbelt conservatism, see Cunningham, *Cowboy Conservatism*; Shermer, *Sunbelt Capitalism*. It is noteworthy that more recently several scholars challenge the perception of the Sunbelt as a conservative region. See Nickerson and Dochuk, *Sunbelt Rising*; Cadava, *Standing on Common Ground*. On the impact of racism on conservatism, see Schulman, *From Cotton Belt to Sunbelt*; Crespino, *In Search of Another Country*; Lassiter, *The Silent Majority*; Lowndes, *From the New Deal to the New Right*.

12. Several historians have examined the origins of modern conservatism in areas outside the Sunbelt. See Formisano, *Boston against Busing*; O'Connor, "The Privatized City"; Sullivan, *New York State*; Gadsden, *Between North and South*; Greason, *Suburban Erasure*.

13. Tocqueville, *Democracy in America*; Schlesinger, "Biography of a Nation of Joiners"; Putnam, *Bowling Alone*.

14. Daniel Rodgers referred to the late twentieth century as the "age of fracture," when conceptions of human nature stressed individual choice, agency, performance, and desire, rather than the aggregate aspects of human life. Rodgers, *Age of Fracture*, 3. See also Kruse and Zelizer, *Fault Lines*.

Chapter 1

1. *Republican Progress*, no. 6, June 20, 1949, box 9, folder "1949–1952—National Republican Congressional Committee—Public Relations Director (3)," Robert Humphreys Papers, DDEL.

2. "The Story of 'Document X,'" n.d., box 10, folder "1952—Campaign and Election—Document 'X' by Robert Humphreys (2)," Humphreys Papers. See also Kelley, *Professional Public Relations*, 1, 151.

3. Greenberg, "A New Way of Campaigning," 186.

4. Sabato, *The Rise of Political Consultants*, 8.

5. Nimmo, *The Political Persuaders*, 35. Political scientists have addressed political consultants in US politics. Kelley, *Professional Public Relations*; Sabato, *The Rise of Political Consultants*; Jamieson, *Packaging the Presidency*; Greenberg, *Republic of Spin*; Sheingate, *Building a Business of Politics*. See also Schneider and Teske, "Toward a Theory of the Political Entrepreneur"; Sheingate, "Political Entrepreneurship"; Friedenberg, *Communication Consultants*; Baumgartner, *Modern Presidential Electioneering*; Medvic, *Political Consultants*; Lathrop, *The Campaign Continues*; Dulio, *For Better or Worse?*; Newman and Davies, *Winning Elections*; Shea and Burton, *Campaign Craft*; Johnson, *No Place for Amateurs*. Several political consultants recounted their activities. See Baus and Ross, *Politics Battle Plan*; Shadegg, *The New How*; Strother, *Falling Up*; Rove, *Courage and Consequence*.

6. Brenton Malin delineates debates over media technology and its effects on emotion in American history. Malin, *Feeling Mediated*. On debates specifically over political consultants' media, see Godwin and Mitchell, "The Implications of Direct Mail."

7. In many studies, "political consultant" and "political entrepreneur" are used interchangeably. For example, Schneider and Teske, "Toward a Theory of the Political Entrepreneur," 737–47; Sheingate, "Political Entrepreneurship," 185–203.

8. Hofstadter, *Anti-Intellectualism*, 233.

9. Friedenberg, *Communication Consultants*, 2–4.

10. Weston, *The Presidential Election of 1828*, 102.

11. For more detailed strategies in the 1828 election, see Friedenberg, *Communication Consultants*, 5–11; Kelley, *Professional Public Relations*, 28–29; Thurber, "Introduction to the Study of Campaign Consultants," 4.

12. Holli, *The Wizard of Washington*, 40.

13. Herrnson, "Hired Guns and House Races," 67. Political parties in the nineteenth century were a coalition of local organizations without permanent institutions. For instance, according to Thomas S. Barclay, the Democratic Party created the Executive Committee as a lasting institution for the maintenance of organization, publicity, and research for the first time in 1929. Also, as Jody C. Baumgartner said, the Democratic National Committee, which was founded in 1848, did not have a permanent headquarters until 1985, and the Republican National Committee was founded in 1854, but its headquarters was formed and disbanded in every campaign until 1970. See Barclay, "The Publicity Division"; Baumgartner, *Modern Presidential Electioneering*, 22.

14. Henry Litchfield West, "American Politics: The President and the Campaign," *Forum* 15, no. 5 (November 1908): 421.

15. Sheingate, *Building a Business of Politics*, 25–31; Lathrop, *The Campaign Continues*, 17; Herrnson, "Hired Guns and House Races," 67.

16. Applegate, *The Rise of Advertising*, 85–98; Sheingate, *Building a Business of Politics*, 29–30.

17. Friedenberg, *Communication Consultants*, 16–17.

18. Holli, *The Wizard of Washington*, 40–41, 57–60.

19. Kelley, *Professional Public Relations*, chap. 2; Sheingate, *Building a Business of Politics*, chap. 5; Nimmo, *The Political Persuaders*, 35–37; Friedenberg, *Communication Consultants*, 18.

20. Lears, *Fables of Abundance*, 247–49; Stole, *Advertising at War*, especially chaps. 5 and 6; Scott, *Comics and Conflict*, chap. 2.

21. Kelley, *Professional Public Relations*, 35.

22. Adam Sheingate, for instance, pointed out Republican ties with business. See Sheingate, *Building a Business of Politics*, 152.

23. "Forward," box 14, folder "1958—Campaign and Election (1)," Humphreys Papers.

24. Letter from Charles G. Thoma to Guy G. Gabrielson, March 2, 1950, box 5, folder "Republican National Committee—Finance Committee (2)," Arthur E. Summerfield Papers, DDEL.

25. Letter from Emil Hurja to President Dwight Eisenhower, March 30, 1953, box 5, folder "Campaign 1953–7," Records of the Office of the Chairman of the Republican National Committee (Leonard W. Hall), DDEL. See also Holli, *The Wizard of Washington*, chaps. 5 and 6.

26. Minutes of Republican National Strategy Committee Meeting, December 13, 1949, box 5, folder "Republican National Strategy Committee—Minutes (1)," Summerfield Papers; News Release by the Republican National Committee, July 30, 1952, box 9, folder "1952–1953—Republican National Committee—Public Relations Director (1)," Humphreys Papers.

27. For the public relations strategy of the Eisenhower campaign in 1952, see Barnouw, *The Golden Web*, 298–99; Blake, *Liking Ike*; Kelley, *Professional Public Relations*, chaps. 5 and 6; Jamieson, *Packaging the Presidency*, chap. 2, especially 42–45; Greenberg, *Republic of Spin*, 276–85.

28. Edward Maurice Glick, "The Campaign Background," 43, box 13, folder "1956—Campaign and Election (3)," Humphreys Papers.

29. Glick, "The Campaign Background," 43.

30. Glick, "The Campaign Background," 44.

31. "Campaign Plan, 1952," 3, box 10, folder "Campaign and Election—Document 'X' by Robert Humphreys (1)," Humphreys Papers.

32. "Campaign Plan, 1952," 4.

33. "Campaign Plan, 1952," 5–12.

34. Nimmo, *The Political Persuaders*, 53.

35. "Campaign Plan, 1952," 13–15.

36. The TV Plans Board to Gov. Adams, Messrs. Summerfield, Williams and Associates, n.d., box 7, folder "Eisenhower-Lodge Campaign Materials, 1952-TV (1)," Maxwell M. Rabb Papers, DDEL. Batten, Barton, Durstine and Osborn (BBD&O) was the main architect of Eisenhower's telethon programs and televised speeches. For its activities in detail, see Kelley, *Professional Public Relations*, 160–69; Barnouw, *The Golden Web*, 298–99; Jamieson, *Packaging the Presidency*, 42–43, 82, 87; Greenberg, "A New Way of Campaigning," 191–201; Blake, *Liking Ike*, 72–74.

37. Angus Campbell, Gerald Gurin, and Warren E. Miller, "Television and the Election," May 1953, box I:13, folder 1 "1952, presidential campaign," Democratic Study Group Records, Manuscripts and Archives Division, Library of Congress. This report was based on a two-year study of political behavior financed by the Carnegie Corporation. The Survey Research Center conducted the research by asking 1,714 citizens of voting age.

38. The TV Plans Board to Gov. Adams, Messrs. Summerfield, Williams and Associates, n.d., box 10, folder "Lodge Campaign Material, 1952 (6)," Rabb Papers.

39. Jamieson, *Packaging the Presidency*, 43.

40. News Release, April 8, 1952, box 158, folder "Publicity—1952 Presidential Campaign," Records of the Democratic National Committee, HSTL.

41. Jamieson, *Packaging the Presidency*, 42–43.

42. "The Operating Structure of the Republican Party Nationally: An Outline of the Functions of the Republican National, Senatorial and Congressional Committees," n.d., 1, box 12, folder "1954–1959—Republican National Committee—Campaign Director (1)," Humphreys Papers.

43. "Campaign Plan," n.d., box 13, folder "1956—Campaign and Election (1)," Humphreys Papers.

44. Tom Fitzsimmons, "Operation Huckster," *New Republic*, April 26, 1954, 5.

45. Letter from Kay Martin to Leonard W. Hall, June 17, 1954, box 6, folder "Campaign 1954–7 (2)," Records of the Office of the Chairman of the RNC (Hall).

46. "Never Underestimate the Question of a Woman," n.d., box 130, folder "Public Relations 1954–42-C (Radio, TV, Movies)," Records of Office of the Chairman of the RNC (Hall); Memo from Leonard W. Hall, July 26, 1954, Records of Office of the Chairman of the RNC (Hall).

47. Rymph, *Republican Women*, 131–59; Lichtenstein, *State of the Union*, chap. 4; Pells, *The Liberal Mind*, 119–21, 135–38, 392–98; Gerald Mayer, "Union Membership Trends in the United States," *CRS Report for Congress*, August 31, 2004, 22.

48. The expenditures on television and radio campaigns were almost the same in 1952 with $3 million spent for television and $3.1 million for radio. However, after the 1952 election, the cost of television always overwhelmed that of radio. Republicans surpassed Democrats in amounts of money for political broadcasts every election over the years: $3.5 million to $2.6 million in 1952, $5.4 million to $4.1 million in 1956, $7.6 million to $6.2 million in 1960. See Heard, *The Costs of Democracy*, 22; Alexander, *Financing the 1968 Election*, 95; Steinberg, *TV Facts*, 283.

49. "Re: Financing Your Television Shows," box 9, folder "1949–1952—National Republican Congressional Committee—Public Relations Director (3)," Humphreys Papers.

50. "Democrats Stress Strategy of Precinct Contacts for 1950," *Washington Post*, January 1, 1950.

51. *Congressional Quarterly*, November 3, 1950, 1219.

52. Robert J. McCully, "Carlton G. Ketchum: A Memorial," *Western Pennsylvania Historical Magazine* 67, no. 4 (October 1984): 384–86.

53. "Fund-Raising Manual," March 1950, box 5, folder "Republican National Committee—Finance Committee (2)," Summerfield Papers.

54. Memo from Carlton G. Ketchum to State Finance Chairmen, May 4, 1950, box 5, folder "Republican National Committee—Finance Committee (1)," Summerfield Papers.

55. Minutes of Meeting of Republican National Committee, February 6, 1950, box 5, folder "Republican National Strategy Committee—Minutes (1)," Summerfield Papers.

56. "GOP Funds Triple Cash of Democrats," *Chicago Sun Times*, September 23, 1952; "Republicans' Funds Double Democrats,'" *New York Herald Tribune*, September 23, 1952; National Citizens For Eisenhower Congressional Committee, "Finance Committee—1954, Detailed Report of Operations," box 2, folder "National Citizens For Eisenhower Congressional Committee—Finance Committee 1954—Final Report," Campaign Series, Dwight D. Eisenhower Papers as President, DDEL.

57. "Grass Roots Plea," *Kansas City Times*, September 18, 1952.

58. Jack Turcott, "Dem Fund Forced, Say Unionists," *New York Daily News*, October 30, 1952.

59. Godwin, *One Billion Dollars*, 3; Greenberg, "A New Way of Campaigning," 198.

60. Walter Weintz, "Direct Mail," n.d., box 6, folder "Campaign 1954–7 (3)," Records of the Office of the Chairman of the RNC (Hall).

61. For the activities and importance of Citizens for Eisenhower, see Mason, "Citizens for Eisenhower."

62. National Citizens For Eisenhower Congressional Committee, "Finance Committee—1954, Detailed Report of Operations," 40–41, box 2, folder "National Citizens For Eisenhower Congressional Committee-Finance Committee 1954—Final Report," Campaign Series, Eisenhower Papers as President.

63. National Citizens For Eisenhower Congressional Committee, 5, 41–43.

64. In Illinois, direct mail fundraising was the most successful: 4,125 contributors responded to direct mails and sent $23,010.12 to the National Citizens for Eisenhower, whereas non-direct mail solicitation raised $31,803.00 from 95 donors in the state. In New York State, direct mail collected $19,241.34 from 1,250 contributors, and other means raised $238,859.68 from 957. In California, Citizens received $5,494.14 from 501 contributors, while 201 donors contributed $56,155.00. See box 2, folder "Contributors to NCECC-1954 Received through Solicitation Credited to State of Origin, Contributors to NCECC 1954," Campaign Series, Eisenhower Papers as President.

65. National Citizens For Eisenhower Congressional Committee, box 2, folder "Finance Committee—1954, Detailed Report of Operations," 40–41, Campaign Series, Eisenhower Papers as President.

66. Democratic National Committee Newspaper Ad, August 31, 1954, box 158, folder "Committee Finances, 1954," Records of the DNC.

67. *New York Times*, July 12, 1954, 2.

68. "A New Declaration of Independence Needs Signing," box 158, folder "Committee Finances, 1954," Records of the DNC; *New York Times*, October 18, 1954, 15.

69. Box 61, folder "Campaign Material, Sample of (1 of 3)," Stephen A. Mitchell Papers, HSTL.

70. Herbert J. Waters, "The Humphrey Story: Report of a Successful Re-election Campaign," n.d., 5, box 61, folder "Campaign Material, Sample of (2 of 3)," Mitchell Papers.

71. Fitzsimmons, "Operation Huckster," 7.

72. Greenberg, "A New Way of Campaigning," 208.

73. "Campaign Plan, 1952," 13, box 10, folder "Campaign and Election—Document 'X' by Robert Humphreys (1)," Humphreys Papers; McGinniss, *The Selling of the President, 1968*, 27.

74. "Political Public Relations," n.d., box 9, folder "1952–1953—Republican National Committee—Public Relations Director (2)," Humphreys Papers.

75. "Political Salesmanship," December 7, 1954, box 12, folder "1954—Campaign and Election (2)," Humphreys Papers.

76. "How to Sell a Candidate: 1952," *Sponsor*, March 24, 1952, 34.

77. Fitzsimmons, "Operation Huckster," 5.

78. Kelley, *Professional Public Relations*, vii, 214–16.

79. Glick, "The Campaign Background," 10.

80. Glick, "The Campaign Background," 51.

81. Kelley, *Professional Public Relations*, 212.

82. Frank, *The Conquest of Cool*, 35–38.

83. Riesman, *The Lonely Crowd*; Whyte, *The Organization Man*. Other contemporary intellectuals examined the mass society in the 1950s. For instance, Kornhauser, *The Politics of Mass Society*; Bell, *End of Ideology*, 222–62; Keniston, "Alienation and the Decline of Utopia."

84. Packard, *The Hidden Persuaders*, 181–200. See also Lears, *Fables of Abundance*, 252–56; Frank, *The Conquest of Cool*, 9–13, 40–42; Blake, *Liking Ike*, chap. 5.

85. Adlai Stevenson, "Address Accepting the Presidential Nomination at the Democratic National Convention in Chicago," August 17, 1956, Gerhard Peters and John T. Wooley, The American Presidency Project, accessed February 19, 2022, https://www.presidency.ucsb.edu/documents/address-accepting-the-presidential-nomination-the-democratic-national-convention-chicago-0.

Chapter 2

1. Summerfield, *U.S. Mail*, 11.

2. Summerfield, *U.S. Mail*, 27, 202, 14.

3. "Missile Mail," July 2008, US Postal Service, accessed September 7, 2017, https://about.usps.com/who-we-are/postal-history/missile-mail.pdf; Nancy A. Pope, "Regulus Missile Mail," June 2006, Smithsonian National Postal Museum, accessed February 19, 2021, https://postalmuseum.si.edu/collections/object-spotlight/regulus-missile-mail.

4. US Postal Service, *The United States Postal Service*, 54–55, accessed September 7, 2017, https://about.usps.com/publications/pub100.pdf; Robert McGill Thomas Jr., "J. Edward Day, 82, Postmaster Who Brought In the ZIP Code," *New York Times*, November 1, 1996, B15; Anny Curtin, "Flashing across the Country: Mr. Zip and the ZIP Code Promotional Campaign," Smithsonian National Postal Museum, accessed February 19, 2021, https://www.si.edu/newsdesk/releases/flashing-across-country-mr-zip-and-zip-code-promotional-campaign; US Postal Service Office of Inspector General, "The Untold Story of the ZIP Code," April 1, 2013, accessed February 19, 2022, https://www.uspsoig.gov/sites/default/files/document-library-files/2015/rarc-wp-13-006_0.pdf.

5. Lester Wunderman, "1995 Nov. 1, The World of Direct Mail: Past, Present and Future, Postal Conference, Toronto," 5, box 20, Lester Wunderman Papers, DU. Wunderman was considered the father of direct marketing because he named the new marketing strategy "direct marketing" in 1961 and detailed the idea in 1967. See Wunderman, "1995 Nov. 1, The World of Direct Mail," 1.

6. John R. McAlpine, *Direct Mail: Two Mediums Not One* (1951), 1, box DG11, J. Walter Thompson Company Records, Publications Collection, DU.

7. James D. Woolf, "The $64 Question in Direct Mail Selling," *Advertising Age*, February 25, 1952.

8. Norman H. Strouse, "Advertising Agency Answers the Challenge of Direct Mail," September 30, 1953, box 45, folder "1952. Speech. Advertising Agency Answers the Challenge of Direct Mail," J. Walter Thompson Company Records, Writings and Speeches, DU.

9. Wunderman, "1995 Nov. 1, The World of Direct Mail," 6.

10. Wunderman, "1995 Nov. 1, The World of Direct Mail," 15.

11. The Education Committee of the Direct Mail Advertising Association, "A Digest of Direct Mail Advertising," January 1963, box 61, folder "Advertising—Media—Direct Mail," J. Walter Thompson Company Records, Advertising Vertical Files, DU.

12. Charles E. Garvin, "Direct Mail's Big Challenge: To Meet Changing Market Requirements," *Reporter of Direct Mail Advertising*, May 1958, 57–58, box 11, folder "1958. Article. Direct Mail's Big Challenge: To Meet Changing Market Requirements," J. Walter Thompson Company Records, Writings and Speeches. See also Derry F. Daly, Roger Franklin, and J. Ronald Hess, "Some Important Things I Believe a Young Account Representative Should Know about Direct Mail Advertising," October 1968, box 8, folder "1968. Other Writing. Direct Mail Advertising," J. Walter Thompson Company Records, Writings and Speeches; McAlpine, *Direct Mail*, 3–4.

13. Lester Wunderman, "1967 Mar. 3, Mail Order: The Coming Revolution in Marketing, Advertising Club of New York," 14–15, box 19, Wunderman Papers.

14. McAlpine, *Direct Mail*, 3–4.

15. Wunderman, "1995 Nov. 1, The World of Direct Mail," 6.

16. John Crichton, Speech "How to Dispel the Mystery and keep the Magic," October 15, 1964, 2, box 61, folder "Advertising—Media—Direct Mail," J. Walter Thompson Company Records, Advertising Vertical Files.

17. Wunderman, "1995 Nov. 1, The World of Direct Mail," 10–12.

18. Wunderman, "1967 Mar. 3, Mail Order," 7–9.

19. Dan Seymour, Speech "Agency Looks at Direct Mail," November 7, 1968, box 44, folder "1968. Speech. Agency Looks at Direct Mail," J. Walter Thompson Company Records, Writings and Speeches.

20. Wunderman, "1995 Nov. 1, The World of Direct Mail," 12. See also Marshall Ganz, "Voters in the Crosshairs: How Technology and the Market Are Destroying Politics," *American Prospect* 16 (Winter 1994): 100–109.

21. Godwin, *One Billion Dollars of Influence*, 2; Issenberg, *The Victory Lab*, 9, 47–48; Viguerie, *The New Right*, 21.

22. Hendershot, *What's Fair on the Air?*, 182.

23. A history of using mail for delivering messages to voters in American political elections dated back to the early twentieth century. According to Kenneth Goodwin, Woodrow Wilson was one of the first political candidates who employed mass mailing in his campaign. William Jennings Bryan also tried to utilize solicitation letters in search of one million contributors in his 1916 campaign, but his fundraising draft failed, obtaining only twenty thousand responses. While several politicians attempted to use mail to no avail, political scientists began to study the effects of political mail on voter turnout during the 1920s. The political scientist Harold Gosnell at the University of Chicago, for instance, tested the effectiveness of mail by sending letters that encouraged Chicago residents to vote. Gosnell found out that turnout increased 1 percent in the 1924 presidential election. In the 1950s, as the first chapter of this book indicates, the Dwight Eisenhower campaign and the Republican National Committee maneuvered direct mail for public opinion poll and fundraising. See Godwin, *One Billion Dollars of Influence*, 3, 8; Johnson, *No Place for Amateurs*, 150; Green and Gerber, *Get Out the Vote*, 60–61.

24. The Trustees of Indiana University, "Oram Group, Inc. Records, 1938–1992," Ruth Lilly Special Collections and Archives, IUPUI University Library, Indiana University/Purdue University, Indianapolis, Indiana, accessed February 19, 2022, https://special.ulib.iupui.edu/collections/philanthropy/mss057.

25. Memorandum, n.d., box 24, folder 16, "Spanish Refugee Relief Committee, 1937–1940," Oram Group, Inc. Records.

26. Appeal from Citizens Committee on Displaced Persons, January 6, 1950, box 8, folder 23 "Appeals, 1947–1950," Oram Group, Inc. Records.

27. Memo from Fund Raising Campaign for the Citizen's Committee for Displaced Persons, May 21, 1947, box 8, folder 29 "Correspondence, 1947–1950," Oram Group, Inc. Records.

28. Appeal from American Association for the United Nations, September 7, 1948, box 4, folder 19 "Appeals, 1947," Oram Group, Inc. Records.

29. The Center for the Study of Democratic Institutions, October 25, 1962, box 7, folder 19, "Appeals, 1963–1964," Oram Group, Inc. Records.

30. Appeal from the United Nations Fund of the American Association for the United Nations, Inc., n.d., box 4, folder 18, "American Association for the United Nations, Appeals, 1946," Oram Group, Inc. Records.

31. Sabato, *The Rise of Political Consultants*, 241. See also Shea and Burton, *Campaign Craft*, chap. 9.

32. Appeal from American Association for the United Nations, September 2, 1947, box 4, folder 19 "Appeals, 1947," Oram Group, Inc. Records.

33. Appeal from American Association for the United Nations, May 22, 1951, box 4, folder 23 "Appeals, 1951," Oram Group, Inc. Records.

34. Appeal from the Center for the Study of Democratic Institutions, October 25, 1962, box 7, folder 19, "Appeals, 1963–1964," Oram Group, Inc. Records.

35. Memo from Harold L. Oram to Walter H. Judd, et al., box 4, folder 7, "Aid Refugee Chinese Intellectuals, Board Correspondence, 1952–1955," Oram Group, Inc. Records; Appeals of November 1968, April 1969, and December 26, 1969, box 11, folder 8 "Appeals, 1967–1969, 1973–1974," Oram Group, Inc. Records.

36. Cited in Gasman and Drezner, "A Maverick in the Field," 465.

37. Neal Blackwell Freeman, "The Marvin Liebman Story," *New Guard* (May 1966): 12. For the early years of Marvin Liebman's political activism, see Liebman, *Coming Out Conservative*, 19–80; Liebman (Marvin) Interview, Transcript, July 18, 1992, box 27, folder 36, Oram Group, Inc. Records; "Marvin Liebman—Professional and Bibliographical Notes," box 139, folder "Liebman, Marvin—Biographical Sketch," Marvin Liebman Papers, HIA; Neal, "The Marvin Liebman Story," 12–14.

38. Liebman, *Coming Out Conservative*, 19–80.

39. Liebman, *Coming Out Conservative*, 80.

40. Liebman, *Coming Out Conservative*, 82.

41. Liebman, *Coming Out Conservative*, 84, 95, 102.

42. Liebman, *Coming Out Conservative*, 83–85, 94–96.

43. Appeal from Frank Kingdon, February 20, 1942, box 13, folder 7 "Appeals, 1942, 1950, 1954, 1956–1957," Oram Group, Inc. Records; Appeal from Richard E. Byrd, May 5, 1954, Oram Group, Inc. Records; Appeal from Angier Biddle Duke, April 14, 1958, box 13, folder 8 "Appeals, 1958–1961," Oram Group, Inc. Records; Appeal from Abram G. Becker, February 25, 1954, box 13, folder 14 "General Correspondence, 1949–1954, 1956–1957," Oram Group, Inc. Records; Liebman, *Coming Out Conservative*, 85–89.

44. Memo from Harold L. Oram to Aid Refugee Chinese Intellectuals, Inc., February 14, 1952, box 166, folder 1 "Aid to Refugee Chinese Intellectuals, Correspondence/General, 1951–1952 April," Walter Judd Papers, HIA; Memo from Ernest K. Moy, September 16, 1951, box 167, folder 4 "Aid to Refugee Chinese Intellectuals, Correspondence/Internal, 1951 Sept.-1952 April," Walter H. Judd Papers, HIA; Memo from Walter H. Judd to Alexander Grantham, n.d., box 166, folder 2 "Aid to Refugee Chinese

Intellectuals, Correspondence/General, 1952 May-Dec.," Judd Papers; Liebman, *Coming Out Conservative*, 92–104.

45. Letter from Walter H. Judd to university presidents, n.d., box 166, folder 1 "Aid to Refugee Chinese Intellectuals, Correspondence/General, 1951–1952 April," Judd Papers; Memo from Walter H. Judd to John F. Schwering, January 9, 1953, box 166, folder 1 "Aid to Refugee Chinese Intellectuals, Correspondence/General, 1951–1952 April," Judd Papers; Memo from Walter H. Judd to E. C. Congdon, January 23, 1953, box 166, folder 3 "Aid to Refugee Chinese Intellectuals, Correspondence/General, 1953 Jan-June," Judd Papers; Letter from Walter H. Judd to Eli Lilly, February 25, 1952, box 166, folder 1 "Aid to Refugee Chinese Intellectuals, Correspondence/General, 1951–1952 April," Judd Papers.

46. Memo from Harold L. Oram to ARCI Executive Committee, October 29, 1952, box 168, folder 1 "Aid to Refugee Chinese Intellectuals, Correspondence/Internal, 1952 Sept.-Dec.," Judd Papers; Memo from Harold L. Oram to Walter H. Judd, March 28, 1952, box 168, folder 2 "Aid to Refugee Chinese Intellectuals, Correspondence/Internal, 1953," Judd Papers.

47. Letter from Arthur H. Riss to Walter H. Judd, February 3, 1952, box 166, folder 3 "Aid to Refugee Chinese Intellectuals, Correspondence/General, 1953 Jan-June," Judd Papers.

48. Letter from Walter H. Judd to Arthur H. Riss, February 25, box 166, folder 3 "Aid to Refugee Chinese Intellectuals, Correspondence/General, 1953 Jan-June," Judd Papers.

49. Memo from Marvin Liebman to ARCI and ABMAC Executive Committees, n.d., box 168, folder 3 "Aid to Refugee Chinese Intellectuals, Correspondence/Internal, 1954," Judd Papers; Liebman, *Coming Out Conservative*, 97.

50. Minutes of Meeting, April 9, 1953, box 170, folder 1 "Aid to Refugee Chinese Intellectuals, Meeting Minutes & Agenda,1952–1953," Judd Papers; Liebman, *Coming Out Conservative*, 102–103.

51. Liebman, *Coming Out Conservative*, 105–11. The name of the organization was initially the Committee for One Million. However, Liebman disbanded the group in January 1955 and changed its name to the Committee of One Million when he reorganized it in March 1955. See Memo, Marvin Liebman, April 1, 1960, box 38, folder "Committee of One Million, 1958/1959," Alfred Kohlberg Papers, HIA.

52. Appeal, August 1956, box 87, folder "Committee of One Million (Against the Admission of Red China to the United Nations) General Information," Group Research, Inc. Records, Rare Book & Manuscript Library, Columbia University.

53. Appeal from Marvin Liebman, September 23, 1964, box 78, folder "Election, mailing, 1964," Liebman Papers.

54. Appeal from Marvin Liebman, April 6, 1960, box 87, folder "Committee of One Million (Against the Admission of Red China to the United Nations) Letters from Headquarters," Group Research, Inc. Records.

55. John O'Kearney, "Lobby of a Million Ghosts," *Nation*, January 23, 1960, 76; Memo to the Steering Committee of The Committee of One Million, 1958, box 9, folder 11 "General Correspondence, 1953–1963," Oram Group, Inc. Records; Liebman, *Coming Out Conservative*, 107.

56. Memo from Marvin Liebman, January 13, 1954, box 39, folder "Committee of One Million (to 1956)," Kohlberg Papers; Memo from the Steering Committee of the Committee of One Million to Harold L. Oram, March 4, 1955, box 9, folder 10 "General Correspondence, 1953–1963," Oram Group, Inc. Records; Memo from the Steering Committee to the Friends of the Committee of One Million, box 39, folder "Committee of One Million (to 1956)," Kohlberg Papers.

57. Ad, "Shall the Chinese Communists Shoot Their Way into the United Nations?" *New York Times*, April 12, 1955, 19; Memo from Marvin Liebman to Daniel A. Poling, January 19, 1959, box 110, folder "Liebman, Marvin," Kohlberg Papers.

58. Appeal, August 1956, box 87, folder "Committee of One Million (Against the Admission of Red China to the United Nations) General Information," Group Research, Inc. Records; O'Kearney, "Lobby of a Million Ghosts," 76.

59. Bowen, *The Roots of Modern Conservatism*, 35–55, 193, 199; Lichtman, *White Protestant Nation*, 140–41, 146–47, 203–204.

60. For an overview of *National Review*, see Nash, *The Conservative Intellectual Movement*, 197–233; Judis, *William F. Buckley*; Hart, *The Making of the American Conservative Mind*; Frisk, *If Not Us, Who?*; Nash, *Reappraising the Right*, 202–24; Lichtman, *White Protestant Nation*, 209–11.

61. Liebman, *Coming Out Conservative*, 109–10.

62. Lichtman, *White Protestant Nation*, 210.

63. For the importance of *National Review* for modern conservatism, see Nash, *The Conservative Intellectual Movement*, 230; Lichtman, *White Protestant Nation*, 216. George Nash pointed to the role played by several Jewish Americans in founding *National Review*. See Nash, *Reappraising the Right*, 202–24.

64. Lichtman, *White Protestant Nation*, 235.

65. Liebman, *Coming Out Conservative*, 106, 96, 131–42.

66. For an overview of Young Americans for Freedom, see Andrew, *The Other Side of the Sixties*; Schneider, *Cadres for Conservatism*; Klatch, *A Generation Divided*. A couple of conservatives also narrated their own activities in YAF. See, for example, Rusher, *The Rise of the Right*; Edwards, *The Conservative Revolution*; Liebman, *Coming Out Conservative*.

67. Schneider, *Cadres for Conservatism*, 21, 28.

68. Andrew, *The Other Side of the Sixties*, 53–74; Schneider, *Cadres for Conservatism*, 31–38.

69. Klatch, *A Generation Divided*, 97–133; Schneider, *Cadres for Conservatism*, 34.

70. Rusher, *The Rise of the Right*, 114; Liebman, *Coming Out Conservative*, 150–53.

71. Schneider, *Cadres for Conservatism*, 47, 50–52.

72. A problem revolving around the study of Richard Viguerie's direct mail fundraising is the shortage of primary sources. Indeed, while many researchers of conservatism have touched on Viguerie's activism, the books and articles rely primarily on interviews with him and his autobiographies, such as Viguerie, *The New Right*, and Viguerie and Franke, *America's Right Turn*. Alf Tomas Tønnessen monographed an exceptional

work focusing on Viguerie as a key political consultant in the conservative movement. Tønnessen, *How Two Political Entrepreneurs*. For works on Viguerie's direct mail, see Critchlow, *The Conservative Ascendancy*, 128–31; Schneider, *The Conservative Century*, 143–44; Crawford, *Thunder on the Right*, 6, 42–44; Andrew, *The Other Side of the Sixties*, 219–20; Schoenwald, *A Time for Choosing*, 160; Bjerre-Poulsen, *Right Face*, 178–81; Clymer, *Drawing the Line at the Big Ditch*, 53–54, 59, 67, 69; Link, *Righteous Warrior*, 145–46, 194; Williams, *God's Own Party*, 165–66, 168–69, 171, 175.

73. Viguerie, *The New Right*, 28–30.

74. Viguerie, *The New Right*, 29–30.

75. Letter from Marvin Liebman to William A. Rusher, September 9, 1977, box 52, folder 10 "General Correspondence, Liebman, Marvin, 1972–1980," William A. Rusher Papers, Manuscripts and Archives Division, Library of Congress; Liebman, *Coming Out Conservative*, 153; Viguerie, *The New Right*, 30–31.

76. Klatch, *A Generation Divided*, 38–40; Bjerre-Poulsen, *Right Face*, 165–66.

77. Perlstein, *Before the Storm*, 162–63; Viguerie, *The New Right*, 31.

78. Viguerie and Franke, *America's Right Turn*, 94–96.

79. "YAF Fundraising Packages (1960–Present)," box 46, folder 1 "Financial Records, 1970–1973," Young Americans for Freedom Records, HIA. This material shows the overview of YAF's direct mail campaigns from fall 1961 to April 1972, documenting each appeal, the names of senders, and the issues over the years.

80. Appeal from Richard Viguerie, November 1961, box 41, folder 6 "Campaign, 1960–1969," YAF Records (emphasis added).

81. Appeal from Richard Viguerie, March 22, 1962, box 41, folder 6 "Campaign, 1960–1969," YAF Records (emphasis added).

82. Appeal from Richard Viguerie, December 5, 1962, box 41, folder 6 "Campaign, 1960–1969," YAF Records.

83. Andrew, *The Other Side of the Sixties*, 80; Schneider, *The Conservative Century*, 96; Bjerre-Poulsen, *Right Face*, 172–78.

84. Appeal from Richard Viguerie, n.d., box 41, folder 6 "Campaign, 1960–1969," YAF Records.

85. Appeal from Richard Viguerie, December 5, 1962, box 41, folder 6 "Campaign, 1960–1969," YAF Records.

Chapter 3

1. "Who Barry Goldwater Is," *U.S. News & World Report* 57, no. 4, July 27, 1964, 37–39.

2. Edwards, *The Conservative Revolution*, 138–39; Rusher, *The Rise of the Right*, 174.

3. For the struggle over "respectable" conservatism, see Critchlow, *The Conservative Ascendancy*, 81; Bjerre-Poulsen, *Right Face*, 185–208; Hendershot, *What's Fair on the Air?*, 6–7, 59–60; Hemmer, *Messengers of the Right*, 189–97.

4. For Barry Goldwater's biography and early career, see Shermer, "Origins of the Conservative Ascendancy"; Shermer, *Barry Goldwater*, 1–8.

5. "Goldwater Aide Pushes Campaign," *New York Times*, September 2, 1962, 34. For a detailed biography of Stephen Shadegg, see "Biographical Sketch, Stephen C. Shadegg," February 6, 1958, box 3H496, folder "1958 Senate Campaign: General Files: Shadegg," Stephen Shadegg/Barry Goldwater Collection, the Dolph Briscoe Center for American History, the University of Texas at Austin. On Shadegg's roles in the Goldwater campaign in 1952, see Shadegg, *What Happened to Goldwater?*, 18; Shadegg, *The New How*, 26–30, 53, 67; Perlstein, *Before the Storm*, 24–26, 39–41.

6. Pamphlet, "The Measure of a Man," n.d., box 3H476, folder "1952 Senate Campaign: Press Release Advertisements," Shadegg/Goldwater Collection.

7. Advertisement, "Fear or Faith," August 11, 1952, box 3H476, folder "1952 Senate Campaign: Newspaper Advertisements," Shadegg/Goldwater Collection (emphasis in original).

8. Advertisement, "Eisenhower Will Be President of the United States," November 3, 1952, box 3H476, folder "1952 Senate Campaign: Newspaper Advertisements," Shadegg/Goldwater Collection.

9. Shadegg, *The New How*, 28–30.

10. Letter from Stephen Shadegg to Barry Goldwater, February 28, 1956, box 3H479, folder "Office File: Correspondence, Steve Shadegg, 1955–1958," Shadegg/Goldwater Collection.

11. Quoted in Donaldson, *Liberalism's Last Hurrah*, 9.

12. Shermer, "Origins of the Conservative Ascendancy," 695–702; Perlstein, *Before the Storm*, 24–26; Lichtman, *White Protestant Nation*, 228–29.

13. Letter from Barry Goldwater to Stephen C. Shadegg, March 2, 1954, box 3H479, folder "Office File: Correspondence, Steve Shadegg, 1952–1954," Shadegg/Goldwater Collection; Letter from Barry Goldwater to Stephen Shadegg, May 10, 1956, box 3H479, folder "Office File: Correspondence, Steve Shadegg, 1955–1958," Shadegg/Goldwater Collection.

14. Letter from George G. Mitchell to Barry Goldwater, July 15, 1958, box 3H488, folder "1958 Senate Campaign: Campaign Literature: Printing Rates, Solicitations, Postcards, Mailing Services, Show Cards," Shadegg/Goldwater Collection.

15. Appeal from Friends of Barry Goldwater, n.d., box 3H488, folder "1958 Senate Campaign: Campaign Literature: Campaign Letters (Mass Mailings)," Shadegg/Goldwater Collection; Appeal from Physicians for Barry Goldwater, July 1958, Shadegg/Goldwater Collection; Appeal from Democrats for Arizona, August 1958, Shadegg/Goldwater Collection; Appeal from Lawyers for Goldwater Committee, n.d., Shadegg/Goldwater Collection; Appeal from Attorneys for Goldwater Committee, n.d., Shadegg/Goldwater Collection; Appeal from Bi-Partisan Small Business Committee for Barry Goldwater, Shadegg/Goldwater Collection.

16. Appeal from Barry Goldwater, n.d., box 3H488, folder "1958 Senate Campaign: Campaign Literature: Campaign Letters (Mass Mailings)," Shadegg/Goldwater Collection.

17. Shadegg, *The New How*, 70–71.

18. Letter from Stephen Shadegg to Barry Goldwater, February 21, 1957, box 3H480, folder "1958 Senate Campaign: Correspondence, Shadegg and Goldwater, August 1957–Oct. 1958," Shadegg/Goldwater Collection.

19. Letter from Stephen Shadegg to Barry Goldwater, July 25, 1958, box 3H480, folder "1958 Senate Campaign: Correspondence, Shadegg and Goldwater, August 1957–Oct. 1958," Shadegg/Goldwater Collection.

20. Appeal, October 25, 1958, box 3H488, folder "1958 Senate Campaign: Campaign Literature: Campaign Letters (Mass Mailings)," Shadegg/Goldwater Collection.

21. Appeal, John Ong, n.d., box 3H488, folder "1958 Senate Campaign: Campaign Literature: Campaign Letters (Mass Mailings)," Shadegg/Goldwater Collection.

22. Appeal from Barry Goldwater to John Doe, box 3H488, folder "1958 Senate Campaign: Campaign Literature: Campaign Letters (Mass Mailings)," Shadegg/Goldwater Collection.

23. Appeal, October 25, 1958, box 3H488, folder "1958 Senate Campaign: Campaign Literature: Campaign Letters (Mass Mailings)," Shadegg/Goldwater Collection.

24. Appeal from Democrats for Arizona, August 1958, box 3H488, folder "1958 Senate Campaign: Campaign Literature: Campaign Letters (Mass Mailings)," Shadegg/Goldwater Collection.

25. Appeal from Stephen Shadegg, March 11, 1958, box 3H488, folder "1958 Senate Campaign: Campaign Literature: Campaign Letters (Mass Mailings)," Shadegg/Goldwater Collection.

26. Letter from Stephen Shadegg to Barry Goldwater, June 24, 1958, box 3H480, folder "1958 Senate Campaign: Correspondence, Shadegg and Goldwater, August 1957–Oct. 1958," Shadegg/Goldwater Collection.

27. Appeal, Bert Fireman, October 24, 1958, box 3H488, folder "1958 Senate Campaign: Campaign Literature: Campaign Letters (Mass Mailings)," Shadegg/Goldwater Collection.

28. Appeal, Friends of Barry Goldwater, n.d., box 3H488, folder "1958 Senate Campaign: Campaign Literature: Campaign Letters (Mass Mailings)," Shadegg/Goldwater Collection.

29. Shadegg, *The New How*, 71.

30. Shadegg, *What Happened to Goldwater*, 25.

31. Schoenwald, *A Time for Choosing*, 126; Hemmer, *Messengers of the Right*, 139–43; Perlstein, *Before the Storm*, 61–68; Rusher, *The Rise of the Right*, 88.

32. Andrew, *The Other Side of the Sixties*, 47–48, 53–74; Schneider, *Cadres for Conservatism*, 27–38; Liebman, *Coming Out Conservative*, 145–58; Rusher, *The Rise of the Right*, 87–93.

33. It is well-known that the "consensus" scholars, such as Daniel Bell, Richard Hofstadter, and Seymour Martin Lipset, criticized the rise of the "radical right" in their volume. See Westin, "The John Birch Society." See also McGirr, *Suburban Warriors*, 75–79; Bennett, *The Party of Fear*, 315–23; Mulloy, *The World of the John Birch Society*.

34. Cited in Epstein and Forster, *The Radical Right*, 153. Epstein and Forster scruti-nized the structure and membership of the John Birch Society. Epstein and Forster, *The Radical Right*, chaps. 11–15.

35. Nickerson, *Mothers of Conservatism*, 142–48; Hart, "The Truth in Time," 98, 138; Hemmer, *Messengers of the Right*, 169.

36. The Reminiscences of F. Clifton White, 17, box 119, folder 29 "'The Goldwater Nomination, The Reminiscences of F. Clinton White,' 1965 (1 of 2)," Personal and Po-litical Papers of Senator Barry M. Goldwater, Arizona State University Library.

37. Lichtman, *White Protestant Nation*, 245–46; Liebman, *Coming Out Conservative*, 165–66; Rusher, *The Rise of the Right*, 99–110; William Middendorf, *A Glorious Disaster*, 12–17. On the grassroots efforts to draft Goldwater, see Brennan, "Winning the War"; Phillips-Fein, *Invisible Hands*, 115–49; McGirr, *Suburban Warriors*, 111–46. For the stud-ies on the role of women in grassroots conservatism, see Critchlow, *Phyllis Schlafly*, chap. 5; Rymph, *Republican Women*, 160–87; Nickerson, *Mothers of Conservatism*, 157–68.

38. Letter from Stephen C. Shadegg to Ed Murray and Rex Barley, December 29, 1960; J. Edward Murray to Stephen C. Shadegg, January 6, 1961, box 3H506, folder "Cor-respondence, Shadegg and Goldwater, Jan.–Aug. 1961," Shadegg/Goldwater Collection.

39. Hemmer, *Messengers of the Right*, 163.

40. Shadegg, *What Happened to Goldwater*, 63–68.

41. Shadegg, *What Happened to Goldwater*, 63–64, 86–91.

42. Background Memo; Biography of Denison Kitchel; Biography of Daniel C. Gainey; Biography of G. R. Herberger; Biography of Richard G. Kleindienst, box 120, folder 25 "Background, 1960–1963," Papers of Goldwater; "Goldwater for President Committee Organizational Structure," box 513, folder "1964 Presidential Campaign: Handbooks, Manuals, and Kits," Shadegg/Goldwater Collection.

43. *Life*, July 24, 1964, 23; "Key Men of the 'Goldwater Team,'" *U.S. News & World Report* 56, no. 25, June 22, 1964, 20.

44. Laurence Stern, "Barry's Men Pack Tax-Free Institution," *Washington Post*, Au-gust 23, 1964. See also a biography of William J. Baroody, box 95, folder 10 "National Association of Manufacturers," William J. Baroody Papers, Manuscripts and Archives Division, Library of Congress.

45. Interview with Lee Edwards, December 1964, 4–5, 10–11, box 3J9, folder "Publi-cations: Shadegg Book, What Happened to Goldwater?: Research Notes: Conversations with and Notes from Individuals Involved in the Campaign, Lee Edwards," Shadegg/ Goldwater Collection. See also Critchlow, *The Conservative Ascendancy*, 118–20; Licht-man, *White Protestant Nation*, 207–208. William Baroody himself and Stephen Sha-degg in his book, *What Happened to Goldwater*, revealed that Baroody was working for Goldwater quite closely. The fact became a problem for AEI's status as a tax-exempt institution. A pundit mentioned, "In short, Shadegg's 'inside-story' of the campaign (including the 'draft' phase) would certainly seem to justify a careful look into AEI's ac-tivities relative to Goldwater through 1963 and 1964. If they haven't done so, appropriate Internal Revenue Service personnel ought to give some study to the book, and then to

AEI." See George Rucker to Harry Olsher, October 25, 1965, box 13, folder "American Enterprise Institute for Public Policy Research General, Washington, DC," Group Research, Inc. Records, Rare Book & Manuscript Library, Columbia University; Shadegg, *What Happened to Goldwater*, 66–68.

46. "Handbook for Victory," box 513, folder "1964 Presidential Campaign: Handbooks, Manuals, and Kits," Shadegg/Goldwater Collection.

47. "Instructions for Organizing a Special Group Committee For Goldwater-Miller," n.d., box 513, folder "1964 Presidential Campaign: Handbooks, Manuals, and Kits, 'Citizens For Goldwater-Miller Victory Manual,'" Shadegg/Goldwater Collection.

48. Lisa McGirr and Michelle Nickerson have demonstrated that women played a central role in grassroots activities for Goldwater and conservatism in Southern California. McGirr, *Suburban Warriors*, 3–4, 124, 138; Nickerson, *Mothers of Conservatism*, chap. 5.

49. Nickerson, *Mothers of Conservatism*, 145–56; Brenner, "Shouting at the Rain," 246–47.

50. Hart, "The Truth in Time," 219–24.

51. Epstein and Forster, *The Radical Right*, 92, 143–44; McGirr, *Suburban Warriors*, 127, 144–45.

52. Letter from Mrs. Henry J. Cadell to Seth M. Fitchet, October 17, 1963; Letter from Seth M. Fitchet to Mrs. Henry J. Cadell, November 1, 1963, box 119, folder 18 "Finance Committee: Contributors F-J, 1963–1964," Papers of Goldwater.

53. Letter from John J. Kennedy to Mrs. R. F. Lange, September 25, 1963, box 120, folder 25 "Background, 1960–1963," Papers of Goldwater.

54. "Handbook for Victory," box 513, folder "1964 Presidential Campaign: Handbooks, Manuals, and Kits," Shadegg/Goldwater Collection.

55. Memo from Marvin Liebman to Rita Bree and All Concerned, July 29, 1964, box 90, folder "Goldwater—Misc.," Marvin Liebman Papers, HIA.

56. Alexander, *Financing the 1964 Election*, 73–76, 119.

57. Memo from Marvin Liebman to Jeremiah Milbank Jr., February 21, 1964, box 90, folder "Goldwater for President," Liebman Papers.

58. Memo from Marvin Liebman to Barry T. Leithead, August 26, 1964, box 92, folder "Goldwater Campaign," Liebman Papers.

59. Memo from Marvin Liebman to Finance Committee, April 9, 1964, box 88, folder "National Goldwater Rally," Liebman Papers.

60. "Campaign Manual: Goldwater for President—New York," box 91, folder "Goldwater—Confidential Reports," Liebman Papers.

61. Letter from Ernest Hillman to Harry Rosenzweig, August 7, 1963, box 119, folder 18 "Finance Committee: Contributors F–J, 1963–1964," Papers of Goldwater.

62. Letter from William C. Morris to Harry Rosenzweig, May 4, 1963, box 119, folder 19 "Finance Committee: Contributors K–M, 1963–1964," Papers of Goldwater.

63. Letter from Harry Rosenzweig to William C. Morris, July 28, 1964, Papers of Goldwater.

64. Letter from A. L. Hall to Barry Goldwater, August 26, 1964, box 119, folder 18 "Finance Committee: Contributors F–J, 1963–1964," Papers of Goldwater.

65. Letter from Leon R. Clausen to Harry Rosenzweig, June 4, 1964, box 119, folder 17 "Finance Committee: Contributors A–D, 1963–1964," Papers of Goldwater.

66. Draft Text of Statement, n.d., box 90, folder "Fighting Aces for Goldwater," Liebman Papers.

67. Letter from Doug Campbell to Reed Chambers and E. V. Rickenbacker, October 22, 1964, box 90, folder "Fighting Aces for Goldwater," Papers of Goldwater; Letter from John M. Smith to Reed Chambers and E. V. Rickenbacker, October 19, 1964, Papers of Goldwater.

68. William F. Buckley Jr., "The Question of Robert Welch," *National Review*, February 13, 1962, 87. See also Critchlow, *The Conservative Ascendancy*, 58–59; Lichtman, *White Protestant Nation*, 239–40.

69. Andrew, *The Other Side of the Sixties*, 102–104, 193; Schneider, *Cadres for Conservatism*, 42, 48–49.

70. Greenberg, *Republic of Spin*, 368–73; Jamieson, *Packaging the Presidency*, 198–203; Hemmer, *Messengers of the Right*, 174.

71. Hendershot, *What's Fair on the Air?*, 176; Jamieson, *Packaging the Presidency*, 187–89, 193–97.

72. Shadegg, *What Happened to Goldwater*, 247.

73. Jamieson, *Packaging the Presidency*, 183, 208–19.

74. Letter from Ralph W. Applegate to Harry Rosenzweig, May 25, 1964, box 119, folder 17 "Finance Committee: Contributors A–D, 1963–1964," Papers of Goldwater; "To Senator Barry Goldwater," n.d., box 119, folder 15 "Finance Committee: California Supporters, 1964–1965," Papers of Goldwater.

75. McGirr, *Suburban Warriors*, 142–43.

76. Rusher, *The Rise of the Right*, 162.

77. Brennan, "Winning the War," 63; McGirr, *Suburban Warriors*, 143.

78. Phillips, *The Emerging Republican Majority*, 23–24.

79. Alexander, *Financing the 1968 Election*, 95; Heard, *The Costs of Democracy*, 22.

80. Nimmo, *The Political Persuaders*, 63–64; Congressional Quarterly Inc., "Campaign Spending Reports for 1964," January 7, 1965, box 4, folder "Campaign Fund Raising, Campaign Costs. General 1964," Records of the Democratic National Committee, LBJL. See also Goldberg, *Barry Goldwater*, 219; Schoenwald, *A Time for Choosing*, 160; Edwards, *The Conservative Revolution*, 138; Middendorf, *A Glorious Disaster*, xi, 136.

81. "Handbook for Victory," box 513, folder "1964 Presidential Campaign: Handbooks, Manuals, and Kits," Shadegg/Goldwater Collection.

82. *Orange County Register*, November 11, 1964, D3.

83. Rusher, *The Rise of the Right*, 161–62.

84. Johnson, *No Place for Amateurs*, 150.

85. Citizens for Goldwater mail, n.d., box 77, folder "Citizens for Goldwater," Group Research, Inc. Records.

86. Appeal, March 6, 1964, box 7, folder 19 "Appeals, 1963–1964," Oram Group, Inc. Records, Ruth Lilly Special Collections and Archives, IUPUI University Library, Indiana University/Purdue University.

Chapter 4

1. Viguerie, *The New Right*, 32–33.

2. Viguerie and Franke, *America's Right Turn*, 112.

3. For the roles played by Ray C. Bliss in party organization, see Green, *Politics, Professionalism, and Power*; Hershey and Green, *Mr. Chairman*.

4. Lichtman, *White Protestant Nation*, 240. See also Bjerre-Poulsen, *Right Face*, 197–208; Critchlow, *The Conservative Ascendancy*, 78–81; Hendershot, *What's Fair on the Air?*, 6–7, 59–60; Hemmer, *Messengers of the Right*, 189–97.

5. "Bliss Gains Support," *New York Times*, December 29, 1964, 12.

6. "Determined Republican: Raymond Charles Bliss," *New York Times*, January 13, 1965, 38.

7. Hershey and Green, *Mr. Chairman*, 25–64.

8. "G.O.P. Can Come Back: Bliss Scoffs at Republicans Are Minority," *Chicago Tribune*, January 14, 1965, 4.

9. "Bliss Confident GOP Can Resolve Differences," *Los Angeles Times*, March 2, 1965, 3.

10. David S. Broder, "Bliss Rides the Elephant," *New York Times Magazine*, March 21, 1965, 49.

11. Don Irwin, "GOP Chairman Brewing Trouble for Democrats," *Los Angeles Times*, May 16, 1965, 28.

12. Broder, "Bliss Rides the Elephant," 57.

13. On the role of direct mail fundraising in Bliss's model of party organization, see Bibby, "Party Leadership," 23, 27. For Republicans' fundraising in the Bliss era, see also Robert B. Semple Jr., "Skill Replaces Ideology at G.O.P. Headquarters under Bliss," *New York Times*, February 1, 1968, 24.

14. "G.O.P. Can Come Back: Bliss Scoffs at Republicans Are Minority," *Chicago Tribune*, January 14, 1965, 4.

15. David S. Broder, "G.O.P. Shifts Focus under Bliss Rule," *New York Times*, January 31, 1966, 16.

16. Broder, "Bliss Rides the Elephant," 49.

17. William F. Buckley Jr., "Bliss' Job: Keep Party Together," *Los Angeles Times*, April 7, 1965, A6.

18. William F. Buckley Jr., "Ray Bliss' Agonizing Dilemma," *Los Angeles Times*, July 7, 1965, A6.

19. Russell Freeburg, "Bliss Starts Shuffle of G.O.P. Staff Jobs," *Chicago Tribune*, March 31, 1965, B11.

20. On the Free Society Association and other conservative splinter groups in the 1960s, see Schoenwald, *A Time for Choosing*, 221–50.

21. Cabell Phillips, "Bliss Denounces Goldwater Unit as Peril to Party," *New York Times*, June 19, 1965, 1.

22. Liebman, *Coming Out Conservative*, 159.

23. Memo from Kenneth Wells Parkinson to Donald C. Bruce, December 4, 1965, box 131, folder 11 "American Conservative Union, By-Laws and Constitution, ca. 1964–68," William A. Rusher Papers, Manuscripts and Archives Division, Library of Congress.

24. Telegram from Marvin Liebman, December 5, 1964, box 57, folder "American Conservative Union, 1962–1966," Marvin Liebman Papers, HIA.

25. Schoenwald, *A Time for Choosing*, 234.

26. News Release, the American Conservative Union, June 23, 1965, box 58, folder "American Conservative Union, 1962–1966," Liebman Papers.

27. Proposal for the American Conservative Union, January 11, 1966, box 59, folder "American Conservative Union, 1962–1966," Liebman Papers.

28. For the relationship between the American Conservative Union and Young Americans for Freedom, see Schoenwald, *A Time for Choosing*, 234; Liebman, *Coming Out Conservative*, 158–59.

29. Confidential Proposal from David R. Jones to the Board of Directors of the American Conservative Union, February 11, 1966, box 59, folder "American Conservative Union, 1962–1966," Liebman Papers.

30. Marvin Liebman, "Goals of the American Conservative Union," n.d., box 57, folder "American Conservative Union, 1962–1966," Liebman Papers.

31. Schoenwald, *A Time for Choosing*, 238–39; Lichtman, *White Protestant Nation*, 261; Rusher, *The Rise of the Right*, 183.

32. Bell, *The Radical Right*; Hofstadter, "The Pseudo-Conservative Revolt"; Epstein and Forster, *The Radical Right*.

33. Schoenwald, *A Time for Choosing*, 234.

34. Marvin Liebman, "Goals of the American Conservative Union."

35. Memo from William A. Rusher to William F. Buckley Jr., et al., August 26, 1965, box 35, folder "Inter-Office Memo (2)," William F. Buckley Jr. Papers, Manuscripts and Archives, Yale University Library.

36. Memo from Donald C. Bruce to Marvin Liebman, January 23, 1965, box 58, folder "American Conservative Union, 1962–1966," Liebman Papers.

37. American Conservative Union, Notes on Reports Filed with Clerk, House of Representatives, 1st quarter 1965, box 9, folder "American Conservative Union Financial, Washington, DC," Group Research, Inc. Records, Rare Book & Manuscript Library, Columbia University.

38. Memo, Donald C. Bruce to Directors and Members of Advisory Assembly, January 14, 1965, box 58, folder "American Conservative Union, 1962–1966," Liebman Papers.

39. William A. Rusher to William F. Buckley, February 2, 1965, box 35, folder "Inter-office memos, Jan 1965–Jun 1965," Buckley Papers.

40. Agenda, ACU Board of Directors Meeting, January 28, 1965, box 58, folder "American Conservative Union, 1962–1966," Liebman Papers.

41. "Fund Raising Program for the American Conservative Union," September 17, 1965, box 132, folder 5 "American Conservative Union, Fundraising Activities, 1965–70," Rusher Papers.

42. Memo from William A. Rusher to William F. Buckley, March 3, 1965, Buckley Papers.

43. Memo from William Buckley to William Rusher, March 15, 1965, Buckley Papers.

44. "Fund Raising Program for the American Conservative Union."

45. For Viguerie's remark on "ideological direct mail," see Viguerie and Franke, *America's Right Turn*, 112.

46. Robert Walters, "Conservative GOP Splinter Ignores Bliss, Asks for Funds," *Washington Star*, August 19, 1965.

47. Appeal from American Conservative Union, August 14, 1965, box 9, folder "American Conservative Union, Washington, DC, 1965–8," Group Research, Inc. Records.

48. Appeal from American Conservative Union.

49. Memo from Marvin Liebman to David R. Jones, April 26, 1966, Liebman Papers.

50. Proposal for American Conservative Union, January 11, 1966, box 59, folder "American Conservative Union, 1962–1966," Liebman Papers.

51. Anti-Defamation League of B'nai and B'rith, "The John Birch Society—1966," *Facts Domestic Report* 17, no. 1 (February 1966): 357, box 434, folder "Group Research Directory Organizations (F–P)," Group Research, Inc. Records; *National Review*, October 19, 1965, 913–28.

52. This report analyzed that 30 percent of all mail concerned the John Birch Society, while 29 percent was on ACU programs, 16 percent urged consolidation of all conservative organizations to reduce duplication of effort, 18.5 percent mentioned the possibility of a third party, and 5.5 percent made some mention to "liberals" and "commies" in the ACU. See "Report on Fund Raising Mailings, Finance Division," February 14, 1966, box 132, folder 5 "American Conservative Union, Fundraising Activities, 1965–70," Rusher Papers.

53. Memo from Frank Wucatz to National Review, n.d., box 39, folder "John Birch Society (correspondence, pamphlets, newsclipped)," Buckley Papers.

54. Memo from Thomas J. Davis to William F. Buckley, February 24, 1966, box 39, folder "John Birch Society (correspondence, pamphlets, newsclipped)," Buckley Papers.

55. For the denunciation and decline of the JBS by the end of the 1960s, see, for example, McGirr, *Suburban Warriors*, 218–23; Schoenwald, *A Time for Choosing*, 176–78; Hendershot, *What's Fair on the Air?*, 59–60.

56. Rusher, *The Rise of the Right*, 182–83.

57. Memo from William J. Gill to Donald C. Bruce, March 17, 1965, box 132, folder 6 "American Conservative Union, General Correspondence, Jan–Spt. 1965," Rusher Papers.

58. Memo from Leo Synnestvedt to Donald C. Bruce, June 2, 1965, box 132, folder 6 "American Conservative Union, General Correspondence, Jan–Spt. 1965," Rusher Papers.

59. Memo from William F. Buckley to All Concerned, n.d., box 35, folder "Inter-office memos, Jul 1965–Dec 1965, n.d.," Buckley Papers.

60. Memo from William A. Rusher to Donald C. Bruce et al., September 10, 1965, box 135, folder 7 "American Conservative Union, Political Action Committee, Correspondence, 1965," Rusher Papers.

61. Rusher, *The Rise of the Right*, 182. See also Schoenwald, *A Time for Choosing*, 235–36, 239–40, 242.

62. Memo from William A. Rusher to Leo Synnestvedt, November 23, 1965, box 132, folder 7 "American Conservative Union, General Correspondence, Oct-Dec. 1965," Rusher Papers.

63. Rusher, *The Rise of the Right*, 183.

64. On conservatives who requested authorization to found local chapters, see memo from John L. Jones to William A. Rusher, March 15, 1968, box 135, folder 10 "American Conservative Union, Political Action Committee, Correspondence, 1968–69," Rusher Papers. For Rusher's rejection, see William A. Rusher to Jerry Harkins, January 7, 1969, Rusher Papers; Memo from William A. Rusher to Mrs. Richard Sundeleaf, February 24, 1970, Rusher Papers.

65. Memo from William A. Rusher to Donald C. Bruce et al., September 10, 1965, box 135, folder 7 "American Conservative Union, Political Action Committee, Correspondence, 1965," Rusher Papers.

66. Memo from John Davenport to the Members of the Advisory Assembly of the American Conservative Union, February 21, 1966, box 58, folder "American Conservative Union, 1962–1966," Liebman Papers.

67. Rusher, *The Rise of the Right*, 183.

68. Letter from Neil McCaffrey to William Rusher, January 20, 1983, box 57, folder 7 "McCaffrey, Neil, 1968–1988," Rusher Papers.

69. Letter from Neil McCaffrey to Lewis L. Strauss, March 28, 1963, box 88, folder 14 "Conservative Book Club, 1963–1965," William J. Baroody Papers, Manuscripts and Archives Division, Library of Congress.

70. Hemmer, *Messengers of the Right*, 183–84; Lee Edwards and Anne Edwards, "How Publishers (and Readers) Learned to Love Conservative Books," *Daily Signal*, April 13, 2015, https://www.dailysignal.com/2015/04/13/how-publishers-and-readers-learned-to-love-conservative-books/. For the cooperation of the Conservative Book Club and the American Conservative Union in direct mail fundraising, see memo from Marvin Liebman to Donald C. Bruce, May 20, 1965, box 57, folder "ACU," Liebman Papers.

71. Neil McCaffrey to Lewis L. Strauss, March 28, 1963, box 88, folder 14 "Conservative Book Club, 1963–1965," Baroody Papers.

72. Hemmer, *Messengers of the Right*, 180, 183–85.

73. Viguerie and Franke, *America's Right Turn*, 127, 95.

74. Appeal from Richard Viguerie, n.d., box 41, folder 6 "Campaign, 1960–1969," Young Americans for Freedom Records, HIA. For the conflicts of Young Americans for Freedom and the National Student Association, see Schneider, *Cadres for Conservatism*, 60–63.

75. Appeal from David R. Jones, September 7, 1969, box 41, folder 6 "Campaign, 1960–1969," YAF Records.

76. Appeal from Herbert A. Philbrick to Jorge E. Ferrer, July 31, 1970, box 41, folder 6 "Campaign, 1960–1969," YAF Records.

77. Appeal from Clarence Manion to Maria L. Berges, October 22, 1969, box 41, folder 6 "Campaign, 1960–1969," YAF Records.

78. Memo from David R. Jones to William A. Rusher, May 13, 1968, box 132, folder 10 "American Conservative Union, General Correspondence, 1968," Rusher Papers.

79. Memo from David R. Jones to Members of the Board of Directors, July 14, 1968, box 132, folder 5 "American Conservative Union, Fundraising Activities, 1965–70," Rusher Papers.

80. Memo from David R. Jones to Members of the Board of Directors, July 14, 1968.

81. Memo from David R. Jones to Members of the Board of Directors, September 13, 1968, box 132, folder 5 "American Conservative Union, Fundraising Activities, 1965–70," Rusher Papers.

82. Joint Appeal, February 1969, box 9, folder "American Conservative Union, Washington, DC, 1969–70," Group Research, Inc. Records.

83. Memo from John L. Jones to All ACU Board Members, n.d., box 132, folder 5 "American Conservative Union, Fundraising Activities, 1965–70," Rusher Papers.

84. For an overview of the Democratic Study Group, see Democratic Study Group Records, 1912–1995, Manuscripts and Archives Division, Library of Congress, accessed December 25, 2018, https://www.loc.gov/item/mm81057125/.

85. Campaign Activity Report, n.d., box I:56, folder 11 "Information about DSG," DSG Records.

86. "Fundraising," 1964, box I:29, folder 9 "Miscellany, 1956, 1964–1971," DSG Records.

87. Mary Meehan, "How to Shake the Money Tree," June 1970 (revised in January 1972), box II:15, folder 8 "Fund Raising, Chronological file, 1969–1979," DSG Records.

88. Viguerie, *The New Right*, 34.

89. Memo from Robert C. Odle Jr. to Jeb S. Magruder, November 24, 1971, box 18, folder 17 "(JSM) Direct Mail & Telephone Operations [16]," Jeb Stuart Magruder Papers, Richard Nixon Presidential Library.

90. Appeal from Martin Luther King, Sr., n.d., box 11, folder 8 "Appeals, 1967–1969, 1973–1974," Oram Group, Inc. Records, Ruth Lilly Special Collections and Archives, IUPUI University Library, Indiana University/Purdue University.

91. Appeal from J. William Fulbright, April 1969, Oram Group, Inc. Records. Harold L. Oram, Inc. mailed out another direct mailing signed by George S. McGovern in December 1969. Much of the content was the same in the two appeals with the signatures of Fulbright and McGovern, indicating that the staff of Oram, Inc., not the prominent

figures, crafted the message on the letters. See Appeal from George S. McGovern, December 26, 1969, Oram Group, Inc. Records.

92. Appeal from David Riesman, November 1968, Oram Group, Inc. Records.

93. Appeal from Bayard Rustin, n.d., box II:15, folder 8 "Fund Raising, Chronological file, 1969–1979," DSG Records.

94. Cohen, *American Maelstrom*; Donaldson, *Liberalism's Last Hurrah*.

95. Lichtman, *White Protestant Nation*, 276.

96. On the viewpoints of William Rusher and F. Clifton White, see Rusher, *The Rise of the Right*, 209, 213. For Viguerie's remark, see Viguerie and Franke, *America's Right Turn*, 87.

97. Phillips, *The Emerging Republican Majority*, 23–24, 32–33, 38–39.

98. McGinniss, *The Selling of the President, 1968*, esp. 27–28.

99. McGinniss, *The Selling of the President, 1968*, 81–82, 161.

100. Greenberg, *Republic of Spin*, 386–87; Sheingate, *Building a Business of Politics*, 146.

101. Memo from Jeb S. Magruder to the Attorney General, June 30, 1971, box 10, folder 11 "(JSM) Advertising [7]," Magruder Papers; Stanley E. Cohen, "Washington Beat," *Advertising Age*, July 19, 1971, 60, Magruder Papers.

102. For an overview of the November Group, see Jamieson, *Packaging the Presidency*, 289–91.

103. Memo from Stephen H. Winchell to Robert C. Odle, April 14, 1971, box 18, folder 9 "(JSM) Direct Mail & Telephone Operations [8]," Magruder Papers; Memo from James L. Martin to Harry S. Dent, April 27, 1971, Magruder Papers; Memo from Robert C. Odle Jr. to Lee Nunn, May 13, 1971, Magruder Papers.

104. Memo for the Attorney General, January 24, 1972, box 18, folder 8 "(JSM) Direct Mail & Telephone Operations [7]," Magruder Papers.

105. Memo from Gregg Petersmeyer to Jeb S. Magruder, September 10, 1971, box 19, folder 1 "(JSM) Direct Mail & Telephone Operations [17]," Magruder Papers.

106. Memo from L. Robert Morgan to Clark MacGregor, July 27, 1972, box 18, folder 2 "(JSM) Direct Mail & Telephone Operations [1]," Magruder Papers.

107. Memo from Bob Morgan to Jeb Magruder, June 6, 1972, box 18, folder 3 "(JSM) Direct Mail & Telephone Operations [2]," Magruder Papers; Memo from Robert H. Marik to Clark MacGregor, n.d., box 18, folder 3 "(JSM) Direct Mail & Telephone Operations [2]," Magruder Papers.

108. Miroff, *The Liberals' Moment*, 168–69; Hart, *Right from the Start*, 42–43.

109. White, *The Making of the President, 1972*, 280.

110. Hart, *Right from the Start*, 118. See also Miroff, *The Liberals' Moment*, 167–69.

111. McGovern, *An American Journey*, 19.

112. White, *The Making of the President, 1972*, 280.

113. Miroff, *The Liberals' Moment*, 65–66.

Chapter 5

1. Alexander Heard, "A New Approach to Campaign Finances," *New York Times Magazine*, October 6, 1963, 244.

2. For the observations on increasing campaign finance and big donors, see "Ike and Truman Join Bipartisan Fund Plea," *New York Herald Tribune*, June 9, 1964, 22. For the remark on advertisers in political campaigns, see Walter Pincus, "Campaign Fund Law Will Revolutionize Politics," *Philadelphia Inquirer*, November 27, 1966.

3. Heard, "A New Approach to Campaign Finances."

4. Mutch, *Campaigns, Congress, and Courts*; Mutch, *Buying the Vote*; Zelizer, "Seeds of Cynicism"; La Raja, *Small Change*. Robert Mutch's 1988 book was the first work to chronicle a history of campaign finance reform in the United States. Mutch has stressed the central significance of scandals, particularly Watergate, in accelerating the reform movement. Alternatively, Julian Zelizer has focused on the role of "the coalition of reformers," including experts, foundations, and philanthropists, in framing legal discussions. While touching on scandals revolving around political fundraising, Zelizer criticizes that Mutch dismissed a series of reform laws long before the Watergate scandal. Arguing against Zelizer's public interest model, Raymond La Raja has succinctly pointed out partisanship and factionalism in the congressional debates in the 1960s. La Raja makes his case that Congress passed campaign reform bills not when legislators were aware of public interest, but when partisanship between Democrats and Republicans or intraparty factionalism helped push for the legislations. However, generally speaking, their studies on campaign finance reform are constrained to Congress without investigating the impacts on social movements. Building on these works, my argument in this chapter and the next is that the "Democratic reforms" ironically encouraged the financial and political power of conservatives that successfully collected small money from the mass.

5. "Kennedy as a Party Fund-Raiser," *San Francisco Chronicle*, August 6, 1963.

6. Joseph Young, "Federal Workers Charge Pressure on $100 Tickets," *Washington Star*, November 6, 1962, A-1.

7. For the Hatch Act, see Azzaro, "The Hatch Act Modernization Act."

8. Young, "Federal Workers Charge Pressure on $100 Tickets," A-4.

9. Young, "Federal Workers Charge Pressure on $100 Tickets," A-1.

10. "Demo 'Shakedown' Probe Asked," *Indianapolis Star*, January 16, 1963.

11. Edward T. Folliard, "Party Denies Pressure in Ticket Sale," *Washington Post*, January 16, 1963.

12. Folliard, "Party Denies Pressure in Ticket Sale."

13. Jerry Kluttz, "Federal Aide Scorns Bid to $100 Gala," *Washington Post*, January 18, 1963.

14. Edward T. Folliard, "$1 Million Salute Given to JFK!" *Boston Globe*, January 19, 1963, 1, 3.

15. For more on the Citizens' Research Foundation and Herbert Alexander, see, for example, Gloria Cornette, "Herbert E. Alexander," The Campaign Finance Institute, accessed June 21, 2018, http://cfinst.org/HerbertEAlexander/Bio.aspx. See also Zelizer, "Seeds of Cynicism," 80–81.

16. Letter from Alexander Heard to the President, June 24, 1964, box 110, folder "PL3 4_20_64—7_25_64," White House Central Files, LBJL.

17. Letter from Herbert E. Alexander to the President, February 6, 1964, box 110, folder "PL3 Fund Raising 11_22_63—4_19_64," White House Central Files.

18. Zelizer, "Seeds of Cynicism," 81.

19. Letter from Lyndon B. Johnson to Alexander Heard, July 13, 1964, box 110, folder "PL3 4_20_64—7_25_64," White House Central Files.

20. Memo from Herbert E. Alexander to Jack Valenti, March 5, 1964, box 110, folder "PL3 Fund Raising 11_22_63—4_19_64," White House Central Files.

21. Julius Duscha, "Parties Seek Small Gifts from Many," *Washington Post*, June 14, 1964, L3.

22. "2 Parties Plan Mail Appeal to Raise Campaign Funds," *Washington Evening Star*, June 9, 1964.

23. Chester Bulgier, "Polk & Co. Experiment to Ask Public to Share Cost of Politics," *Detroit News*, June 10, 1964.

24. "Ike and Truman Join Bipartisan Fund Plea," *New York Herald Tribune*, June 9, 1964, 1, 22.

25. James Robinson, "Ike-Adlai Campaign for Widely Based Party Gifts Flops," *Washington Post*, September 24, 1964, B2.

26. "An Important Letter," *Minneapolis Star*, June 10, 1964.

27. Robinson, "Ike-Adlai Campaign for Widely Based Party Gifts Flops."

28. "The Campaign Fund Problem Is Unsolved," *Providence Sunday Journal*, October 11, 1964.

29. Rowland Evans and Robert Novak, "Inside Report: The Democratic Deficit," *Washington Post*, September 23, 1965.

30. Richard L. Lyons, "'Fat Cats' Leaving GOP," *Washington Post*, October 28, 1965, G5.

31. "Democrats Led in Large Donors," *New York Times*, October 26, 1965, 30.

32. On the President's Club, see Alexander, *Financing the 1964 Election*, 9; Mutch, *Buying the Vote*, 125–26; Phillips-Fein, *Invisible Hands*, 141.

33. Lyons, "'Fat Cats' Leaving GOP," G5.

34. Eileen Shanahan, "Campaign Marked by Shifts in Patterns of Fund-Giving to Republicans and Democrats," *New York Times*, October 14, 1964, 27.

35. Jerry Landauer, "Political Fund-Raising: A Murky World," *Wall Street Journal*, June 28, 1967, 14.

36. Sixty-eight corporations purchased ad pages in December 1965, then the figure increased to 168 by the next month. See Robert S. Boyd, "68 Firms Finance Johnson

Booster Book," *Washington Post*, December 8, 1965, A2; Walter R. Mears, "Political Parties Find New Source of Revenue in Magazine Advertising," *Oregonian*, January 6, 1966, 12.

37. Walter Pincus, "Democrats to Solicit Business Ads Again," *Washington Star*, September 8, 1965, A-1, A-5.

38. "Dead Letter," *Washington Post*, December 18, 1965.

39. Mears, "Political Parties Find New Source," 12.

40. Editorial, "Advertising the Great Society," *New York Times*, December 13, 1965, 38.

41. Walter Pincus, "Weltner Balks at Fund Books," *Washington Evening Star*, December 13, 1965, A-1, A-8.

42. "Democrats to Give Up $600,000 Ad Profit," *Plain Dealer*, March 7, 1966; "GOP Abandons Ad Book Plan," *Washington Evening Star*, March 17, 1966.

43. Mears, "Political Parties Find New Source of Revenue," 12.

44. Congressional Quarterly, Inc., "Campaign Financing Reforms Sought by President," January 14, 1966, box 152, folder "Johnson, Pres. Lyndon: Campaign Finances 1966. Funds Reform Proposal in State of Union Message, Jan. 12, 1966," Records of the Democratic National Committee, LBJL. On the Republicans' endorsement of the campaign finance reform, see Editorial, "End Campaign Cheating," *Chicago Sun-Times*, January 30, 1966.

45. For Senator John J. Williams's remarks, see Joseph R. Daughen, "The Williams Amendment: Political 'Blackmail' Ends," *Evening Bulletin*, March 15, 1966, B-33. For Senator Everett McKinley Dirksen's comment, see Congressional Quarterly, Inc., "New Political Ad Law May Hurt Party Finances," March 17, 1966, box 4, folder "Campaign Fund Raising. 1966. Reform," DNC Collection. On the rescission of the Williams amendment, see La Raja, *Small Change*, 69.

46. Zelizer, "Seeds of Cynicism," 84–85.

47. La Raja, *Small Change*, 69–71; Zelizer, "Seeds of Cynicism," 84–85; Mutch, *Buying the Vote*, 128–29.

48. Walter Pincus, "Campaign Fund Law Will Revolutionize Politics," *Philadelphia Inquirer*, November 27, 1966.

49. Zelizer, "Seeds of Cynicism," 86.

50. " . . . and a Bad Signing," *New York Times*, November 15, 1966, 46.

51. Ted Knap, "No Dessert at Political Dinners?" *Washington Daily News*, August 24, 1967.

52. "Election Finances Still Under Debate," *Washington Post*, December 28, 1967. For the 1967 Ashmore–Goodell bill, see Zelizer, "Seeds of Cynicism," 76, 87.

53. Zelizer, "Seeds of Cynicism," 84.

54. McGinniss, *The Selling of the President, 1968*, 39.

55. "Daily, California Agency Chief, to Head Nixon's House Agency Setup," box 10, folder 15 "(JSM) Advertising #1 [1]," Jeb Stuart Magruder Papers, Richard Nixon Presidential Library.

56. Alexander, *Financing the 1968 Election*, 95; Heard, *The Costs of Democracy*, 22.

57. Alexander, *Money in Politics*, 60–61.

58. La Raja, *Small Change*, 45.

59. Congress, House, Committee on House Administration, Subcommittee on Elections, Hearing on Federal Election Reform, Ninety-Third Congress, First Session (November 29, 1973), 385, quoted in Gillon, *"That's Not What We Meant to Do,"* 267n1.

60. McFarland, *Common Cause*. On the role of Common Cause in campaign finance reform, see also Zelizer, "Seeds of Cynicism," 90–92; Gillon, *"That's Not What We Meant to Do,"* 200–202.

61. Mutch, *Campaigns, Congress, and Courts*, 45; Zelizer, "Seeds of Cynicism," 92.

62. La Raja, *Small Change*, 72–75.

63. "Conservative Fund-Raisers: New Hope for 1974," *Congressional Quarterly*, September 7, 1974, 2437.

64. Zelizer, "Seeds of Cynicism," 97.

65. Gillon, *"That's Not What We Meant to Do,"* 203.

66. For key provisions of the campaign finance reforms in 1971 and 1974, see La Raja, *Small Change*, 78–79.

67. Appeal from Ronald B. Dear, April 29, 1974, box 8, folder "American Conservative Union, Washington, DC, 1974–5," Group Research, Inc. Records, Rare Book & Manuscript Library, Columbia University.

68. John Quincy Adams, "Discussion Paper: The Deficiencies of the Federal Election Campaign Act and Its Amendments," n.a., 21, box D17, folder "Federal Election Campaign Act Amendments of 1976—American Association of Political Consultants Recommendation," President Ford Committee Records, GRFL.

69. Adams, "Discussion Paper," 6.

70. Adams, "Discussion Paper," 13. The "marketplace of ideas" was a common conception in the Cold War era. Nancy Bernhard demonstrated that two assumptions, one that the commercial marketplace guaranteed free debates and the other that the US government valued a free marketplace of ideas, were closely connected. Particularly in the Second Red Scare of the 1950s, the concept had "a quality of irrefutability." Niels Bjerre-Poulsen also pointed out that the "consensus scholars," such as Seymour Martin Lipset, accused right-wing extremists of rejecting the belief in an open marketplace of ideas. See Bernhard, *U.S. Television News*, 7; Bjerre-Poulsen, *Right Face*, 197–203.

71. "Recommendations to the Federal Election Commission on the Federal Election Campaign Act of 1974 prepared by the American Association of Political Consultants," n.a., 1, box D17, folder "Federal Election Campaign Act Amendments of 1976—American Association of Political Consultants Recommendation," President Ford Committee Records.

72. Tomas Tønnessen, *How Two Political Entrepreneurs*, 73. See also Sabato, *The Rise of Political Consultants*, 224; Issenberg, *The Victory Lab*, 53.

Chapter 6

1. "The Right Wing," *AFL-CIO Special Report*, n.d., box 2, folder "AFL-CIO," Group Research, Inc. Records, Rare Book & Manuscript Library, Columbia University; "The Right Wing: Part II," *AFL-CIO Special Report*, n.d., Group Research, Inc. Records.

2. E. J. Dionne Jr., "Labor, in Trade Battle, Sends a Bleak TV Message," *New York Times*, March 6, 1987, A16.

3. George Meany, "Danger from the Right," *AFL-CIO News*, September 10, 1977, 4, Group Research, Inc. Records.

4. "The Right Wing."

5. For an overview of the New Right, see, for example, Lichtman, *White Protestant Nation*, 307–308, 310; Critchlow, *The Conservative Ascendancy*, 128–31, 136; Bennett, *The Party of Fear*, 392–94; Gottfried and Fleming, *The Conservative Movement*, 83–84.

6. The term "New Right" has been coined several times over the course of the twentieth century. According to political commentator Kevin Phillips, the "New Right" referred to seven cohorts of conservatives: (1) traditionalist intellectuals such as Richard Weaver during the 1940s, (2) supporters of McCarthyism in the early 1950s, (3) William F. Buckley Jr. and *National Review* writers, (4) the John Birch Society, (5) Irving Kristol's neoconservatives, (6) libertarians, and (7) the allies of Richard Viguerie and Paul Weyrich. For the taxonomy of the New Right, see Lichtman, *White Protestant Nation*, 308. Additionally, in 1969, M. Stanton Evans used the phrase of the "New Right" to describe young conservatives who fought against the New Left activists. See Viguerie and Franke, *America's Right Turn*, 53.

The New Right movement often includes the Religious Right since Paul Weyrich founded the Moral Majority with Baptist minister Jerry Falwell in 1979. Evangelicals and New Right activists, including Weyrich, Viguerie, Howard Phillips, and Terry Dolan, worked intimately with each other. However, in this book, I distinguish the religious conservatives and the political New Right, regarding the Christian right as an ally, rather than part, of the New Right.

7. Gary McMillan, "What Is the New Right Up To?" *Boston Globe*, December 17, 1978, A4.

8. Christopher Buchanan, "New Right: 'Many Times More Effective' Now," *Congressional Quarterly*, December 24, 1977, 2649.

9. Memo from Stephen H. Winchell to Pete Hoke, John Daly, Robert Delay, and Ed Mayer, June 5, 1975, Paul M. Weyrich Papers, American Heritage Center, University of Wyoming.

10. Letter from William A. Rusher to Terry Dolan, Howard Phillips, Richard Viguerie, and Paul Weyrich, April 23, 1981, William A. Rusher Papers, Manuscript and Archives Division, Library of Congress.

11. Viguerie, *The New Right*, 50.

12. *Right Report* 3, no. 19 (October 7, 1974), Wilcox Collection of Contemporary Political Movements, Kenneth Spencer Research Library, University of Kansas. Gerald Ford shortly realized that Vice President Nelson Rockefeller was a major problem in his administration as Rockefeller generated resentment among right-wing Republicans. On October 28, 1975, the two met in the Oval Office and Ford convinced Rockefeller to request the president to remove himself from the 1976 ticket. Ford regretted this decision for years, confessing that it was "one of the few cowardly things I did in my life." See Ford, *A Time to Heal*, 327–28.

13. Viguerie, *The New Right*, 51.

14. For the biography of Paul Weyrich, see Tønnessen, *How Two Political Entrepreneurs*, 27–34.

15. Paul M. Weyrich, "Weyrich on Weyrich: Here's the Rest of the Story," *Conservative Digest* 7, no. 10 (October 1981): 20.

16. Lichtman, *White Protestant Nation*, 310.

17. Stephen Isaacs wrote a series of articles in the *Washington Post* describing the roles played by Joseph Coors in 1970s conservatism. See Stephen Isaacs, "Coors Beer—and Politics—Move East," *Washington Post*, May 4, 1975, A1, A4; Stephen Isaacs, "Coors Bucks Network 'Bias,'" *Washington Post*, May 5, 1975, A1, A3; Stephen Isaacs, "Coors-Backed Unit Seeks Defeat of Hill 'Radicals,'" *Washington Post*, May 6, 1975, A1, A6; Stephen Isaacs, "Coors' Capital Connection," *Washington Post*, May 7, 1975, A1, A5, A6.

18. Bob Poole, "Conservatives Already at Work," *Richmond Times Dispatch*, April 27, 1975.

19. Stanhope Gould, "Coors Brews the News," *Columbia Journalism Review*, March/April 1975, 17–29; Isaacs, "Coors Beer—and Politics—Move East," A4; Isaacs, "Coors' Capital Connection," A1.

20. Bennett, *The Party of Fear*, 393–94; Gottfried and Fleming, *The Conservative Movement*, 97–98; Lichtman, *White Protestant Nation*, 311.

21. Interview with Morton Blackwell, Arlington, Virginia, October 19, 2015. See also Resume, Morton Blackwell, September 10, 1975, box 9, folder "Keene, Dave—Miscellaneous, 1974–1976," Citizens for Reagan Records, HIA.

22. Gottfried and Fleming, *The Conservative Movement*, 99–100.

23. Crawford, *Thunder on the Right*, 51.

24. Alan Ehrenhalt, "'New Right' Plans Move to Change Congress," *CP Magazine*, October 23, 1976, 3027.

25. John Fialka, "The Godfather of the 'New Right' Feels the Torch Is Passing," *Washington Star*, June 23, 1975.

26. Rich Jaroslovsky, "New-Right Cashier," *Wall Street Journal*, October 6, 1978, 41.

27. Alan Crawford, "Richard Viguerie's Bid for Power," *Nation*, January 29, 1977, 105. For the biography of Alan Pell Crawford, see Saloma, *Ominous Politics*, 47.

28. Crawford, "Richard Viguerie's Bid for Power," 106.

29. Ehrenhalt, "'New Right' Plans Move to Change Congress," 3027.

30. Ehrenhalt, "'New Right' Plans Move to Change Congress," 3028.

31. Ehrenhalt, "'New Right' Plans Move to Change Congress," 3028.

32. James M. Perry, "The Right Wing Got Plucked," *National Observer*, November 26, 1976, 14.

33. Milton Ellerin and Alisa Kesten, "The New Right: A Background Memorandum," n.d., box 119, folder 2 "Reference Files, New Right, 1969–81," Rusher Papers.

34. Viguerie, *The Establishment vs. The People*, esp. 36, 55. See also Lichtman, *White Protestant Nation*, 308.

35. Ehrenhalt, "'New Right' Plans Move to Change Congress," 3028–29.

36. *American Political Report* 7, no. 3 (October 28, 1977), box 6, folder 6 "vol. 21, Aug-Dec 1977 (2 of 2)," Paul M. Weyrich Scrapbooks, Manuscripts and Archives Division, Library of Congress.

37. Crawford, "Richard Viguerie's Bid for Power," 106.

38. On the antielite populism of the New Right, see for example Bennett, *The Party of Fear*, 398–400. For the history of American populism, see Kazin, *The Populist Persuasion*; Formisano, *For the People*. While Formisano examined populist movements from the early Republic to the 1840s, Kazin delineated the tradition of populism ranging from the People's Party in the 1890s to the New Right of the 1970s.

39. Crawford, *Thunder on the Right*, 5, 292–93, 303–10.

40. Quoted in Lichtman, *White Protestant Nation*, 309.

41. Allan F. Yoder, "Right's Rites of Passage," *Bergen County Record*, June 1978.

42. Lichtman, *White Protestant Nation*, 309.

43. Ehrenhalt, "'New Right' Plans Move to Change Congress," 3029.

44. Perry, "The Right Wing Got Plucked," 14.

45. "Why the 'New Right' Isn't Doing Well at the Polls," *Business Week*, October 30, 1978, 160.

46. William A. Rusher, "Raising Conservative Bucks," *National Review*, December 8, 1978, 1532.

47. Perry, "The Right Wing Got Plucked," 14.

48. Perry, "The Right Wing Got Plucked," 14.

49. Nick Kotz, "King Midas of 'the New Right,'" *Atlantic*, November 1978, 61.

50. Lou Cannon, "Tapping the Little Guy: Conservative Broaden Financial Base," *Washington Post*, March 6, 1977.

51. Jaroslovsky, "New-Right Cashier," 41.

52. "Conservative Fund-Raisers: New Hope for 1974," *Congressional Quarterly Magazine*, September 7, 1974, 2440.

53. Jaroslovsky, "New-Right Cashier," 41.

54. Perry, "The Right Wing Got Plucked," 1.

55. "Right-Wing Wins Another Upset," *NCEC Campaign Report*, September 1976, 1, 3.

56. "Conservative Fund-Raisers: New Hope for 1974," 2438. For the relationship of Richard Viguerie with Billy James Hargis, see also Hendershot, *What's Fair on the Air?*, 182.

57. Frank Mayer quoted in Kazin, *The Populist Persuasion*, 237. See also Judis, *William F. Buckley, Jr.*, 283–87.

58. On the overview of Viguerie's direct mail operations on Wallace's behalf, see "Conservative Fund-Raisers: New Hope for 1974," 2438. For the amount of funds raised, see Crawford, "Richard Viguerie's Bid for Power," 105. On the increasing number of Democrats in Viguerie's mailing lists, see Perry, "The Right Wing Got Plucked," 14.

59. Jaroslovsky, "New-Right Cashier," 1.

60. Perry, "The Right Wing Got Plucked," 14.

61. Letter from John P. Sears to John Alex McCone, August 4, 1975, box 61, folder "July & August 1975," Citizens for Reagan Records.

62. For Bruce W. Eberle's background, see "Some background notes on Bruce Eberle," Group Research, Inc., May 1977, Group Research, Inc. Records. According to the Group Research document, Bruce W. Eberle & Associates was located in Chantilly, Virginia, in June 1974 but moved to Vienna, Virginia, by August 1974. On Marvin Liebman's remark, see letter from Marvin Liebman to William A. Rusher, September 9, 1977, box 52, folder 10 "General Correspondence, Liebman, Marvin, 1972–80," Rusher Papers.

63. Letter from Lyn Nofziger to David LeRoy, October 24, 1975, box 9, folder 8 "Formation of the Citizens for Reagan (CFR) announcement, 1975," Citizens for Reagan Records. See also *Rocky Mountain News*, July 6, 1977, 39.

64. Dear Fellow Sportsman, n.d., box 13, folder 13 "solicitation letters, 1976," Citizens for Reagan Records.

65. Dear Friends, n.d., box 13, folder 13 "solicitation letters, 1976," Citizens for Reagan Records.

66. Dear Fellow Republicans, n.d., box 13, folder 13 "solicitation letters, 1976," Citizens for Reagan Records (emphasis in original).

67. Letter from Wilbert Hallock to Ronald Reagan, n.d., box 60, folder 15 "Responses of John P. Sears to contribution letters—Primary after March 31 speech, 1976 March 15–April 30," Citizens for Reagan Records.

68. Letter from Frank Gard Jameson to Paul Laxalt, July 25, 1975, box 61, folder 5 "California, July & August 1975," Citizens for Reagan Records.

69. Alan Ehrenhalt, "'New Right' Plans Move to Change Congress," *CP Magazine*, October 23, 1976, 3028.

70. Memo from Paul M. Weyrich to Robert A. Walker and Richard A. Viguerie, October 3, 1975, box 43, folder 13 "Correspondence, 1975," Weyrich Papers.

71. Ehrenhalt, "'New Right' Plans Move to Change Congress," 3028.

72. Richard A. Viguerie, "An Alternative Plan," *Conservative Digest*, August 1976.

73. "Final Fundraising Letter for Approval for State Parties in Tennessee, New Jersey, Oklahoma and Connecticut," n.d., box 18, folder "Presidential/Republican National Committee/Congressional Fundraising Letters (1)," Robert P. Visser Papers, GRFL.

74. "Final Fundraising Letter for Approval for State Parties"; Appeal from Gerald Ford to Barry N. Roth, August 10, 1976, box 18, folder "Presidential/Republican National Committee/Congressional Fundraising Letters (1)," Visser Papers; Appeal from Gerald Ford, August 18, 1976, Visser Papers.

75. For populism in the 1976 presidential election, see for example Mieczkowski, *Gerald Ford*, 338–40. See also Williams, *God's Own Party*, 121–32; Flippen, *Jimmy Carter*; Freedman, "The Religious Right."

76. Crawford, "Richard Viguerie's Bid for Power," 105–106.

77. Viguerie, "An Alternative Plan."

78. "Why the 'New Right' Isn't Doing Well at the Polls," 158, 160.

79. For the negotiations between the United States and Panama over the Panama Canal issue, see Clymer, *Drawing the Line*, 6–9.

80. Clymer, *Drawing the Line*, 6–9.

81. Clymer, *Drawing the Line*, 9.

82. Alan Abelson, "Up and Down Wall Street," *Barron's National Business and Financial Weekly*, September 12, 1977, 1.

83. Clymer, *Drawing the Line*, 34.

84. Letter from Frank McDonald to Paul Laxalt, August 15, 1975, box 61, folder 5 "California, July & August 1975," Citizens for Reagan Records.

85. Clymer, *Drawing the Line*, 42.

86. Bernard Gwertzman, "Carter Says He Will Probably Meet Brezhnev in 1977, Possibly in U.S.," *New York Times*, December 28, 1976, 1.

87. Clymer, *Drawing the Line*, 43.

88. Clymer, *Drawing the Line*, 50–52.

89. Critchlow, *Phyllis Schlafly*, 256–57.

90. "The Proposed Treaty: Preliminary Thoughts," *National Review*, September 2, 1977, 981.

91. James Burnham, "The Protracted Conflict," *National Review*, September 16, 1977, 1043.

92. Burnham, "The Protracted Conflict," 1072.

93. S. I. Hayakawa, "After the Canal Treaties," *New York Times*, October 25, 1977, 37.

94. William J. Lanouette, "The Panama Canal Treaties—Playing in Peoria and in the Senate," *National Journal*, no. 41, October 8, 1977, 1556, 1559–60.

95. Peter Kiernan, "'New Right' Counts on Groundswell of Discontent," *Christian Science Monitor*, May 18, 1978.

96. "Canal Treaty an Issue?" *Herald News*, October 6, 1977.

97. Joe Aaron, "Panama Canal Issue Rallies Conservatives," *Green Bay Press-Gazette*, November 15, 1977.

98. Appeal from Ronald Reagan, December 7, 1977, box 24, folder 1 "Memos to the committee, 1977," Weyrich Papers.

99. Appeal from Ronald Reagan, December 7, 1977; Lanouette, "The Panama Canal Treaties," 1557.

100. Rudy Abramson, "Conservatives Against the Canal Treaties Planning a Multi-Media Blitz for January," *Los Angeles Times*, November 7, 1977, 5.

101. Letter from Kevin Walters to Jimmy Carter, September 8, 1977, box 2, folder "Direct Mail Samples—Panama Canal [O/A 2944]," Valerio Giannini Files, Jimmy Carter Presidential Library.

102. Letter from Minna O. Schaefer to Jimmy Carter, September 10, 1977, box 2, folder "Direct Mail Samples—Panama Canal [O/A 2944]," Giannini Files.

103. Abramson, "Conservatives Against the Canal Treaties," 5.

104. *American Political Report* 7, no. 3 (October 28, 1977).

105. Christopher Buchanan, "New Right: 'Many Times More Effective' Now," *Congressional Quarterly*, December 24, 1977, 2650.

106. Buchanan, "New Right," 2649.

107. McMillan, "What Is the New Right Up To," A1, A4.

108. Michael Knight, "Presidential Is Visiting Three States Where Democrats Face Problems," *New York Times*, February 18, 1978, 11; Michael Knight, "1980 Primary Off to Early Start for G.O.P. in New Hampshire," *New York Times*, December 2, 1978, 12.

109. McIntyre, *The Fear Brokers*, 7, 91, 60.

110. Robert Bruce Harris, "History of the Congressional Club," 1979, 3, box 91, folder "The Congressional Club," Group Research, Inc. Records.

111. For the biography of Jesse Helms, see Link, *Righteous Warrior*; Thrift, *Conservative Bias*. See also Paul Taylor, "Helms Modernizes GOP Political Machine for the Electronic Age," *Washington Post*, October 15,1982, A2.

112. "North Carolina's Congressional Club Working Hard for Strong America," *Conservative Digest*, December 1980, 17.

113. On the role of Viguerie's direct mail in the Congressional Club, see Link, *Righteous Warrior*, 145–46. For Jesse Helms's assistance in the establishment of the Conservative Caucus and the National Conservative Political Action Committee, see Lichtman, *White Protestant Nation*, 310–11.

114. Wilentz, *The Age of Reagan*, 66–68; Link, *Righteous Warrior*, 150–58.

115. Harris, "History of the Congressional Club," 2.

116. John F. Stacks, "The Machine That Jesse Built," *Nation*, September 14, 1981, 39; "North Carolina's Congressional Club Working Hard for Strong America," 17; Link, *Righteous Warrior*, 194.

117. Appeal from Ronald Reagan, March 11, 1977, box 159, folder "Helms, Jesse (Sen.), R-NC," Group Research, Inc. Records; Appeal from Jesse Helms, September 15, 1978, Group Research, Inc. Records.

118. Fialka, "The Godfather of the 'New Right' Feels the Torch Is Passing"; Stacks, "The Machine That Jesse Built," 39.

119. "Reagan's Relations with Hard-Liners Are Strained," *Honolulu Star-Bulletin*, April 27, 1978.

120. Bruce W. Eberle to Mike Deaver, January 23, 1979, box 105, folder "Direct Mail," Ronald Reagan 1980 Presidential Campaign Papers, Ronald Reagan Presidential Library; Bruce W. Eberle & Association, Inc., "Fund Raising Proposal Prepared For: 1980

Reagan Presidential Campaign," May 15, 1978, box 100, folder "Campaign Finance—Fundraising (1)," Ronald Reagan 1980 Presidential Campaign Papers.

121. For the background of L. Robert Morgan, see for example, letter from L. Robert Morgan to Lyn Nofziger, January 16, 1979, box 105, folder "Direct Mail," Ronald Reagan 1980 Presidential Campaign Papers. For Morgan's remark on Phil Joanou and SFM, see letter from L. Robert Morgan to Ed Meese, July 19, 1979, Ronald Reagan 1980 Presidential Campaign Papers.

122. Campaign 80 Marketing Plan, August 8, 1980, box 101, folder "Campaign '80 Marketing Plan, 8/8/1980 (1)," Ronald Reagan 1980 Presidential Campaign Papers.

123. Appeal from Ronald Reagan to Ed Meese, January 2, 1980, box 111, folder "Solicitation Letters (1)," Ronald Reagan 1980 Presidential Campaign Papers. Ed Meese was a staff member of the Reagan campaign. See Memo from Roger J. Stone to Ed Meese, April 4, 1980, box 100, folder "Campaign Finance—Fundraising (2)," Ronald Reagan 1980 Presidential Campaign Papers.

124. Appeal from John T. Dolan to Ed Meese, January 25, 1980, box 111, folder "Solicitation Letters (2)," Ronald Reagan 1980 Presidential Campaign Papers.

125. Appeal from Bob Bauman, August 14, 1980, box 7, folder "American Conservative Union, Washington, DC, 1980," Group Research, Inc. Records.

126. Memo from David A. Schwartz to Richard O'Reilly, October 15, 1980, box 221, folder "[Advertising Strategy]," Ronald Reagan 1980 Presidential Campaign Papers.

127. Anthony R. Dolan, "The Opposition Campaign Some Proposals," August 4, 1980, box 229, folder "Advertising—Anti-Carter (3)," Ronald Reagan 1980 Presidential Campaign Papers.

128. Richard A. Viguerie, "Conservatives Must Work Hard and Vote for Ronald Reagan for President," *Conservative Digest* 6, no. 9 (September 1980): 48.

129. Richard A. Viguerie, "Conservatives Owe Much to Reagan, Direct Mail," *Conservative Digest* 6, no. 11 (November 1980): 39–40.

130. Annelise Anderson, The 1976 Presidential Election Budget and Control, n.d., box 100, folder "Reagan for President Finances (1)," Ronald Reagan 1980 Presidential Campaign Papers.

Epilogue

1. American Opinion Bookstore Manual, 27, box 1, folder 1 "Manual," John Birch Society Records, John Hay Library, Brown University.

2. Letter from Wallis W. Wood to Arthur Maranjian, March 6, 1975, box 5, folder 9 "Wholesale Book Division, 1973–1976," JBS Records.

3. Howard Phillips, "Reagan's 'New Beginning,'" L. Tom Perry Special Collections, Brigham Young University.

4. Richard A. Viguerie, "Can the President Hold On to His Conservative Base?" *Conservative Digest* 7, no. 3 (March 1981): 39–40.

5. Phillips, "Reagan's 'New Beginning.'"

6. Richard A. Viguerie, "President's Problem Is With Personnel, Not Policy," *Conservative Digest* 7, no. 2 (February 1981): 39–40; John D. Lofton Jr., "An Open Letter to President Reagan," *Conservative Digest* 7, no. 2 (February 1981): 1–2.

7. Richard A. Viguerie, "President's Choice of O'Connor Could Be Politically Damaging to New Republican Coalition," *Conservative Digest* 7, no. 8 (August 1981): 40.

8. "Goldwater Tells Opponents of O'Connor Nomination to 'Back Off,'" *New York Times*, July 10, 1981, A11.

9. Richard A. Viguerie, "An Open Letter to the President," *Conservative Digest* 8, no. 2 (February 1982): 31–32.

10. Richard A. Viguerie, "It's Not Too Late for Reagan," *Conservative Digest* 8, no. 12 (December 1982): 56; Richard A. Viguerie, "Conservatives Need to Play Their Game," *Conservative Digest* 9, no. 1 (January 1983): 56.

11. Rusher, *The Rise of the Right*, 314.

12. Williams, *God's Own Party*, 194–98; Young, *We Gather Together*, 210–22.

13. Phillips, "Reagan's 'New Beginning'"; Edwards, *The Conservative Revolution*, 239.

14. Tønnessen, *How Two Political Entrepreneurs*, 286–89; Gottfried and Fleming, *The Conservative Movement*, 93; Diamond, *Spiritual Warfare*, 59–60.

15. Sabato, *The Rise of Political Consultants*, 223–24. See also Issenberg, *The Victory Lab*.

16. For the use of direct mail by environmental organizations, see Bosso, "The Color of Money," 113–15; Shaiko, *Voices and Echoes*, 93–103. On the growth of the direct mail industry, see Shaiko, *Voices and Echoes*, 93–94; Bosso, *Environment, Inc.* 105–18.

17. Natasha Singer, "Mapping, and Sharing, the Consumer Genome," *New York Times*, June 16, 2012. In October 2018, Acxiom sold the Acxiom Marketing Solutions division, which dealt with the datasets of consumers' information. Acxiom reorganized itself under the brand of LiveRamp, focusing its resources on "offline matching" that helps connect offline data to online patterns of activity. See "Acxiom Marketing Solutions Sale Now Complete," Press Release Details, LiveRamp, October 1, 2018, https://investors.liveramp.com/news-and-events/press-release-details/2018/Acxiom-Marketing-Solutions-Sale-Now-Complete/default.aspx.

18. Stephen Gausch, "Direct Mail Is Far from Dead for Most Credit Card Issues," Acxiom, March 1, 2019, https://www.acxiom.com/blog/direct-mail-is-far-from-dead-for-most-credit-card-issuers/.

19. For the works on Democrats' use of digital networking for their political campaigns since the 1990s, see Kreiss, *Taking Our Country Back*; Karpf, *The MoveOn Effect*.

20. "Ted Cruz Using Firm that Harvested Data on Millions of Unwitting Facebook Users," *Guardian*, December 11, 2015, https://www.theguardian.com/us-news/2015/dec/11/senator-ted-cruz-president-campaign-facebook-user-data.

21. Matthew Rosenberg, Nicholas Confessore, and Carole Cadwalladr, "How Trump Consultants Exploited the Facebook Data of Millions," *New York Times*, March 17, 2018, https://www.nytimes.com/2018/03/17/us/politics/cambridge-analytica-trump-campaign.html.

22. "Revealed: 50 Million Facebook Profiles Harvested for Cambridge Analytica in Major Data Breach," *Guardian*, March 17, 2018, https://www.theguardian.com/news/2018/mar/17/cambridge-analytica-facebook-influence-us-election; Matthew Rosenberg and Sheera Frenkel, "Facebook's Role in Data Misuse Sets Off Storms on Two Continents," *New York Times*, March 18, 2018, https://www.nytimes.com/2018/03/18/us/cambridge-analytica-facebook-privacy-data.html; Mattathias Schwartz, "Facebook Failed to Protect 30 Million Users from Having Their Data Harvested by Trump Campaign Affiliate," *Intercept*, March 31, 2017, https://theintercept.com/2017/03/30/facebook-failed-to-protect-30-million-users-from-having-their-data-harvested-by-trump-campaign-affiliate/.

23. Carole Cadwalladr, "If You're Not Terrified about Facebook, You Haven't Been Paying Attention," *Guardian*, July 26, 2020, https://www.theguardian.com/commentisfree/2020/jul/26/with-facebook-we-are-already-through-the-looking-glass.

24. Sabato, *The Rise of Political Consultants*, 241.

25. Godwin, *One Billion Dollars of Influence*, 48–49; Marshall Ganz, "Voters in the Crosshairs: How Technology and the Market Are Destroying Politics," *American Prospect* (Winter 1994): 100–109. See also Cosgrove, *Branded Conservatives*, 12, 18, 56–59; Godwin and Mitchell, "The Implications of Direct Mail"; Johnson, "Interest Group Recruitment."

26. Putnam, "Bowling Alone," 75; Putnam, *Bowling Alone*. See also Lin, Cook, and Burt, *Social Capital*; Skocpol, *Diminished Democracy*.

27. For example, the website of Blue State Digital, which conducted fundraising campaigns for Barack Obama in the 2008 presidential election, notes that the organization built up a "massive grassroots movement" through its online fundraising operation. See "How Do You Change the Way Campaigns Are Won?" Obama 2008 Campaign, Digital Case Study, Blue State Digital, accessed February 8, 2019, https://www.bluestatedigital.com/our-work/obama-for-america-2008/.

BIBLIOGRAPHY

Archival Sources

Arizona State University Library, Tempe
Personal and Political Papers of Senator Barry M. Goldwater
Brigham Young University, Harold B. Lee Library, Provo, Utah
L. Tom Perry Special Collections
Brown University Library, Providence, Rhode Island
John Birch Society Records
Jimmy Carter Presidential Library, Atlanta, Georgia
Valerio Giannini Files
Columbia University, Rare Book & Manuscript Library, New York
Group Research, Inc. Records
Duke University, David M. Rubenstein Rare Book & Manuscript Library, Durham, North Carolina (DU)
J. Walter Thompson Company Records
Lester Wunderman Papers
Dwight D. Eisenhower Presidential Library, Abilene, Kansas (DDEL)
Dwight D. Eisenhower Papers as President
Records of the Office of the Chairman of the Republican National Committee (Leonard W. Hall)
Robert Humphreys Papers
Maxwell M. Rabb Papers
Arthur E. Summerfield Papers
Gerald R. Ford Presidential Library, Ann Arbor, Michigan (GRFL)
President Ford Committee Records
Robert P. Visser Papers
Hoover Institution Archives, Stanford, California (HIA)
Citizens for Reagan Records
Lee Edwards Papers
Walter H. Judd Papers
Alfred Kohlberg Papers
Marvin Liebman Papers

Young Americans for Freedom Records
Indiana University/Purdue University, IUPUI University Library, Ruth Lilly Special
    Collections & Archives, Indianapolis
Oram Group, Inc. Records
Lyndon B. Johnson Presidential Library, Austin, Texas (LBJL)
Records of the Democratic National Committee
White House Central Files
Library of Congress, Manuscripts and Archives Division, Washington, DC
William J. Baroody Papers
Democratic Study Group Records
William A. Rusher Papers
Paul M. Weyrich Scrapbooks
Richard Nixon Presidential Library, Yorba Linda, California
Jeb Stuart Magruder Papers
Ronald Reagan Presidential Library, Simi Valley, California
Ronald Reagan 1980 Presidential Campaign Papers
Harry S. Truman Presidential Library, Independence, Missouri (HSTL)
Records of the Democratic National Committee
Stephen A. Mitchell Papers
University of Arkansas, Special Collections Department, Fayetteville
Billy James Hargis Papers
University of Kansas, Kenneth Spencer Research Library, Lawrence
Wilcox Collection of Contemporary Political Movements
University of Texas, Austin, Briscoe Center for American History, Austin
Stephen Shadegg/Barry Goldwater Collection
University of Wyoming, American Heritage Center, Laramie
Paul M. Weyrich Papers
Yale University Library, Manuscripts and Archives, New Haven, Connecticut
William F. Buckley Jr. Papers

Periodicals

Advertising Age
AFL-CIO News
American Political Report
American Prospect
Atlantic
Barron's National Business and Financial Weekly
Bergen County Record (New Jersey)
Boston Globe
Business Week

Chicago Sun-Times
Chicago Tribune
Christian Science Monitor
CP Magazine
Congressional Quarterly
Conservative Digest
Columbia Journalism Review
CRS Report for Congress
Daily Signal
Detroit News
Forum
Green Bay Press-Gazette
Passaic Herald News
Honolulu Star-Bulletin
Indianapolis Star
Kansas City Times
Life
Los Angeles Times
Minneapolis Star
Nation
National Journal
National Observer
National Review
NCEC Campaign Report
New Guard
New Republic
New York Daily News
New York Herald Tribune
New York Times
Orange County Register (California)
Oregonian
Philadelphia Inquirer
Providence Sunday Journal
Richmond Times Dispatch
Right Report
Rocky Mountain News
San Francisco Chronicle
U.S. News & World Report
Public Interest
Republican Progress
Sponsor
Wall Street Journal

Washington Daily News
Washington Evening Star
Washington Post
Washington Star
Western Pennsylvania Historical Magazine

Memoirs

Ford, Gerald R. *A Time to Heal: The Autobiography of Gerald R. Ford*. New York: Harper & Row, 1979.

Liebman, Marvin. *Coming Out Conservative: An Autobiography*. San Francisco: Chronicle Books, 1992.

Viguerie, Richard A. *Conservatives Betrayed: How George W. Bush and Other Big Government Republicans Hijacked the Conservative Cause*. Los Angeles: Bonus Books, 2006.

——. *The Establishment vs. The People*. Chicago: Regnery, 1983.

——. *The New Right: We're Ready to Lead*. Falls Church, VA: Viguerie, 1980.

Viguerie, Richard A., and David Franke. *America's Right Turn: How Conservatives Used New and Alternative Media to Take Over America*. Chicago: Bonus Books, 2004.

Oral History Interviews

Interview with Author

Morton Blackwell, October 19, 2015

Harold Oram Oral History Project Interview, Indiana University/Purdue University

Marvin Liebman, July 18, 1992

Lee Edwards Interviews, Hoover Institution Archives

Morton Blackwell, January 13, 1992
Richard Viguerie, February 5, 1992
Paul Weyrich, February 18, 1992
Paul Weyrich, April 16, 1992
Paul Weyrich, April 17, 1992
Paul Weyrich, May 5, 1996

Books

Alexander, Herbert E. *Financing the 1960 Election*. Princeton, NJ: Citizens Research Foundation, 1962.

———. *Financing the 1964 Election*. Princeton, NJ: Citizens Research Foundation, 1966.

———. *Financing the 1968 Election*. Lexington, MA: Heath Lexington Books, 1971.

———. *Financing Politics: Money, Elections, and Political Reform*. 3rd ed. Washington, DC: CQ Press, 1984.

———. *Money in Politics*. Washington: Public Affairs Press, 1972.

Andrew, John A., III. *The Other Side of the Sixties: Young Americans for Freedom and the Rise of Conservative Politics*. New Brunswick, NJ: Rutgers University Press, 1997.

Applegate, Edd. *The Rise of Advertising in the United States: A History of Innovation to 1960*. Lanham, MD: Scarecrow Press, 2012.

Armstrong, Richard. *The Next Hurrah: The Communications Revolution in American Politics*. New York: Beech Tree Books, 1988.

Bacchetta, P., and Margaret Power, eds. *Right-Wing Women: From Conservatives to Extremists around the World*. New York: Routledge, 2002.

Bailey, Beth L., and Dave Farber, eds. *America in the Seventies*. Lawrence: University Press of Kansas, 2004.

Baker, Kelly. *Gospel According to the Klan: The KKK's Appeal to Protestant America, 1915–1930*. Lawrence: University Press of Kansas, 2011.

Barnhisel, Greg, and Catherine Turner, eds. *Pressing the Fight: Print, Propaganda, and the Cold War*. Amherst: University of Massachusetts Press, 2010.

Barnouw, Erik. *The Golden Web: A History of Broadcasting in the United States*. Vol. II. New York: Oxford University Press, 1968.

———. *The Image Empire: A History of Broadcasting in the United States*. Vol. II. New York: Oxford University Press, 1970.

———. *Tube of Plenty: The Evolution of American Television*. 2nd ed. New York: Oxford University Press, 1990.

Baughman, James L. *The Republic of Mass Culture: Journalism, Filmmaking, and Broadcasting in America since 1941*. 2nd ed. Baltimore: Johns Hopkins University Press, 1997.

Baumgartner, Jody C. *Modern Presidential Electioneering: An Organizational and Comparative Approach*. Westport, CT: Praeger, 2000.

Baus, Herbert M., and William B. Ross. *Politics Battle Plan*. New York: Macmillan, 1968.

Beeby, James M., ed. *Populism in the South Revisited: New Interpretations and New Departures*. Jackson: University Press of Mississippi, 2012.

Bell, Daniel, ed. *The New American Right*. New York: Criterion Books, 1955.

———. *The Radical Right: The New American Right, Expanded and Updated*. Garden City, NY: Doubleday, 1963.

Bell, Daniel. *The End of Ideology: On the Exhaustion of Political Ideas in the Fifties*. Glencoe, IL: Free Press, 1988.

Bellah, Robert Neelly, ed. *Habits of the Heart: Individualism and Commitment in American Life*. Berkeley: University of California Press, 1985.

Bennett, David H. *The Party of Fear: The American Far Right from Nativism to the Militia Movement*. Chapel Hill: University of North Carolina Press, 1988.

Benowitz, June Melby. *Days of Discontent: American Women and Right-Wing Politics, 1933–1945*. DeKalb: Northern Illinois University Press, 2002.

Berlet, Chip, and Matthew Nemiroff Lyons. *Right-Wing Populism in America: Too Close for Comfort*. New York: Guilford Press, 2000.

Bernhard, Nancy E. *U.S. Television News and Cold War Propaganda, 1947–1960*. New York: Cambridge University Press, 1999.

Berry, Jeffrey M. *The Interest Group Society*. Glenview, IL: Scott, Foresman, 1997.

Berry, Jeffrey M., and Sarah Sobieraj. *The Outrage Industry: Political Opinion Media and the New Incivility*. New York: Oxford University Press, 2014.

Bieger, Laura, and Christian Lammert, eds. *Revisiting the Sixties: Interdisciplinary Perspectives on America's Longest Decade*. Frankfurt: Campus Verlag, 2013.

Bjerre-Poulsen, Niels. *Right Face: Organizing the American Conservative Movement, 1945–65*. Copenhagen: Museum Tusculanum Press, 2002.

Blake, David Haven. *Liking Ike: Eisenhower, Advertising and the Rise of Celebrity Politics*. New York: Oxford University Press, 2016.

Blee, Kathleen M. *Women of the Klan: Racism and Gender in the 1920s*. Berkeley: University of California Press, 1991.

Bloodworth, Jeffrey. *Losing the Center: The Decline of American Liberalism, 1968–1992*. Lexington: University Press of Kentucky, 2013.

Bloom, Alexander. *Long Time Gone: Sixties America Then and Now*. New York: Oxford University Press, 2001.

Bloom, Allan David. *The Closing of the American Mind: How Higher Education Has Failed Democracy and Impoverished the Souls of Today's Students*. New York: Simon and Schuster, 1987.

Blumenthal, Sidney. *The Rise of the Counter-Establishment: From Conservative Ideology to Political Power*. New York: Times Books, 1986.

Bosso, Christopher J. *Environment, Inc.: From Grassroots to Beltway*. Lawrence: University Press of Kansas, 2005.

Bowen, Michael. *The Roots of Modern Conservatism: Dewey, Taft, and the Battle for the Soul of the Republican Party*. Chapel Hill: University of North Carolina Press, 2011.

Bracey, Christopher Alan. *Saviors or Sellouts: The Promise and Peril of Black Conservatism, from Booker T. Washington to Condoleezza Rice*. Boston: Beacon Press, 2008.

Braukman, Stacy Lorraine. *Communists and Perverts under the Palms: The Johns Committee in Florida, 1956–1965*. Gainesville: University Press of Florida, 2012.

Brennan, Mary C. *Turning Right in the Sixties: The Conservative Capture of the GOP*. Chapel Hill: University of North Carolina Press, 1995.

———. *Wives, Mothers, and the Red Menace: Conservative Women and the Crusade Against Communism*. Boulder: University Press of Colorado, 2008.

Brinkley, Alan. *Liberalism and Its Discontents*. Cambridge, MA: Harvard University Press, 1998.

———. *Voices of Protest: Huey Long, Father Coughlin, and the Great Depression*. New York: Knopf, 1982.

Brock, Gerald W. *The Second Information Revolution*. Cambridge, MA: Harvard University Press, 2003.

Brown, Richard D. *Knowledge Is Power: The Diffusion of Information in Early America, 1700–1865*. New York: Oxford University Press, 1989.

Broyles, J. Allen. *The John Birch Society, Anatomy of a Protest*. Boston: Beacon Press, 1964.

Bryce, James. *The American Commonwealth*. London: Macmillan, 1888.

Buckley, William F. *Flying High: Remembering Barry Goldwater*. New York: Basic Books, 2008.

Burke, Colin B. *Information and Intrigue: From Index Cards to Dewey Decimals to Alger Hiss*. Cambridge, MA: MIT Press, 2014.

Burke, Edmund, David P. Fidler, and Jennifer M. Welsh. *Empire and Community: Edmund Burke's Writings and Speeches on International Relations*. Boulder, CO: Westview Press, 1999.

Burns, Jennifer. *Goddess of the Market: Ayn Rand and the American Right*. New York: Oxford University Press, 2009.

Byrne, Jeb. *Out in Front: Preparing the Way for JKF and LBJ*. Albany: State University of New York Press, 2010.

Cadava, Geraldo L. *Standing on Common Ground: The Making of a Sunbelt Borderland*. Cambridge, MA: Harvard University Press, 2013.

Calhoun, Craig, ed. *Habermas and the Public Sphere*. Cambridge, MA: MIT Press, 1992.

Calhoun, Craig. *The Roots of Radicalism: Tradition, the Public Sphere, and Early Nineteenth-Century Social Movements*. Chicago: University of Chicago Press, 2012.

Carpenter, Joel A. *Revive Us Again: The Reawakening of American Fundamentalism*. New York: Oxford University Press, 1997.

Carson, Jamie L. *Ambition, Competition, and Electoral Reform: The Politics of Congressional Elections across Time*. Ann Arbor: University of Michigan Press, 2013.

Chalmers, David Mark. *Hooded Americanism: The History of the Ku Klux Klan*. 3rd ed. Durham, NC: Duke University Press, 1987.

Chandler, Alfred D. *The Visible Hand: The Managerial Revolution in American Business*. Cambridge, MA: Belknap Press, 1977.

Chandler, Alfred D., and James W. Cortada, eds. *Nation Transformed by Information: How Information Has Shaped the United States from Colonial Times to the Present*. New York: Oxford University Press, 2000.

Cherny, Robert W., William Issel, and Kieran Walsh Taylor. *American Labor and the Cold War: Grassroots Politics and Postwar Political Culture*. New Brunswick, NJ: Rutgers University Press, 2004.

Clymer, Adam. *Drawing the Line at the Big Ditch: The Panama Canal Treaties and the Rise of the Right*. Lawrence: University Press of Kansas, 2008.

Cohen, Michael A. *American Maelstrom: The 1968 Election and the Politics of Division*. New York: Oxford University Press, 2016.

Connell, Tula A. *Conservative Counterrevolution: Challenging Liberalism in 1950s Milwaukee*. Urbana: University of Illinois Press, 2016.

Cosgrove, Kenneth M. *Branded Conservatives: How the Brand Brought the Right from the Fringes to the Center of American Politics*. New York: P. Lang, 2007.

Cowie, Jefferson. *Stayin' Alive: The 1970s and the Last Days of the Working Class*. New York: New Press, 2010.

Crăiuțu, Aurelian, and Jeremy Jennings, eds. *Tocqueville on America after 1840: Letters and Other Writings*. New York: Cambridge University Press, 2009.

Crawford, Alan. *Thunder on the Right: The "New Right" and the Politics of Resentment*. New York: Pantheon, 1980.

Crenson, Matthew A., and Benjamin Ginsberg. *Downsizing Democracy: How America Sidelined Its Citizens and Privatized Its Public*. Baltimore: Johns Hopkins University Press, 2002.

Crespino, Joseph. *In Search of Another Country: Mississippi and the Conservative Counterrevolution*. Princeton, NJ: Princeton University Press, 2007.

———. *Strom Thurmond's America*. New York: Hill and Wang, 2012.

Critchlow, Donald T. *The Conservative Ascendancy: How the GOP Right Made Political History*. Cambridge, MA: Harvard University Press, 2007.

———. *Phyllis Schlafly and Grassroots Conservatism: A Woman's Crusade*. Princeton, NJ: Princeton University Press, 2005.

———. *When Hollywood Was Right: How Movie Stars, Studio Moguls, and Big Business Remade American Politics*. New York: Cambridge University Press, 2013.

Crossley, Nick, and John Michael Roberts. *After Habermas: New Perspectives on the Public Sphere*. London: Wiley-Blackwell, 2004.

Cunningham, David. *Klansville, U.S.A.: The Rise and Fall of the Civil Rights-Era Ku Klux Klan*. New York: Oxford University Press, 2013.

Cunningham, Sean P. *Cowboy Conservatism: Texas and the Rise of the Modern Right*. Lexington: University Press of Kentucky, 2010.

Dallek, Matthew. *The Right Moment: Ronald Reagan's First Victory and the Decisive Turning Point in American Politics*. New York: Oxford University Press, 2004.

Damrosch, Leopold. *Tocqueville's Discovery of America*. New York: Farrar, Straus and Giroux, 2010.

Davies, Gareth. *See Government Grow: Education Politics from Johnson to Reagan*. Lawrence: University Press of Kansas, 2007.

Decker, Jefferson. *The Other Rights Revolution: Conservative Lawyers and the Remaking of American Government*. New York: Oxford University Press, 2016.

Deery, Phillip. *Red Apple: Communism and McCarthyism in Cold War New York*. Bronx, NY: Fordham University Press, 2014.

Delegard, Kirsten. *Battling Miss Bolsheviki: The Origins of Female Conservatism in the United States*. Philadelphia: University of Pennsylvania Press, 2012.

Delton, Jennifer A. *Rethinking the 1950s: How Anticommunism and the Cold War Made America Liberal*. New York: Cambridge University Press, 2013.

Diamond, Sara. *Roads to Dominion: Right-Wing Movements and Political Power in the United States*. New York: Guilford Press, 1995.

———. *Spiritual Warfare: The Politics of the Christian Right*. Boston: South End Press, 1989.

Diggins, John Patrick. *The Proud Decades: America in War and in Peace, 1941–1960*. New York: Norton, 1988.

———. *Ronald Reagan: Fate, Freedom, and the Making of History*. New York: Norton, 2008.

———. *Up from Communism: Conservative Odysseys in American Intellectual History*. New York: Harper & Row, 1975.

Dillard, Angela D. *Guess Who's Coming to Dinner Now? Multicultural Conservatism in America*. New York: New York University Press, 2001.

Dionne, E. J. *Why Americans Hate Politics*. New York: Simon & Schuster, 1991.

Dochuk, Darren. *From Bible Belt to Sunbelt: Plain-Folk Religion, Grassroots Politics, and the Rise of Evangelical Conservatism*. New York: W. W. Norton, 2011.

Domhoff, G. William. *The Myth of Liberal Ascendancy: Corporate Dominance from the Great Depression to the Great Recession*. Boulder, CO: Paradigm Publishers, 2013.

Donaldson, Gary. *Liberalism's Last Hurrah: The Presidential Campaign of 1964*. Armonk, NY: M. E. Sharpe, 2003.

Doody, Colleen. *Detroit's Cold War: The Origins of Postwar Conservatism*. Urbana: University of Illinois Press, 2013.

Dowland, Seth. *Family Values and the Rise of the Christian Right*. Philadelphia: University of Pennsylvania Press, 2015.

Dubose, Lou, Jan Reid, and Carl M. Cannon. *Boy Genius: Karl Rove, the Brains behind the Remarkable Political Triumph of George W. Bush*. New York: PublicAffairs, 2003.

Dulio, David A. *For Better or Worse? How Political Consultants Are Changing Elections in the United States*. Albany: State University of New York Press, 2004.

Dupont, Carolyn Renée. *Mississippi Praying: Southern White Evangelicals and the Civil Rights Movement, 1945–1975*. New York: NYU Press, 2013.

Edwards, Lee. *The Conservative Revolution: The Movement that Remade America*. New York: Free Press, 1999.

———. *The Essential Ronald Reagan: A Profile in Courage, Justice, and Wisdom*. Lanham, MD: Rowman & Littlefield, 2005.

———. *Goldwater: The Man Who Made a Revolution*. Washington, DC: Regnery, 1995.

———. *Missionary for Freedom: The Life and Times of Walter Judd*. New York: Paragon House, 1990.

———. *Ronald Reagan, a Political Biography.* Rev., updated, and expanded ed. Houston, TX: Nordland Pub. International, 1980.

Edwards, Rebecca. *Angels in the Machinery: Gender in American Party Politics from the Civil War to the Progressive Era.* New York: Oxford University Press, 1997.

Eisenstadt, Abraham Seldin, ed. *Reconsidering Tocqueville's Democracy in America.* New Brunswick, NJ: Rutgers University Press, 1988.

Epstein, Benjamin R., and Arnold Forster. *The Radical Right: Report on the John Birch Society and Its Allies.* New York: Vintage Books, 1967.

Evans, Rowland, and Robert D. Novak. *The Reagan Revolution.* New York: Dutton, 1981.

Farber, David R., and Jeff Roche, eds. *The Conservative Sixties.* New York: Peter Lang, 2003.

Fetner, Tina. *How the Religious Right Shaped Lesbian and Gay Activism.* Minneapolis: University of Minnesota Press, 2008.

Fischer, David Hackett. *The Revolution of American Conservatism.* New York: Harper & Row, 1965.

Flamm, Michael W. *Law and Order: Street Crime, Civil Unrest, and the Crisis of Liberalism in the 1960s.* New York: Columbia University Press, 2005.

Flippen, J. Brooks. *Jimmy Carter, the Politics of Family, and the Rise of the Religious Right.* Athens: University of Georgia Press, 2011.

Formisano, Ronald P. *Boston against Busing: Race, Class, and Ethnicity in the 1960s and 1970s.* 2nd ed. Chapel Hill: University of North Carolina Press, 2004.

———. *For the People: American Populist Movements from the Revolution to the 1850s.* Chapel Hill: University of North Carolina Press, 2008.

Frank, Thomas. *The Conquest of Cool: Business Culture, Counterculture, and the Rise of Hip Consumerism.* Chicago: University of Chicago Press, 1997.

———. *What's the Matter with Kansas? How Conservatives Won the Heart of America.* New York: Metropolitan Books, 2004.

Fraser, Steve, and Joshua Benjamin Freeman. *Audacious Democracy: Labor, Intellectuals, and the Social Reconstruction of America.* Boston: Houghton Mifflin, 1997.

Frederickson, Kari A. *The Dixiecrat Revolt and the End of the Solid South, 1932–1968.* Chapel Hill: University of North Carolina Press, 2001.

Friedenberg, Robert V. *Communication Consultants in Political Campaigns: Ballot Box Warriors.* Westport, CT: Praeger, 1997.

Friedman, Murray. *The Neoconservative Revolution: Jewish Intellectuals and the Shaping of Public Policy.* New York: Cambridge University Press, 2005.

Frisk, David B. *If Not Us, Who? William Rusher, National Review, and the Conservative Movement.* Wilmington, DE: ISI Books, 2011.

Gadsden, Brett V. *Between North and South: Delaware, Desegregation, and the Myth of American Sectionalism.* Philadelphia: University of Pennsylvania Press, 2013.

Gifford, Laura Jane. *The Center Cannot Hold: The 1960 Presidential Election and the Rise of Modern Conservatism.* DeKalb: Northern Illinois University Press, 2009.

Gifford, Laura Jane, and Daniel K. Williams, eds. *The Right Side of the Sixties: Re-examining Conservatism's Decade of Transformation*. New York: Palgrave Macmillan, 2012.

Gillon, Steven M. *Politics and Vision: The ADA and American Liberalism, 1947–1985*. New York: Oxford University Press, 1987.

———. *"That's Not What We Meant to Do": Reform and Its Unintended Consequences in Twentieth-Century America*. New York: W. W. Norton, 2000.

Gitelman, Lisa. *Paper Knowledge: Toward a Media History of Documents*. Durham, NC: Duke University Press, 2014.

Gitlin, Todd. *The Sixties: Years of Hope, Days of Rage*. New York: Bantam Books, 1993.

Glenn, Brian J., and Steven Michael Teles, eds. *Conservatism and American Political Development*. New York: Oxford University Press, 2009.

Godwin, R. Kenneth. *One Billion Dollars of Influence: The Direct Marketing of Politics*. Chatham, NJ: Chatham House Publishers, 1988.

Goldberg, Robert Alan. *Barry Goldwater*. New Haven, CT: Yale University Press, 1995.

Goldstein, Robert Justin. *Little "Red Scares": Anti-Communism and Political Repression in the United States, 1921–1946*. Surrey: Ashgate, 2014.

Gonzales, Manuel G., and Richard Delgado. *The Politics of Fear: How Republicans Use Money, Race, and the Media to Win*. Boulder, CO: Paradigm, 2006.

Gottfried, Paul. *Conservatism in America: Making Sense of the American Right*. New York: Palgrave, 2007.

Gottfried, Paul, and Thomas Fleming. *The Conservative Movement*. Boston: Twayne, 1988.

Graves, Karen. *And They Were Wonderful Teachers: Florida's Purge of Gay and Lesbian Teachers*. Urbana: University of Illinois Press, 2009.

Greason, Walter. *Suburban Erasure: How the Suburbs Ended the Civil Rights Movement in New Jersey*. Madison, NJ: Fairleigh Dickinson University Press, 2013.

Green, Donald P., and Alan S. Gerber. *Get Out the Vote: How to Increase Voter Turnout*. 2nd ed. Washington, DC: Brookings Institution Press, 2008.

Green, John C., ed. *Politics, Professionalism, and Power: Modern Party Organization and the Legacy of Ray C. Bliss*. Lanham, MD: University Press of America, 1994.

Greenberg, David. *Republic of Spin: An Inside History of the American Presidency*. New York: W. W. Norton, 2016.

Habermas, Jürgen. *The Structural Transformation of the Public Sphere: An Inquiry into a Category of Bourgeois Society*. Cambridge, MA: MIT Press, 1989.

Hacker, Jacob S., and Paul Pierson. *Off Center: The Republican Revolution and the Erosion of American Democracy*. New Haven, CT: Yale University Press, 2005.

Hall, Simon. *American Patriotism, American Protest: Social Movements since the Sixties*. Philadelphia: University of Pennsylvania Press, 2010.

Harding, Susan Friend. *The Book of Jerry Falwell: Fundamentalist Language and Politics*. Princeton, NJ: Princeton University Press, 2000.

Hardisty, Jean V. *Mobilizing Resentment: Conservative Resurgence from the John Birch Society to the Promise Keepers.* Boston: Beacon Press, 1999.

Hart, Gary Warren. *Right from the Start: A Chronicle of the McGovern Campaign.* New York: Quadrangle, 1973.

Hart, Jeffrey Peter. *The Making of the American Conservative Mind:* National Review *and Its Times.* Wilmington, DE: ISI Books, 2005.

Hartz, Louis. *The Liberal Tradition in America: An Interpretation of American Political Thought since the Revolution.* New York: Harcourt, Brace, 1955.

Hawley, George. *Right-Wing Critics of American Conservatism.* Lawrence: University Press of Kansas, 2016.

Hayward, Steven F. *The Age of Reagan, 1964–1980: The Fall of the Old Liberal Order.* Roseville, CA: Forum, 2001.

Heard, Alexander. *The Costs of Democracy.* Garden City, NY: Doubleday, 1962.

Heineman, Kenneth J. *God Is a Conservative: Religion, Politics, and Morality in Contemporary America.* New York: NYU Press, 1998.

Heldrich, Gerard C. *The Painting of Elmer: Gertz v. John Birch Society.* Los Angeles: Authors Unlimited, 1989.

Hemmer, Nicole. *Messengers of the Right: Conservative Media and the Transformation of American Politics.* Philadelphia: University of Pennsylvania Press, 2016.

Hendershot, Cynthia. *Anti-Communism and Popular Culture in Mid-Century America.* Jefferson, NC: McFarland, 2003.

Hendershot, Heather. *What's Fair on the Air? Cold War Right-Wing Broadcasting and the Public Interest.* Chicago: University of Chicago Press, 2011.

Hershey, William L., and John Clifford Green. *Mr. Chairman: The Life and Times of Ray C. Bliss.* Akron, OH: University of Akron Press, 2017.

Himmelstein, Jerome L. *To the Right: The Transformation of American Conservatism.* Berkeley: University of California Press, 1990.

Hixson, William B. *Search for the American Right Wing: An Analysis of the Social Science Record, 1955–1987.* Princeton, NJ: Princeton University Press, 1992.

Hofstadter, Richard. *Anti-Intellectualism in American Life.* New York: Knopf, 1963.

Holli, Melvin G. *The Wizard of Washington: Emil Hurja, Franklin Roosevelt, and the Birth of Public Opinion Polling.* New York: Palgrave, 2002.

Howard, Philip N. *New Media Campaigns and the Managed Citizen.* New York: Cambridge University Press, 2006.

Howison, Jeffrey D. *The 1980 Presidential Election: Ronald Reagan and the Shaping of the American Conservative Movement.* New York: Routledge Taylor & Francis Group, 2014.

Hustwit, William P. *James J. Kilpatrick: Salesman for Segregation.* Chapel Hill: University of North Carolina Press, 2013.

Hutchins, Lavern C. *The John Birch Society and United States Foreign Policy.* New York: Pageant Press, 1968.

Igo, Sarah E. *The Known Citizen: A History of Privacy in Modern America.* Cambridge, MA: Harvard University Press, 2018.

Inglehart, Ronald. *Culture Shift in Advanced Industrial Society*. Princeton, NJ: Princeton University Press, 1990.

Ionescu, Ghiţa, and Ernest Gellner, eds. *Populism: Its Meaning and National Characteristics*. New York: Macmillan, 1969.

Issenberg, Sasha. *The Victory Lab: The Secret Science of Winning Campaigns*. New York: Broadway Books, 2013.

Isserman, Maurice, and Michael Kazin. *America Divided: The Civil War of the 1960s*. 2nd ed. New York: Oxford University Press, 2004.

Jackall, Robert, and Janice M. Hirota. *Image Makers: Advertising, Public Relations, and the Ethos of Advocacy*. Chicago: University of Chicago Press, 2000.

Jamieson, Kathleen Hall. *Packaging the Presidency: A History and Criticism of Presidential Campaign Advertising*. 3rd ed. New York: Oxford University Press, 1996.

Jamieson, Kathleen Hall, and Joseph N. Cappella. *Echo Chamber: Rush Limbaugh and the Conservative Media Establishment*. New York: Oxford University Press, 2008.

Jeansonne, Glen. *Women of the Far Right: The Mothers' Movement and World War II*. Chicago: University of Chicago Press, 1996.

Jenkins, Philip. *Decade of Nightmares: The End of the Sixties and the Making of Eighties America*. New York: Oxford University Press, 2006.

John Birch Society. *The Blue Book of the John Birch Society*. Edited by Robert Welch. Belmont, MA, 1961.

John, Richard R. *Spreading the News: The American Postal System from Franklin to Morse*. Cambridge, MA: Harvard University Press, 1995.

Johnson, Dennis W. *No Place for Amateurs: How Political Consultants Are Reshaping American Democracy*. 2nd ed. New York: Routledge, 2007.

Jones, Daniel Stedman. *Masters of the Universe: Hayek, Friedman, and the Birth of Neoliberal Politics*. Princeton, NJ: Princeton University Press, 2012.

Judis, John B. *William F. Buckley, Jr., Patron Saint of the Conservatives*. New York: Simon and Schuster, 1988.

Jumonville, Neil. *Critical Crossings: The New York Intellectuals in Postwar America*. Berkeley: University of California Press, 1991.

Karpf, David. *The MoveOn Effect: The Unexpected Transformation of American Political Advocacy*. New York: Oxford University Press, 2012.

Katagiri, Yasuhiro. *Black Freedom, White Resistance, and Red Menace: Civil Rights and Anticommunism in the Jim Crow South*. Baton Rouge: Louisiana State University Press, 2014.

Kazin, Michael. *The Populist Persuasion: An American History*. 2nd ed. Ithaca, NY: Cornell University Press, 1998.

Kelley, Stanley. *Professional Public Relations and Political Power*. Baltimore: Johns Hopkins University Press, 1956.

Kessel, John H. *The Goldwater Coalition: Republican Strategies in 1964*. Indianapolis: Bobbs-Merrill, 1968.

Kidd, Quentin. *Civic Participation in America*. New York: Palgrave Macmillan, 2011.

Kielbowicz, Richard Burket. *News in the Mail: The Press, Post Office, and Public Information, 1700–1860s*. New York: Greenwood Press, 1989.

Killen, Andreas. *1973 Nervous Breakdown: Watergate, Warhol, and the Birth of Post-Sixties America*. New York: Bloomsbury, 2006.

Kimmage, Michael. *The Conservative Turn: Lionel Trilling, Whittaker Chambers, and the Lessons of Anti-Communism*. Cambridge, MA: Harvard University Press, 2009.

Kirkpatrick, Rob. *1969, the Year Everything Changed*. New York: Skyhorse Publishing, 2009.

Klatch, Rebecca E. *A Generation Divided: The New Left, the New Right, and the 1960s*. Berkeley: University of California Press, 1999.

———. *Women of the New Right*. Philadelphia: Temple University Press, 1987.

Kling, Rob, Spencer Olin, and Mark Poster, eds. *Postsuburban California: The Transformation of Orange County since World War II*. Berkeley: University of California Press, 1991.

Kolkey, Jonathan Martin. *The New Right, 1960–1968: With Epilogue, 1969–1980*. Washington, DC: University Press of America, 1983.

Kornbluh, Mark Lawrence. *Why America Stopped Voting: The Decline of Participatory Democracy and the Emergence of Modern American Politics*. New York: NYU Press, 2000.

Kornhauser, William. *The Politics of Mass Society*. Glencoe, IL: Free Press, 1959.

Kovel, Joel. *Red Hunting in the Promised Land: Anticommunism and the Making of America*. New York: Basic Books, 1994.

Kreiss, Daniel. *Taking Our Country Back: The Crafting of Networked Politics from Howard Dean to Barack Obama*. New York: Oxford University Press, 2012.

Kruse, Kevin Michael. *One Nation Under God: How Corporate America Invented Christian America*. New York: Basic Books, 2015.

———. *White Flight: Atlanta and the Making of Modern Conservatism*. Princeton, NJ: Princeton University Press, 2005.

Kruse, Kevin Michael, and Thomas J. Sugrue. *The New Suburban History*. Chicago: University of Chicago Press, 2006.

Kruse, Kevin Michael, and Julian E. Zelizer. *Fault Lines: A History of the United States since 1974*. New York: W. W. Norton, 2019.

Kuhn, Thomas S. *The Structure of Scientific Revolutions*. Chicago: University of Chicago Press, 1962.

La Raja, Raymond J. *Small Change: Money, Political Parties, and Campaign Finance Reform*. Ann Arbor: University of Michigan Press, 2008.

Ladd, Everett Carll. *The Ladd Report*. New York: Free Press, 1999.

Lassiter, Matthew D. *The Silent Majority: Suburban Politics in the Sunbelt South*. Princeton, NJ: Princeton University Press, 2007.

Lassiter, Matthew D., and Joseph Crespino, eds. *The Myth of Southern Exceptionalism*. New York: Oxford University Press, 2010.

Lathrop, Douglas A. *The Campaign Continues: How Political Consultants and Campaign Tactics Affect Public Policy*. Westport, CT: Praeger, 2003.

Lears, T. J. Jackson. *Fables of Abundance: A Cultural History of Advertising in America.* New York: Basic Books, 1994.

Lee, Michael J. *Creating Conservatism: Postwar Words that Made an American Movement.* East Lansing: Michigan State University Press, 2014.

Lesher, Stephan. *George Wallace: American Populist.* Reading, MA: Addison-Wesley, 1994.

Lewis, Andrew R. *The Rights Turn in Conservative Christian Politics: How Abortion Transformed the Culture Wars.* Cambridge, UK: Cambridge University Press, 2017.

Lewis, Angela K. *Conservatism in the Black Community to the Right and Misunderstood.* New York: Routledge, 2012.

Lewis, Penny. *Hardhats, Hippies, and Hawks: The Vietnam Antiwar Movement as Myth and Memory.* Ithaca, NY: ILR Press, 2013.

Lichtenstein, Nelson. *State of the Union: A Century of American Labor.* Revised ed. Princeton, NJ: Princeton University Press, 2013.

Lichtenstein, Nelson, and Elizabeth Tandy Shermer, eds. *The Right and Labor in America: Politics, Ideology, and Imagination.* Philadelphia: University of Pennsylvania Press, 2012.

Lichtman, Allan J. *White Protestant Nation: The Rise of the American Conservative Movement.* New York: Atlantic Monthly Press, 2008.

Lichtman, Robert M. *The Supreme Court and McCarthy-Era Repression: One Hundred Decisions.* Urbana: University of Illinois Press, 2012.

Lin, Nan, Karen Cook, and Ronald S. Burt. *Social Capital: Theory and Research.* New York: Aldine de Gruyter, 2001.

Link, William A. *Righteous Warrior: Jesse Helms and the Rise of Modern Conservatism.* New York: St. Martin's Press, 2008.

Lints, Richard. *Progressive and Conservative Religious Ideologies: The Tumultuous Decade of the 1960s.* Burlington, VT: Ashgate, 2010.

Little, Thomas J. *The Origins of Southern Evangelicalism: Religious Revivalism in the South Carolina Lowcountry, 1670–1760.* Columbia: University of South Carolina Press, 2013.

Lloyd, Mark. *Prologue to a Farce: Communication and Democracy in America.* Urbana: University of Illinois Press, 2007.

Lora, Ronald. *Conservative Minds in America.* Chicago: Rand McNally, 1971.

Lora, Ronald, and William Henry Longton, eds. *The Conservative Press in Twentieth-Century America.* Westport, CT: Greenwood Press, 1999.

Lowndes, Joseph E. *From the New Deal to the New Right: Race and the Southern Origins of Modern Conservatism.* New Haven, CT: Yale University Press, 2008.

Lyons, Paul. *New Left, New Right, and the Legacy of the Sixties.* Philadelphia: Temple University Press, 1996.

Maciag, Drew. *Edmund Burke in America: The Contested Career of the Father of Modern Conservatism.* Ithaca, NY: Cornell University Press, 2013.

Malin, Brenton. *Feeling Mediated: A History of Media Technology and Emotion in America.* New York: NYU Press, 2014.

Martin, Isaac William. *The Permanent Tax Revolt: How the Property Tax Transformed American Politics*. Stanford, CA: Stanford University Press, 2008.

———. *Rich People's Movements: Grassroots Campaigns to Untax the One Percent*. New York: Oxford University Press, 2013.

Martin, William C. *With God on Our Side: The Rise of the Religious Right in America*. New York: Broadway Books, 1996.

Matzko, Paul. *The Radio Right: How a Band of Broadcasters Took on the Federal Government and Built the Modern Conservative Movement*. New York: Oxford University Press, 2020.

McAllister, Matthew P. *The Commercialization of American Culture: New Advertising, Control, and Democracy*. Thousand Oaks, CA: Sage Publications, 1996.

McAllister, Ted V. *Revolt against Modernity: Leo Strauss, Eric Voegelin, and the Search for a Postliberal Order*. Lawrence: University Press of Kansas, 1996.

McCurry, Stephanie. *Confederate Reckoning: Power and Politics in the Civil War South*. Cambridge, MA: Harvard University Press, 2010.

McFarland, Andrew S. *Common Cause: Lobbying in the Public Interest*. Chatham, NJ: Chatham House Publishers, 1984.

McGinniss, Joe. *The Selling of the President, 1968*. New York: Trident Press, 1969.

McGirr, Lisa. *Suburban Warriors: The Origins of the New American Right*. Princeton, NJ: Princeton University Press, 2001.

McGovern, George. *An American Journey: The Campaign Speeches of George McGovern*. New York: Random House, 1974.

McIntyre, Thomas J. *The Fear Brokers*. New York: Pilgrim Press, 1979.

McPherson, James Brian. *The Conservative Resurgence and the Press: The Media's Role in the Rise of the Right*. Evanston, IL: Northwestern University Press, 2008.

Medvic, Stephen K. *Political Consultants in U.S. Congressional Elections*. Columbus: Ohio State University Press, 2001.

Middendorf, John William. *A Glorious Disaster: Barry Goldwater's Presidential Campaign and the Origins of the Conservative Movement*. New York: Basic Books, 2006.

Mieczkowski, Yanek. *Gerald Ford and the Challenges of the 1970s*. Lexington: University Press of Kentucky, 2005.

Miroff, Bruce. *The Liberals' Moment: The McGovern Insurgency and the Identity Crisis of the Democratic Party*. Lawrence: University Press of Kansas, 2007.

Moffett, George D. *The Limits of Victory: The Ratification of the Panama Canal Treaties*. Ithaca, NY: Cornell University Press, 1985.

Moore, James, and Wayne Slater. *The Architect: Karl Rove and the Master Plan for Absolute Power*. New York: Crown Publishers, 2006.

Moore, Leonard Joseph. *Citizen Klansmen: The Ku Klux Klan in Indiana, 1921–1928*. Chapel Hill: University of North Carolina Press, 1991.

Morgan, Edward P. *What Really Happened to the 1960s: How Mass Media Culture Failed American Democracy*. Lawrence: University Press of Kansas, 2010.

Moss, Richard. *Creating the New Right Ethnic in 1970s America: The Intersection of Anger and Nostalgia*. Lanham, MD: Fairleigh Dickinson University Press, 2017.

Mulloy, D. J. *The World of the John Birch Society: Conspiracy, Conservatism and the Cold War*. Nashville: Vanderbilt University Press, 2014.

Musser, Charles. *Politicking and Emergent Media: US Presidential Elections of the 1890s*. Berkeley: University of California Press, 2016.

Mutch, Robert E. *Buying the Vote: A History of Campaign Finance Reform*. New York: Oxford University Press, 2014.

———. *Campaigns, Congress, and Courts: The Making of Federal Campaign Finance Law*. New York: Praeger, 1988.

Nadler, Anthony, and A. J. Bauer, eds. *News on the Right: Studying Conservative News Cultures*. New York: Oxford University Press, 2020.

Nash, George H. *The Conservative Intellectual Movement in America since 1945*. New York: Basic Books, 1976.

———. *Reappraising the Right: The Past and Future of American Conservatism*. Wilmington, DE: ISI Books, 2009.

Newman, Bruce I., and Philip Davies, eds. *Winning Elections with Political Marketing*. New York: Haworth Press, 2006.

Nickerson, Michelle M. *Mothers of Conservatism: Women and the Postwar Right*. Princeton, NJ: Princeton University Press, 2012.

Nickerson, Michelle M., and Darren Dochuk, eds. *Sunbelt Rising: The Politics of Place, Space, and Region*. Politics and Culture in Modern America. Philadelphia: University of Pennsylvania Press, 2011.

Nielsen, Kim E. *Un-American Womanhood: Antiradicalism, Antifeminism, and the First Red Scare*. Columbus: Ohio State University Press, 2001.

Nielsen, Rasmus Kleis. *Ground Wars: Personalized Communication in Political Campaigns*. Princeton, NJ: Princeton University Press, 2012.

Nimmo, Dan D. *The Political Persuaders: The Techniques of Modern Election Campaigns*. Englewood Cliffs, NJ: Prentice-Hall, 1970.

Nisbet, Robert A. *Twilight of Authority*. New York: Oxford University Press, 1975.

Nugent, Margaret Latus, and John R. Johannes, eds. *Money, Elections, and Democracy: Reforming Congressional Campaign Finance*. Boulder, CO: Westview Press, 1990.

Osgood, Kenneth Alan, and Derrick E. White, eds. *Winning While Losing: Civil Rights, the Conservative Movement, and the Presidency from Nixon to Obama*. Gainesville: University Press of Florida, 2014.

Packard, Vance Oakley. *The Hidden Persuaders*. New York: D. McKay, 1957.

Parry, Manon. *Broadcasting Birth Control: Mass Media and Family Planning*. New Brunswick, NJ: Rutgers University Press, 2013.

Pasley, Jeffrey L. *The First Presidential Contest: 1796 and the Founding of American Democracy*. Lawrence: University Press of Kansas, 2013.

Patterson, James T. *Congressional Conservatism and the New Deal: The Growth of the Conservative Coalition in Congress, 1933–1939*. Lexington: University of Kentucky Press, 1967.

Peck, Reece. *Fox Populism: Branding Conservatism as Working Class*. New York: Cambridge University Press, 2019.

Pegram, Thomas R. *One Hundred Percent American: The Rebirth and Decline of the Ku Klux Klan in the 1920s*. Chicago: Ivan R. Dee, 2011.

Pells, Richard H. *The Liberal Mind in a Conservative Age: American Intellectuals in the 1940s and 1950s*. New York: Harper & Row, 1985.

Perlstein, Rick. *Before the Storm: Barry Goldwater and the Unmaking of the American Consensus*. New York: Hill and Wang, 2001.

———. *The Invisible Bridge: The Fall of Nixon and the Rise of Reagan*. New York: Simon and Schuster, 2014.

Phillips, Howard. *The New Right at Harvard*. Vienna, VA: Conservative Caucus, 1983.

Phillips, Kevin P. *The Emerging Republican Majority*. New Rochelle, NY: Arlington House, 1969.

———. *Post-Conservative America: People, Politics, and Ideology in a Time of Crisis*. New York: Random House, 1982.

Phillips-Fein, Kim. *Invisible Hands: The Making of the Conservative Movement from the New Deal to Reagan*. New York: W. W. Norton, 2009.

Phillips-Fein, Kim, and Julian E. Zelizer, eds. *What's Good for Business: Business and American Politics since World War II*. New York: Oxford University Press, 2012.

Pierson, Paul, and Theda Skocpol. *The Transformation of American Politics: Activist Government and the Rise of Conservatism*. Princeton, NJ: Princeton University Press, 2007.

Putnam, Robert D. *Bowling Alone: The Collapse and Revival of American Community*. New York: Simon and Schuster, 2000.

Qualter, Terence H. *Advertising and Democracy in the Mass Age*. New York: St. Martin's Press, 1991.

Regnery, Alfred S. *Upstream: The Ascendance of American Conservatism*. New York: Threshold Editions, 2008.

Ribuffo, Leo P. *The Old Christian Right: The Protestant Far Right from the Great Depression to the Cold War*. Philadelphia: Temple University Press, 1983.

Riesman, David. *The Lonely Crowd: A Study of the Changing American Character*. New Haven, CT: Yale University Press, 1950.

Robin, Corey. *The Reactionary Mind: Conservatism from Edmund Burke to Sarah Palin*. New York: Oxford University Press, 2011.

Rodgers, Daniel T. *Age of Fracture*. Cambridge, MA: Belknap Press of Harvard University Press, 2011.

Rohler, Lloyd. *George Wallace: Conservative Populist*. Westport, CT: Praeger, 2004.

Rosen, Elliot A. *The Republican Party in the Age of Roosevelt: Sources of Anti-Government Conservatism in the United States*. Charlottesville: University of Virginia Press, 2014.

Rossinow, Douglas C. *The Reagan Era: A History of the 1980s*. New York: Columbia University Press, 2015.

Rove, Karl. *Courage and Consequence: My Life as a Conservative in the Fight*. New York: Threshold Editions, 2010.

Rusher, William A. *The Rise of the Right*. New York: William Morrow, 1984.

Rymph, Catherine E. *Republican Women: Feminism and Conservatism from Suffrage through the Rise of the New Right*. Chapel Hill: University of North Carolina Press, 2006.

Sabato, Larry J. *The Rise of Political Consultants: New Ways of Winning Elections*. New York: Basic Books, 1981.

Saloma, John S. *Ominous Politics: The New Conservative Labyrinth*. New York: Hill and Wang, 1984.

Sandbrook, Dominic. *Mad as Hell: The Crisis of the 1970s and the Rise of the Populist Right*. New York: Alfred A. Knopf, 2011.

Schneider, Gregory L. *Cadres for Conservatism: Young Americans for Freedom and the Rise of the Contemporary Right*. New York: New York University Press, 1998.

———. *The Conservative Century: From Reaction to Revolution*. Lanham, MD: Rowman & Littlefield, 2009.

Schoenwald, Jonathan. *A Time for Choosing: The Rise of Modern American Conservatism*. New York: Oxford University Press, 2001.

Schomp, Gerald. *Birchism Was My Business*. New York: Macmillan, 1970.

Schrecker, Ellen. *Many Are the Crimes: McCarthyism in America*. Boston: Little, Brown, 1998.

Schreiber, Ronnee. *Righting Feminism: Conservative Women and American Politics*. New York: Oxford University Press, 2008.

Schulman, Bruce J. *From Cotton Belt to Sunbelt: Federal Policy, Economic Development, and the Transformation of the South, 1938–1980*. New York: Oxford University Press, 1991.

———. *The Seventies: The Great Shift in American Culture, Society, and Politics*. New York: Free Press, 2001.

Schulman, Bruce J., and Julian E. Zelizer, eds. *Media Nation: The Political History of News in Modern America*. Philadelphia: University of Pennsylvania Press, 2017.

———, and Julian E. Zelizer, eds. *Rightward Bound: Making America Conservative in the 1970s*. Cambridge, MA: Harvard University Press, 2008.

Schuparra, Kurt. *Triumph of the Right: The Rise of the California Conservative Movement, 1945–1966*. Armonk, NY: M. E. Sharpe, 1998.

Scott, Cord A. *Comics and Conflict: Patriotism and Propaganda from WWII through Operation Iraqi Freedom*. Annapolis: Naval Institute Press, 2014.

Segrave, Kerry. *Endorsements in Advertising: A Social History*. Jefferson, NC: McFarland, 2005.

Shadegg, Stephen C. *The New How to Win an Election*. New York: Taplinger, 1972.

———. *What Happened to Goldwater? The Inside Story of the 1964 Republican Campaign*. New York: Holt, Rinehart and Winston, 1965.

Shaiko, Ronald G. *Voices and Echoes for the Environment*. New York: Columbia University Press, 1999.

Shea, Daniel M., and Michael John Burton. *Campaign Craft: The Strategies, Tactics, and Art of Political Campaign Management*. 3rd ed. Westport, CT: Praeger, 2006.

Sheingate, Adam. *Building a Business of Politics: The Rise of Political Consulting and the Transformation of American Democracy*. New York: Oxford University Press, 2016.

Shermer, Elizabeth Tandy, ed. *Barry Goldwater and the Remaking of the American Political Landscape*. Tucson: University of Arizona Press, 2013.

Shermer, Elizabeth Tandy. *Sunbelt Capitalism: Phoenix and the Transformation of American Politics*. Philadelphia: University of Pennsylvania Press, 2013.

Skocpol, Theda. *Diminished Democracy: From Membership to Management in American Civic Life*. Norman: University of Oklahoma Press, 2003.

Skocpol, Theda, and Morris P. Fiorina, eds. *Civic Engagement in American Democracy*. Washington, DC: Brookings Institution Press, 1999.

Spring, Dawn. *Advertising in the Age of Persuasion: Building Brand America 1941–1961*. New York: Palgrave Macmillan, 2011.

Stahl, Jason M. *Right Moves: The Conservative Think Tank in American Political Culture since 1945*. Chapel Hill: University of North Carolina Press, 2016.

Starr, Paul. *The Creation of the Media: Political Origins of Modern Communications*. New York: Basic Books, 2004.

Stebenne, David. *Modern Republican: Arthur Larson and the Eisenhower Years*. Bloomington: Indiana University Press, 2006.

Steinberg, Cobbett S. *TV Facts*. New York: Facts on File, 1980.

Stole, Inger L. *Advertising at War: Business, Consumers, and Government in the 1940s*. Urbana: University of Illinois Press, 2012.

Storrs, Landon R. Y. *The Second Red Scare and the Unmaking of the New Deal Left*. Princeton, NJ: Princeton University Press, 2013.

Straus, Emily E. *Death of a Suburban Dream: Race and Schools in Compton, California*. Philadelphia: University of Pennsylvania Press, 2014.

Strother, Raymond. *Falling Up: How a Redneck Helped Invent Political Consulting*. Baton Rouge: Louisiana State University Press, 2003.

Strub, Whitney. *Perversion for Profit: The Politics of Pornography and the Rise of the New Right*. New York: Columbia University Press, 2011.

Sullivan, Timothy J. *New York State and the Rise of Modern Conservatism: Redrawing Party Lines*. Albany: State University of New York Press, 2009.

Summerfield, Arthur E. *U.S. Mail: The Story of the United States Postal Service*. New York: Holt, Rinehart and Winston, 1960.

Suri, Jeremy. *Power and Protest: Global Revolution and the Rise of Detente*. Cambridge, MA: Harvard University Press, 2003.

Swartz, David R. *Moral Minority: The Evangelical Left in an Age of Conservatism*. Philadelphia: University of Pennsylvania Press, 2012.

Teles, Steven Michael. *The Rise of the Conservative Legal Movement: The Battle for Control of the Law.* Princeton, NJ: Princeton University Press, 2008.

Thrift, Bryan Hardin. *Conservative Bias: How Jesse Helms Pioneered the Rise of Right-Wing Media and Realigned the Republican Party.* Gainesville: University Press of Florida, 2014.

Thurber, James A., and Candice J. Nelson, eds. *Campaign Warriors: The Role of Political Consultants in Elections.* Washington, DC: Brookings Institution Press, 2000.

Tocqueville, Alexis de. *Democracy in America.* Translated by Arthur Goldhammer. New York: Library of America, 2004.

Tønnessen, Alf Tomas. *How Two Political Entrepreneurs Helped Create the American Conservative Movement, 1973–1981: The Ideas of Richard Viguerie and Paul Weyrich.* Lewiston, NY: Edwin Mellen Press, 2009.

Trow, Martin A. *Right-Wing Radicalism and Political Intolerance: A Study of Support for McCarthy in a New England Town.* New York: Arno Press, 1980.

US Federal Election Commission. *Survey of Political Broadcasting: Primary and General Election Campaigns of 1966.* Washington, DC: Government Printing Office, 1967.

US Postal Service. *The United States Postal Service: An American History, 1775–2006.* Washington, DC: Government Relations, US Postal Service, 2007.

Vahan, Richard. *The Truth about the John Birch Society.* New York: Macfadden-Bartell, 1962.

Vinyard, JoEllen McNergney. *Right in Michigan's Grassroots: From the KKK to the Michigan Militia.* Ann Arbor: University of Michigan Press, 2011.

Volle, Jeffrey J. *The Political Legacies of Barry Goldwater and George McGovern: Shifting Party Paradigms.* New York: Palgrave Macmillan, 2010.

Wallace, Aurora. *Media Capital: Architecture and Communications in New York City.* Urbana: University of Illinois Press, 2012.

Weston, Florence. *The Presidential Election of 1828.* Washington, DC: The Ruddick Press, 1938.

Whitaker, Robert W., ed. *The New Right Papers.* New York: St. Martin's Press, 1982.

White, Khadijah Costley. *The Branding of Right-Wing Activism: The News Media and the Tea Party.* New York: Oxford University Press, 2018.

White, Theodore H. *The Making of the President, 1972.* New York: Atheneum Publishers, 1973.

Whyte, William Hollingsworth. *The Organization Man.* New York: Simon and Schuster, 1956.

Wilentz, Sean. *The Age of Reagan: A History, 1974–2008.* New York: Harper, 2008.

Wilkinson, Kyle Grant, and David O'Donald Cullen, eds. *The Texas Right: The Radical Roots of Lone Star Conservatism.* College Station: Texas A&M University Press, 2014.

Williams, Daniel K. *God's Own Party: The Making of the Christian Right.* New York: Oxford University Press, 2010.

Wolfskill, George. *The Revolt of the Conservatives: A History of the American Liberty League, 1934–1940*. Boston: Houghton Mifflin, 1962.

Wunderlin, Clarence E. *Robert A. Taft: Ideas, Tradition, and Party in U.S. Foreign Policy*. Lanham, MD: SR Books, 2005.

Wuthnow, Robert. *Loose Connections: Joining Together in America's Fragmented Communities*. Cambridge, MA: Harvard University Press, 1998.

———. *Rough Country: How Texas Became America's Most Powerful Bible-Belt State*. Princeton, NJ: Princeton University Press, 2014.

Young, Neil J. *We Gather Together: The Religious Right and the Problem of Interfaith Politics*. New York: Oxford University Press, 2015.

Zelizer, Julian E. *On Capitol Hill: The Struggle to Reform Congress and Its Consequences, 1948–2000*. New York: Cambridge University Press, 2004.

Articles and Essays

Alexander, Herbert E. "Rethinking Reform." In *Campaign Money Reform and Reality in the States*, edited by Herbert E. Alexander, 1–13. New York: Free Press, 1976.

Azzaro, Shannon D. "The Hatch Act Modernization Act: Putting the Government Back in Politics." *Fordham Urban Law Journal* 42, no. 3 (March 2015): 781–839.

Barclay, Thomas S. "The Publicity Division of the Democratic Party, 1929–30." *American Political Science Review* 25, no. 1 (1931): 68–72.

Bauer, Raymond A. "The Obstinate Audience: The Influence Process from the Point of View of Social Communication." *American Psychologist* 19 (May 1964): 319–28.

Bell, Daniel. "The Dispossessed." In *The Radical Right: The New American Right, Expanded and Updated*, 2nd ed., edited by Daniel Bell, 1–38. Garden City, NY: Doubleday, 1963.

Bennett, Stephen Earl. "Modes of Resolution of a 'Belief Dilemma' in the Ideology of the John Birch Society." *Journal of Politics* 33, no. 3 (August 1971): 735–72.

Bibby, John F. "Party Leadership, the Bliss Model, and the Development of the Republican National Committee." In *Politics, Professionalism, and Power: Modern Party Organization and the Legacy of Ray C. Bliss*, edited by John C. Green, 19–33. Lanham, MD: University Press of America, 1994.

Blee, Kathleen M. "The Gendered Organization of Hate: Women in the U.S. Ku Klux Klan." In *Right-Wing Women: From Conservatives to Extremists around the World*, edited by Paola Bacchetta and Margaret Power, 101–14. New York: Routledge, 2002.

Bosso, Christopher J. "The Color of Money: Environmental Groups and the Pathologies of Fund Raising." In *Interest Group Politics*, 4th ed., edited by Allan J. Cigler and Burdett A. Loomis, 101–30. Washington, DC: CQ Press, 1995.

Bowen, Michael. "Getting to Goldwater: Robert A. Taft, William F. Knowland, and the Rightward Drift of the Republican Party." In *Barry Goldwater and the*

Remaking of the American Political Landscape, edited by Elizabeth Tandy Shermer, 87–113. Tucson: University of Arizona Press, 2013.

Boyer, Paul. "The Evangelical Resurgence in 1970s American Protestantism." In *Rightward Bound: Making America Conservative in the 1970s*, edited by Bruce J. Schulman and Julian E. Zelizer, 29–51. Cambridge, MA: Harvard University Press, 2008.

Brennan, Mary C. "Winning the War/Losing the Battle: The Goldwater Presidential Campaign and Its Effects on the Evolution of Modern Conservatism." In *The Conservative Sixties*, edited by David R. Farber and Jeff Roche, 63–78. New York: Peter Lang, 2003.

Brody, Richard A. "The Puzzle of Political Participation in America." In *The New American Political System*, edited by Anthony King, 287–324. Washington, DC: American Enterprise Institute for Public Policy Research, 1978.

Burns, Jennifer. "Godless Capitalism: Ayn Rand and the Conservative Movement." *Modern Intellectual History* 1, no. 3 (November 2004): 359–85.

———. "The Three 'Furies' of Libertarianism: Rose Wilder Lane, Isabel Paterson, and Ayn Rand." *Journal of American History* 102, no. 3 (December 2015): 746–74.

Clinton, Wally. "Consumer-Driven Politics: Using Telephones and Direct Mail to Build New Relationships with Voters." *Campaigns & Elections* 23, no. 3 (April 2002): 44.

Collins, Robert M. "The Originality Trap: Richard Hofstadter on Populism." *Journal of American History* 76, no. 1 (June 1989): 150–67.

Conover, Pamela Johnston. "The Mobilization of the New Right: A Test of Various Explanations." *Western Political Quarterly* 36, no. 4 (December 1983): 632–49.

Crespino, Joseph. "Civil Rights and the Religious Right." In *Rightward Bound: Making America Conservative in the 1970s*, edited by Bruce J. Schulman and Julian E. Zelizer, 90–105. Cambridge, MA: Harvard University Press, 2008.

Davies, Gareth. "Towards Big-Government Conservatism: Conservatives and Federal Aid to Education in the 1970s." *Journal of Contemporary History* 43, no. 4 (October 2008): 621–35.

Farber, David. "The Silent Majority and Talk about Revolution." In *The Sixties: From Memory to History*, edited by David Farber, 291–316. Chapel Hill: University of North Carolina Press, 1994.

Freedman, Robert. "The Religious Right and the Carter Administration." *Historical Journal* 48, no. 1 (2005): 231–60.

Gasman, Marybeth, and Noah D. Drezner. "A Maverick in the Field: The Oram Group and Fundraising in the Black College Community during the 1970s." *History of Education Quarterly* 49, no. 4 (November 2009): 465–506.

Gaston, K. Healan. "The Cold War Romance of Religious Authenticity: Will Herberg, William F. Buckley Jr., and the Rise of the New Right." *Journal of American History* 99, no. 4 (March 2013): 1133–58.

Gifford, Laura Jane. "The Education of a Cold War Conservative: Anti-Communist Literature of the 1950s and 1960s." In *Pressing the Fight: Print, Propaganda, and the*

Cold War, edited by Greg Barnhisel and Catherine Turner, 50–67. Amherst and Boston: University of Massachusetts Press, 2010.

Godwin, R. Kenneth, and Robert Cameron Mitchell. "The Implications of Direct Mail for Political Organizations." *Social Science Quarterly* 65, no. 3 (1984): 829–39.

Greenberg, David. "A New Way of Campaigning: Eisenhower, Stevenson, and the Anxieties of Television Politics." In *Liberty and Justice for All? Rethinking Politics in Cold War America*, edited by Kathleen G. Donohue, 185–212. Boston: University of Massachusetts Press, 2012.

Grupp, Fred W. "Personal Satisfaction Derived from Membership in the John Birch Society." *Western Political Quarterly* 24, no. 1 (March 1971): 79–83.

Hacker, Jacob S., and Paul Pierson. "Tax Politics and the Struggle over Activist Government." In *The Transformation of American Politics: Activist Government and the Rise of Conservatism*, edited by Paul Pierson and Theda Skocpol, 256–80. Princeton, NJ: Princeton University Press, 2007.

Hemmer, Nicole. "The Dealers and the Darling: Conservative Media and the Candidacy of Barry Goldwater." In *Barry Goldwater and the Remaking of the American Political Landscape*, edited by Elizabeth Tandy Shermer, 114–43. Tucson: University of Arizona Press, 2013.

Hendershot, Heather. "God's Angriest Man: Carl McIntire, Cold War Fundamentalism, and Right-Wing Broadcasting." *American Quarterly* 59, no. 2 (June 2007): 373–96.

Herrnson, Paul S. "Hired Guns and House Races: Campaign Professionals in House Elections." In *Campaign Warriors: The Role of Political Consultants in Elections*, edited by James A. Thurber and Candice J. Nelson, 65–90. Washington, DC: Brookings Institution Press, 2000.

Hofstadter, Richard. "North America." In *Populism: Its Meaning and National Characteristics*, edited by Ghiţa Ionescu and Ernest Gellner, 9–27. New York: Macmillan, 1969.

———. "Pseudo-Conservatism Revisited." In *The Radical Right: The New American Right, Expanded and Updated*, 2nd ed., edited by Daniel Bell, 81–86. Garden City, NY: Doubleday, 1963.

———. "The Pseudo-Conservative Revolt." In *The Radical Right: The New American Right, Expanded and Updated*, 2nd ed., edited by Daniel Bell, 63–80. Garden City, NY: Doubleday, 1963.

Johnson, Paul E. "Interest Group Recruitment: Finding Members and Keeping Them." In *Interest Group Politics*, edited by Allan J. Cigler and Burdett A. Loomis, 35–62. Washington, DC: CQ Press, 1998.

Keniston, Kenneth. "Alienation and the Decline of Utopia." *American Scholar*, vol. XXIX (Spring 1960): 1–40.

La Raja, Raymond J. "Campaign Finance and Partisan Polarization in the United States Congress." *Duke Journal of Constitutional Law & Public Policy* 9, no. 1 (2014): 223–58.

Lee, Michael J. "The Conservative Canon and Its Uses." *Rhetoric & Public Affairs* 15, no. 1 (Spring 2012): 1–39.

———. "WFB: The Gladiatorial Style and the Politics of Provocation." *Rhetoric & Public Affairs* 13, no. 2 (Summer 2010): 217–50.

Lipset, Seymour Martin. "The Sources of the 'Radical Right—1955.'" In *The Radical Right: The New American Right, Expanded and Updated*, 2nd ed., edited by Daniel Bell, 259–312. Garden City, NY: Doubleday, 1963.

Mason, Robert. "Citizens for Eisenhower and the Republican Party, 1951–1965." *The Historical Journal* 56, no. 2 (June 2013): 513–36.

Mathews, Kristin. "The Medium, the Message, and the Movement: Print Culture and New Left Politics." In *Pressing the Fight: Print, Propaganda, and the Cold War*, edited by Greg Barnhisel and Catherine Turner, 31–49. Amherst and Boston: University of Massachusetts Press, 2010.

McClosky, Herbert. "Conservatism and Personality." *American Political Science Review* 52, no. 1 (March 1958): 27–45.

McEnaney, Laura. "He-Men and Christian Mothers: The America First Movement and the Gendered Meanings of Patriotism and Isolationism." *Diplomatic History* 18, no. 1 (Winter 1994): 47–56.

Moore, Leonard J. "Historical Interpretations of the 1920's Klan: The Traditional View and the Populist Revision." *Journal of Social History* 24, no. 2 (Winter 1990): 341–57.

Murray, Sylvie. "Rethinking Middle-Class Populism and Politics in the Postwar Era: Community Activism in Queens." In *The Middling Sorts: Explorations in the History of the American Middle Class*, edited by Burton J. Bledstein and Robert D. Johnston, 267–79. New York: Routledge, 2001.

Nickerson, Michelle M. "Goldwater's 'Moral Mothers': Miscalculations of Gender in the 1964 Republican Presidential Campaign." In *Barry Goldwater and the Remaking of the American Political Landscape*, edited by Elizabeth Tandy Shermer, 170–90. Tucson: University of Arizona Press, 2013.

———. "Moral Mothers and Goldwater Girls." In *The Conservative Sixties*, edited by David R. Farber and Jeff Roche, 51–62. New York: Peter Lang, 2003.

Nielsen, Kim E. "Doing the 'Right' Right." *Journal of Women's History* 16, no. 3 (Fall 2004): 168–72.

Norrell, Robert J. "Modern Conservatism and the Consequences of Its Ideas." *Reviews in American History* 36, no. 3 (2008): 456–67.

Nye, Joseph S. "In Government We Don't Trust." *Foreign Policy*, no. 108 (October 1997): 99–111.

O'Connor, Alice. "Financing the Counterrevolution." In *Rightward Bound: Making America Conservative in the 1970s*, edited by Bruce J. Schulman and Julian Zelizer, 148–68. Cambridge, MA: Harvard University Press, 2008.

———. "The Privatized City: The Manhattan Institute, the Urban Crisis, and the Conservative Counterrevolution in New York." *Journal of Urban History* 34, no. 2 (2008): 333–53.

Phillips-Fein, Kim. "'As Great an Issue as Slavery or Abolition': Economic Populism, the Conservative Movement, and the Right-to-Work Campaigns of 1958." *Journal of Policy History* 23, no. 4 (2011): 491–512.

———. "Conservatism: A State of the Field." *Journal of American History* 98, no. 3 (December 2011): 723–43.

———. "'If Business and the Country Will Be Run Right:' The Business Challenge to the Liberal Consensus, 1945–1964." *International Labor and Working-Class History*, no. 72 (October 2007): 192–215.

Phillips-Fein, Kim, and Julian E. Zelizer. "Introduction: What's Good for Business." In *What's Good for Business: Business and American Politics since World War II*, edited by Kim Phillps-Fein and Julian E. Zelizer, 3–15. New York: Oxford University Press, 2012.

Pierson, Paul, and Theda Skocpol. "American Politics in the Long Run." In *The Transformation of American Politics: Activist Government and the Rise of Conservatism*, edited by Paul Pierson and Theda Skocpol, 3–16. Princeton, NJ: Princeton University Press, 2007.

Poster, Mark. "Narcissism or Liberation? The Affluent Middle-Class Family." In *Postsuburban California: The Transformation of Orange County since World War II*, edited by Rob Kling, Spencer Olin, and Mark Poster, 190–222. Berkeley: University of California Press, 1991.

Putnam, Robert D. "Bowling Alone: America's Declining Social Capital." *Journal of Democracy* 6, no. 1 (January 1995): 65–78.

Ray, Marcella Ridlen. "Technological Change and Associational Life." In *Civic Engagement in American Democracy*, edited by Theda Skocpol and Morris P. Fiorina, 297–329. Washington, DC: Brookings Institution Press, 1999.

Rydgren, Jens. "The Sociology of the Radical Right." *Annual Review of Sociology* 33 (January 1, 2007): 241–62.

Sabato, Larry J. "Political Consultants and the New Campaign Technology." In *Interest Group Politics*, edited by Allan J. Cigler and Burdett A. Loomis, 145–68. Washington, DC: CQ Press, 1983.

Schlesinger, Arthur M. "Biography of a Nation of Joiners." *American Historical Review* 50, no. 1 (October 1944): 1–25.

Schneider, Mark, and Paul Teske. "Toward a Theory of the Political Entrepreneur: Evidence from Local Government." *American Political Science Review* 86, no. 3 (September 1992): 737–47.

Schreiber, Ronnee. "Playing 'Femball': Conservative Women's Organizations and Political Representation in the United States." In *Right-Wing Women: From Conservatives to Extremists around the World*, edited by Paola Bacchetta and Margaret Power, 211–23. New York: Routledge, 2002.

Sheingate, Adam D. "Political Entrepreneurship, Institutional Change, and American Political Development." *Studies in American Political Development* 17, no. 2 (October 2003): 185–203.

Shermer, Elizabeth Tandy. "Origins of the Conservative Ascendancy: Barry Goldwater's Early Senate Career and the De-Legitimization of Organized Labor." *Journal of American History* 95, no. 3 (December 2008): 678–709.

Skocpol, Theda. "Advocates without Members: The Recent Transformation of American Civic Life." In *Civic Engagement in American Democracy*, edited by Theda Skocpol and Morris P. Fiorina, 461–509. Washington, DC: Brookings Institution Press, 1999.

Thurber, James A. "Introduction to the Study of Campaign Consultants." In *Campaign Warriors: The Role of Political Consultants in Elections*, edited by James A. Thurber and Candice J. Nelson. Washington, DC: Brookings Institution Press, 2000.

Westin, Alan F. "The John Birch Society: 'Radical Right' and 'Extreme Left' in the Political Context of Post World War II." In *The Radical Right: The New American Right, Expanded and Updated*, 2nd ed., edited by Daniel Bell, 201–26. Garden City, NY: Doubleday, 1963.

Williams, Daniel K. "Jerry Falwell's Sunbelt Politics: The Regional Origins of the Moral Majority." *Journal of Policy History* 22, no. 2 (2010): 125–47.

Witwer, David. "Pattern for Partnership: Putting Labor Racketeering on the Nation's Agenda in the Late 1950s." In *The Right and Labor in America: Politics, Ideology, and Imagination*, edited by Nelson Lichtenstein and Elizabeth Tandy Shermer, 207–25. Philadelphia: University of Pennsylvania Press, 2012.

Young, Neil J. "'Worse than Cancer and Worse than Snakes': Jimmy Carter's Southern Baptist Problem and the 1980 Election." *Journal of Policy History* 26, no. 4 (2014): 479–508.

Zelizer, Julian E. "Seeds of Cynicism: The Struggle over Campaign Finance, 1956–1974." *Journal of Policy History* 14, no. 1 (January 2002): 73–111.

Dissertations

Brenner, Samuel Lawrence. "Shouting at the Rain: The Voices and Ideas of Right-Wing Anti-Communist Americanists in the Era of Modern American Conservatism, 1950–1974." PhD diss., Brown University, 2009.

Eow, Gregory Teddy. "Fighting a New Deal: Intellectual Origins of the Reagan Revolution, 1932–1952." PhD diss., Rice University, 2007.

Hart, Randle Joseph. "The Truth in Time: Robert Welch, the John Birch Society and the American Conservative Movement, 1900–1972." PhD diss., University of Toronto, 2007.

Huntington, John S. "Right-Wing Paranoid Blues: The Role of Radicalism in Modern Conservatism." PhD diss., University of Houston, 2016.

Stahl, Jason Michael. "Selling Conservatism: Think Tanks, Conservative Ideology, and the Undermining of Liberalism, 1945–Present." PhD diss., University of Minnesota, 2008.

INDEX

Ketchum, Carlton G., 26
Kimball, Dan A., 111
Kirk, Russell, 50, 94
Kissinger, Henry A., 145–146
Kitchel, Denison, 67–68, 84
Kleindienst, Richard, 67
Knott, Walter, 88
Knowland, William, 49
Korean War, 12, 21, 27, 47–49, 59
Kudner Agency, Inc., 20
Ku Klux Klan (KKK), 74

Lasker, Albert, 17
Laxalt, Paul, 140, 146, 150, 159, 161
Lichenstein, Charles, 74
Liebman, Marvin, 37, 43–53, 55, 58,
    71–72, 78, 80, 85–90, 93, 97, 141;
    American Conservative Union
    (ACU), 85–90; as an anticommunist,
    45–53; early life, 43–45; Goldwater
    campaign, 71–72; relation with
    William F. Buckley, 49–51; relation
    with Richard Viguerie, 52–53; Young
    Americans for Freedom (YAF), 51–52
Lilly, Eli, 46, 88
Lilly Endowment, 46
Lodge, Henry Cabot, 75
Lonely Crowd, The (David
    Riesman), 32–33
Long, Russell, 117
Lyon, Don, 153

Madison Avenue, 7–8, 10, 13, 126, 128;
    advertising agencies on, 73, 158; direct
    mail activists on, 34, 40, 55, 58, 71;
    Eisenhower campaign, 31; relation
    with the Republican Party, 20, 29, 31,
    100, 119
Magruder, Jeb S., 101
Maguire, Richard, 114
Man in Gray Flannel Suit, The (Sloan
    Wilson), 32–33
Manion, Clarence, 64

Martin, Kay, 24
mass mail, 36, 37–41. *See also* direct mail
mass media, 2, 8; Barry Goldwater, 64,
    67, 76–77; contrast with direct mail,
    11, 36–40, 61; criticism of, 29, 31, 124;
    liberal ascendancy in, 3, 58, 81, 161;
    political use of, 20, 23, 25; Richard
    Nixon, 101. *See also* newspaper; radio;
    television.
McCaffrey, Neil, 88, 93–94
McCarthy, Eugene, 81, 97–98
McCarthy, Joseph, 12, 60, 75, 98
McClellan, John, 61
McFarland, Ernest, 59–60, 63
McGinnis, Joe, 99–100, 119
McGovern, George, 43, 81, 160; 1972
    presidential campaign, 102–105; on
    the New Right, 127–128; relation with
    Richard Viguerie, 96–97
McIntyre, Thomas, 153–154
McManus, Charles, 122
Meany, George, 126, 128, 156
Meese, Ed, 159
Mercer, Robert, 167
Metcalf, Lee, 117
Meyer, Frank, 50, 81, 85
Milbank, Jeremiah, 88
Milliken, Roger, 88
missile mail, 35
Mitchell, John, 100
Mitchell, Stephen, A., 28–29
Moon, Sun Myung, 165
Moral Majority, 165
Morgan, L. Robert, 102, 158

National Abortion Rights Action
    League, 166
National Association for the
    Advancement of Colored People
    (NAACP), 41
National Association of Manufacturers
    (NAM), 131
National Audubon Society, 166

CPSIA information can be obtained
at www.ICGtesting.com
Printed in the USA
JSHW020847290822
29831JS00006B/97

9 780700 633418